Benjamin F. Johnson

Friend to the Prophets

I0807887

Benjamin F. Johnson

Friend to the Prophets

E. Dale LeBaron

CFI
Springville, Utah

Dedicated to the heritage passed on to my family by
Benjamin Franklin Johnson (my great-grandfather),
Harriet Naomi Johnson LeBaron (my grandmother),
Homer Neal LeBaron (my father), and
Luella Wight LeBaron (my mother).

© 2008 E. Dale LeBaron

All rights reserved.

No part of this book may be reproduced in any form whatsoever, whether by graphic, visual, electronic, film, microfilm, tape recording, or any other means, without prior written permission of the publisher, except in the case of brief passages embodied in critical reviews and articles.

This is not an official publication of The Church of Jesus Christ of Latter-day Saints. The opinions and views expressed herein belong solely to the author and do not necessarily represent the opinions or views of Cedar Fort, Inc. Permission for the use of sources, graphics, and photos is also solely the responsibility of the author.

ISBN 13: 978-1-59955-171-5

Published by CFI, an imprint of Cedar Fort, Inc.
2373 W. 700 S., Springville, UT 84663
Distributed by Cedar Fort, Inc., www.cedarfort.com

Cover design by Jen Boss
Cover design © 2008 by Lyle Mortimer

Printed in the United States of America

10 9 8 7 6 5 4 3 2 1

Printed on acid-free paper

Contents

Acknowledgments

The writer gratefully acknowledges the encouragement and support of many family members and friends who have contributed to this work. Although space prohibits mentioning them all at this time, I must recognize the following: My grandmother, Harriet Naomi Johnson LeBaron—a daughter of Benjamin, who instilled in me as a boy a love and appreciation for her father, a noble ancestor; my father, Homer Neal LeBaron, whose memory of his grandfather and his love for him deeply inspired me as a youth; and my mother, Luella Wight LeBaron, whose life mission focused on family history and temple work. My mother spent the winter of 1946–47 in the Church Historian's Library in Salt Lake City, typing (on a manual typewriter) the manuscript for *My Life's Review* from Benjamin F. Johnson's large hand-written journal. From the time I was young this book had a deep impact upon my faith and love for the gospel, and my appreciation for my heritage.

Special thanks to my brother Homer, for his generous service for many years in making copies of my thesis on Benjamin Franklin Johnson available and for his dedicated leadership in the Benjamin Franklin Johnson family organization. Thanks also to many others who have shown an interest in the life of Benjamin Franklin Johnson and encouraged the publication of this book.

I also express appreciation to Elma Fugal for her invaluable contribution in editing and preparing the original materials; Angi Cummings and her son, Michael, for help with its final preparation; and Lyndon Cook of Grandin Book Company who is publishing this biography.

In life—as with this publication—the writer is grateful beyond expression for the countless hours of editing, in addition to the support and encouragement, of my eternal companion, Laura May. I am also deeply grateful to our posterity for their love, encouragement and appreciation of this work: Debi & Keri St.Jeor; Angi & Curt Cummings; Curtis & Jan LeBaron; Rachel & Steve Huber; Shawna & Clark Hammond; David LeBaron; and twenty-four beautiful grandchildren, as of this writing.

Introduction

The tree that never had to fight
For sun and sky and air and light,
That stood out in the open plain
And always got its share of rain,
Never became a forest king,
But lived and died a scrubby thing.

The man who never had to toil
By hand or mind mid life's turmoil,
Who never had to win his share
Of sun and sky and light and air
Never became a manly man,
But lived and died as he began.

Good timber does not grow with ease;
The stronger wind, the tougher trees;
The farther sky, the greater length;
The more the storm, the more the strength;
By sun and cold, by rain and snow,
In tree or man good timber grows.

Where thickest stands the forest growth,
We find the patriarchs of both,
And they hold converse with the stars
Whose broken branches show the scars
Of many winds and much of strife.
This is the common law of life.

—Author Unknown

Men's lives are shaped by the challenges they face and how they accept them. Benjamin Franklin Johnson lived a life filled with challenges, most of them accepted and overcome. His life, closely interwoven with the early history of The Church of Jesus Christ of Latter-day Saints, was clearly influenced by Church doctrines and leaders. From the time he embraced the gospel in 1831 at age thirteen, until the time of his death in 1905, he participated in many of the prominent events in the history of the Church. He became a trusted friend of the Prophet Joseph Smith and served in the Council of Fifty from the time of its inception. He was taught the doctrine of plural marriage by the Prophet Joseph Smith and practiced and defended it. With the expulsion of the Saints from Nauvoo and their emigration to the West, Benjamin faced immense challenges as a pioneer and colonizer. In addition to his Church assignments and his never-ending devotion to missionary work, he became a servant of the people, working in public office to elevate the status of the Church and the state of Utah. He became known as one of the most prominent and influential men in the territory (Warrum 905).

The writer has drawn information from many sources. The major source is *My Life's Review* which President Joseph Fielding Smith, President of the Quorum of the Twelve and Church Historian, said was one of the greatest treasure houses of early Church historical information ever left by a single man (Reported by Luella LeBaron to the author). Benjamin's handwritten journal also provided additional information which was not included in *My Life's Review.* Other sources include Church publications, historical documents, newspapers, affidavits, interviews, letters, articles, diaries, and various other writings by or about Benjamin. References from *My Life's Review* used in this book are listed as "MLR" and are taken from editions published prior to 1996.

Benjamin began his personal journal in 1885 at age 67, while hiding to avoid prosecution for plural marriage. The writer recognizes the problem of historical accuracy of events recorded many years after their occurrence. However, Benjamin's narrative reflects a vivid memory which is generally verified by other historical documents, including some of his earlier writings. The details of these events may have been distant, but the colors are rich and with them comes Benjamin's feelings about the events and their prominence in his life. In explaining his reason for writing his story so late in life, Benjamin said:

> I took up another labor that had impressed itself for years upon my mind as a stern and nervous duty—that of writing for the benefit of my children, "A Life Review," to record the principle events of my life. From this duty I shrank for years and tried to excuse myself from it. But a voice within my soul has continually urged me to this effort, which has so long appeared nervous. But now, feeling I have no further

> excuse I commenced to write "A Life Review" from my early childhood (MLR 303).

This biography, *Benjamin Franklin Johnson: Friend to the Prophets*, is a legacy of faith which should impact his posterity and bring eternal blessings as "the hearts of the children...turn to their fathers" (D&C 2:1–3. See also Malachi 4:5–6 and 3 Nephi 25:5–6). May those who read his story, cherish it as illustrated by the following experience of Elder Melvin J. Ballard:

> The last time I visited my dear friend Orson F. Whitney he was in great distress and I knew it was my last visit with him. I was bidding him goodbye and knew the end was at hand. He said, "I am not going to leave my family any stocks, any bonds, any mortgages, or money in the bank. . . The only thing I will leave them is the story of my life."
>
> It is the story of his sacrifices; the story of the price he paid and the struggle that he went through to subscribe to the Gospel of Jesus Christ and to become a servant of the Master, to win and achieve distinction and honors, to develop the gifts and talents that were in him. "There is only one thing I am leaving in this world that is worth anything," he said. "It is my family. If some day they, too, can come where I am I will be rich; I will have everything that life offers that is worth anything."
>
> Do you think he was rich or poor? Well, he left the history of his life to his children. Oh, what a blessing that is! I know what the history of my father has been to me and to all my brothers and sisters. It has been the greatest heritage. If he had left us a million dollars, we would not have appreciated it as we did that history. I have found a hundred, yes a thousand different times when that history has come to me as a comfort and a consolation. It is something to dwell on. And so Brother Whitney takes with him practically everything he worked for and yet he left the history of his life behind him (Ballard, 280–81).

Chapter I

Family Background and Youth

For all who come into this land, there is a place and a page where each may start his own life story, free to write it as he will, in his own hand, by his own works, and according to his own stature. With that freedom, Benjamin Franklin Johnson chose his place and his page. His life's work seems to have been shaped largely by his home life and his family's deep religious convictions.

Benjamin's progenitors were among the first of America's sons to offer their blood as the price for freedom and liberty (*Mormonism as an Issue* 5). Among these patriots was a grandfather who fell at the Battle of Bunker Hill.

Benjamin was born 23 July 1818 in Pomfret, Chataqua County, New York, and was the tenth child in a family of sixteen children born to Ezekiel and Julia Hills Johnson. (See Appendix for names, birth and death information). Benjamin's parents married on 12 January 1801. They were both born in Massachusetts and were descendants of Pilgrims (Terry; Openshaw).

Julia's family were devout Presbyterians. Her father, Joseph Hills, died when she was very young. Her mother, Esther (Ellis) Hills, who then had three children, Julia, Joel, and Nancy, later married Enoch Forbush. From this marriage came Enoch, Joseph, Seneca, and Didamia.

At the age of seventeen, Julia married Ezekiel Johnson. He was about 5'10" tall, of solid build, with light brown hair and piercing blue eyes. He deeply loved his mother, Sethiah Garnzey, but left home at the age of thirteen because of his cruel and abusive stepfather.

Ezekiel travelled around the country for several years and when he finally returned to see his mother he was bereaved to find that she had left the area in search of him. Sadly they did not meet again. The Johnson family has two prized heirlooms from Ezekiel. One is a worn purse stamped with gold leaf which bears the name of James King, his stepfather, and the date 1742. The purse contains a faded document bearing Ezekiel's mother's name. The other treasure is a small, double-barrelled, silver-trimmed shotgun which Ezekiel called "Old Bess" and used for hunting and protection.

The birth information of Julia and Ezekiel's children show that the family lived in five different places in twelve years. Ezekiel was born with a restless spirit which kept him looking for the perfect location. He would usually go ahead of the family to find a good piece of land, and as soon as the homestead was ready, he would return for his family. The wild frontier wielded a strange fascination for him and seemed ever to be calling and challenging him to conquer and subdue. Grappling with difficulties and taming the wilderness gave zest to life. Under Ezekiel's indefatigable hand, a chaos of rugged timberland soon evolved into productive fields with homes of utility and rustic charm.

In June 1813, Ezekiel moved the family from Vermont to Pomfret, New York where they lived for seventeen years. Pomfret was warmer and more beautiful than Vermont. Ezekiel worked hard as a miller and carpenter in order to provide for his large family. The children helped clear the land, raise food, and make clothing.

Ezekiel took little or no interest in religious matters, but the older children attended the Presbyterian church with their mother. It was there that they learned to read by studying the Bible. The Johnsons were a closely knit family, primarily because of Julia's spiritual and emotional strength (*MLR* 7). Her faith is reflected in excerpts from two letters written to her mother in 1814 and 1815. Julia wrote,

> I hope we shall put our trust in [the Lord] and be reconciled to His will for he knows what is best for us. All things shall work together for the good of those who love Him. If we are afflicted it is for our good, for He doth not afflict willingly nor grieve the children of men. Therefore, let us put our trust in Him, for He hath said, "they that put their trust in Him shall be as Mount Zion which shall not be removed....I hope we shall live as we shall wish we had lived when we are called from time to Eternity. I hope we shall be prepared in Heaven to dwell with the righteous forever (Julia Johnson letters).

Joel, the eldest of the children, said that he was so carefully instructed by a devoutly religious mother that he dared not do anything that would displease the Lord or his parents. As soon as Joel could read, Julia gave him a small New Testament which he carried in his pocket (Joel Johnson, Diary).

Through close association with his father, Benjamin developed a love for nature and pioneering. Childhood experiences of gathering nuts, wild fruits, and flowers with his brothers and sisters, and helping his father clear forests, were precious memories throughout his life. Rugged life on the

American frontier also gave Benjamin an appreciation and understanding of work and industry. Family members worked together to make their own clothes from wool and linen, and to make their own cheese, butter, honey, sugar, soap, and candles (*MLR* 8). These experiences proved to be of great value to Benjamin in his later assignments as a colonizer.

After years of struggling to clear the land and striving in vain to raise adequate food for his large family, Ezekiel sought escape through liquor. Being a very sensitive child, Benjamin vividly recalls,

> Neither his labors nor his love for his family seemed to diminish, yet the fiend of unhappiness had entered our home to break the bonds of union between our parents and to destroy the happiness of their children. In looking back over my childhood it almost seems that I was born to be a child of sorrow, for such was my love for both of my parents that because of the troubles and unhappiness my heart at times would seem almost ready to burst with sorrow and grief, and a feeling always seemed with me to wish that I had died at my birth, or that I never had been born (*MLR* 8).

As a young boy, Benjamin was hampered in acquiring much formal education by his acute sensitivity to criticism. When he was nine years old, he and his brother Joseph, who was fifteen months older than Benjamin, were permitted to attend a winter school taught by their older brother Seth. Even here, because of his shyness and susceptibility to slight or ridicule, he tended to withdraw, content to share in the pride of Joseph's accomplishments. So that nothing would interfere with Joseph's success in school, Benjamin chose to assume extra work and duties at home instead of continuing in school. As a result, Joseph excelled scholastically while Benjamin passed up opportunities for formal education (*MLR* 10).

Through Benjamin's study of the Bible at Presbyterian meetings, he learned to read and write (*MLR* 9). He also developed a fear of literal fire and brimstone if he did not "get religion." Hoping to receive forgiveness of his sins and release from the fears of the awful Hell, Benjamin attended the Presbyterian services with devout determination to be faithful. Yet his devotion to his family's religion did not leave him without doubts. Even as a child he was greatly confused by the differences between the many religious faiths. His study of the life and sufferings of the Savior and the Apostles had filled his soul with a desire either to have lived in their day or to have prophets and revelation in his day (*MLR* 9).

Although while in his youth Benjamin was affected by organized religious groups and their teachings, his greatest motivation to be obedient and to love truth came from the love of his parents (*MLR* 10).

A New Religion

In 1829 a strange story appeared in the Pomfret newspaper. It seemed that a young man professed to have received, from an angel, golden plates engraved with a strange language. From these he claimed to have written a new Bible. As Benjamin pondered the possibility of this story being true, he "could hardly refrain from wishing or hoping it might be so" (*MLR* 9).

The following year, Benjamin's older brother David went to Amherst, Ohio to visit their brother Joel. Julia feared that her sons might become deluded by the new doctrines of the Campbellites, a religious group in Ohio led by Sidney Rigdon, and so she wrote them a letter of caution. Her letter was answered with the horrifying news that her sons had joined the "Mormonites." While in Amherst, Joel and David had been baptized into the Church of Christ[1] when Oliver Cowdery and Parley P. Pratt stopped there on their way to teach Lamanites in Missouri (Nibley 68). The boys sent their mother a lengthy letter of explanation and a copy of the Book of Mormon (*MLR* 11).

Because of slanderous reports about Joseph Smith and the strong public opinion against him and his "Golden Bible," the Johnson family feared that the brothers had been duped. To become acquainted with the delusion into which the two boys had fallen, some of the family and close friends began meeting secretly to read the Book of Mormon and letter of explanation. Shortly after receiving the religious material, Seth, the oldest son living at home, wrote Joel a letter in which he stated,

> Strange things indeed I have found in your letter. Alas, how unexpected, how unthought of. Is it true? That I know not...But I have fears, lest this is one of those false prophets ...warned against by the Savior and His Apostles.... The manner of your becoming convinced of the doctrine and book I am not prepared to condemn, but since Satan will, if possible, deceive the very elect, I fear that you may have been deceived. I view it of infinite importance that we try the spirits by which we are moved in such cases, which I earnestly hope you have done. O how careful should we be to embrace nothing but the truth, as it is in Jesus; for says the Apostles though we hear an angel from heaven preach

[1] In 1838 the Church was renamed The Church of Jesus Christ of Latter-day Saints.

> any other gospel to you than what ye have received let him be accursed (Joel Johnson, Diary 8-11).

Although the family feared greatly that Joel and David had been deceived and had joined a movement that would bring great embarrassment to them, they also realized the importance of this new religion if its claims proved to be true. Seth wrote further,

> I judge not neither have I satisfied my mind sufficiently as yet to tell any man what I think on the subject further than to say it is a supernatural work, either divine or infernal. . . [and] never did I receive any intelligence in my life that so affected me as that contained in your letters (Joel Johnson, Diary).

After several family meetings, Benjamin was permitted to study with them. Soon the family's original feelings toward the boys' conversion changed to wonder and interest. Benjamin noticed that the reading "soon led to marveling at the simplicity and purity of what they read, and at the spirit which accompanied it, bearing witness of its truth" (*MLR* 11). Although Benjamin was only thirteen years of age, his background and religious experiences had prepared him for this message. As he listened to what was being read and discussed, a feeling of intense anxiety came over him to learn more. It seemed as if he must hear it all before he could be satisfied; and the principle of faith began to spring up in his heart. He hoped that there really was a living prophet on the earth. His greatest fear was that it would not prove to be true (*MLR* 11-12).

When David and Joel returned home from Ohio, they said they believed this new religion was true. Although they bore a strong testimony, neither they nor Almon W. Babbitt, who accompanied them, were capable of explaining the new teachings publicly. The Johnson family continued to study and when Mormon missionaries, Elders James Brackinbury and Jabez Durfee, called on them, they were warmly received. Elder Brackinbury, a capable teacher impelled by a spirit of divine commission, brought a confirming witness to what the Johnsons already felt. Benjamin's mother and Lyman R. Sherman, a brother-in-law, were soon baptized. However, Ezekiel, who was not interested, would not consent to Benjamin's baptism (*MLR* 12).

The neighborhood reacted immediately against the Johnson family and others who had joined the "Mormonites." Whereas the Johnsons were once among the most respected in their religious society, they were now ridiculed by the ministers and members of other faiths (*MLR* 12). This gave the converts a brief glimpse of the difficulties and trials awaiting them in their new way of life, and the tests came quickly (*MLR* 13).

Elder Brackinbury became violently ill with bilious colic and soon died. This sudden tragedy was a shock to the young and inexperienced members of the Church and a trial of their faith. The death of this powerful missionary increased the persecution. After the funeral and burial, the members of the Church gathered in the Johnson home "to talk and pray and mourn together." While thus assembled, David Johnson felt impressed that some of their enemies were at that moment digging up the body of the deceased elder. Rushing to the grave, the Johnson brothers found three men who had unearthed the coffin and were lifting the corpse from it. When they saw the Johnsons approaching, the men sprang from the grave and fled. One of them was captured and imprisoned (Benjamin Johnson, "Show Us a Sign").

Considerable ridicule was focused upon the Johnson family for yet another reason. One year prior to her conversion, Nancy Johnson had been thrown from a horse and broken her hip. Physicians agreed that it would be impossible for her to ever have use of that leg again. Since the accident, Nancy had used crutches, being unable to place any weight on the injured leg. After the family joined the Church and proclaimed their belief in divine revelation and power, many people scoffed and asked, "Why, if miracles can be performed, do you not heal Sister Nancy?" They said that if Nancy was healed they would all believe (Benjamin Johnson, "Show Us a Sign").

Ezekiel was not at home when his family joined the Church. He was furious that some were baptized without his knowledge or approval. His resentment flamed, and he immediately sold the family property. He then travelled to Chicago and purchased a quarter section of land so he could move the family away from the despised Mormons. He wrote to Julia, giving instructions for the family to join him, but the letter never arrived.

Julia waited in vain for word from her husband. When the family was forced to vacate their property, she took matters into her own hands. In the spring of 1833, she moved the family to Kirtland, Ohio, which was then the gathering place for the Saints.

Chapter II

Experiences in Ohio

The journey to Ohio was a long and difficult one for the Johnson family. Despite a wounded ankle which caused him great pain, Benjamin and his oldest brother Joel walked over two hundred miles to Amherst, Ohio (*MLR* 13-14). Shortly after Benjamin arrived in Ohio, he met the young Prophet Joseph Smith. Benjamin wrote,

> I now became acquainted with the Prophet, he being then hardly more than a boy in appearance; but I soon learned he was a man indeed in wisdom and council, and although younger than he, I had great opportunities to scrutinize his life and habits, and such was the social and religious elements of his unselfish nature that they who knew him the best loved him most. . . To me he was the embodiment and perfection of all that I comprehend in perfect manhood (Benjamin Johnson, "What I Know of Mormonism").

In the meantime, when Ezekiel did not receive a response to his letter, he became concerned, so he sold his newly acquired property, and returned to New York. Learning that his family had left Pomfret and joined the Mormons in Kirtland was a bitter blow to him. Feeling angry and confused, he went to Kirtland and demanded that they join him in relocating. As the family was now settled with the Saints and knowing that her husband was bitter towards the Church, Julia refused to yield to his demands. Ezekiel left Kirtland a "resentful and broken man." He found shelter with a daughter in Mentor, Ohio and half-heartedly toiled at his trade. "From the volcanic fire raging within him, the heated lava of his ill-will erupted daily in bitter invectives and denunciations of the hated religion" (Openshaw).

In spite of his negative feelings towards the Church, Ezekiel continued to manifest a spirit of love for his family and for his fellow men. In speaking of his father and the effect his father had upon his life, Benjamin said,

> Although my father was apparently opposed to the truth, and had developed habits, yet he was a man of the highest organization. As a husband and parent, he was by nature the most tender and affectionate. As a neighbor and friend, most

> obliging and true, and was a man of truth and honor among men. Never was a question known to be raised as to his integrity, for his word was his bond; and in all things he was a gentleman in the fullest sense, except only in the habit of intemperance, which at times would seem to change his whole nature. . . He was beloved and sought after by his friends, and for his words only he was feared and avoided, for with no other blow than words was he ever known to strike anything living (*MLR* 15).

The Johnsons soon became thoroughly involved in the growing Church. Despite the fact that there were relatively few Saints in Kirtland during the fall of 1833, the Prophet received a revelation commanding them to build a temple (*HC* 302-312). The members of the Church were all poor in terms of worldly goods; so much so, that as they prepared to break ground for the foundation, they realized that no one had an earth scraper, and that there were very few plows among them.

The original plan was to build the temple out of brick, and Benjamin and his brother Joel were asked to make them. Their brother David, a tall, muscular young man of twenty-three years, was assigned to gather the wood with which to burn the bricks. In his enthusiasm to fulfill his duty, he overtaxed his strength, took a severe cold, and began bleeding from his lungs. On 30 October 1833, just prior to his death, David gave his last testimony of the truth of the restored Gospel by the gift of tongues. Don Carlos Smith, a friend and companion to David and brother of the Prophet Joseph Smith, interpreted his testimony (*HC* 15-16). David was the first of five family members to die of consumption, later known as tuberculosis.

Soon after work began on the temple, a stone quarry was discovered nearby. Church leaders decided that stone should be used for the temple instead of brick (Fields 17). Joel and Seth Johnson helped lay the cornerstone of the temple in the spring of 1834 (Fields 16).

On the night of 14 November 1833, Benjamin observed a heavenly phenomenon which he interpreted to be a partial fulfillment of the prophecy that "the stars should fall from heaven as a fig tree casteth her untimely figs" (MLR 16). Benjamin wrote,

> My pen is inadequate to give a description of the scene then presented, for the heavens were full of blazing storm, from zenith to horizon, and a view more sublime and terrible the eyes of man may never have seen. To the fearful it struck terror, and even some of the Saints seemed almost paralyzed with fear, for it appeared for a time that both the heavens

> and the earth were on fire. I gazed upon the scene with wondering awe, but with a full realization of its purport as a sign of the last days. I afterwards learned that it occurred on the night following the driving of the Saints from Jackson County, Missouri (Fields 16-17).

Zion's Camp was organized to march a thousand miles to Missouri to help the fleeing Saints, and Benjamin's brother Seth and brother-in-law Lyman R. Sherman were among them (Fields 17). Benjamin wanted to join them, but because he had not yet been baptized, the Prophet Joseph advised him to stay at home. He told Benjamin that no loss would come to him in waiting. He would partake of every hope, desire, and spiritual influence which those around him were experiencing (Jenson 973-75).

During the winter of 1833–34, fifteen-year-old Benjamin attended the district school in Kirtland. That summer, to help his family financially, he apprenticed to Uriah B. Powell in the saddlery business for twenty-four dollars a year plus board. After only a few months, however, the business was dissolved. Benjamin then worked at a sawmill and did carpentry work (Jensen 973–75).

During the summer of 1834, Joseph Smith Sr. visited some of the families to give them patriarchal blessings. Benjamin felt a spiritual strengthening among the Saints as a result of these blessings. The Spirit of the Lord was manifest among them through the gift of tongues, interpretation of tongues, prophecy, and healings (Jensen 17).

During this same time a miracle occurred in the Johnson household. Benjamin said,

> As yet my sister Nancy had never, since her hip had been broken, taken one step unaided by her crutches; but the time had now come for her release. She was commanded by Elder Jared Carter—then a man of mighty faith—to arise, leave her crutches and walk.
>
> She arose in faith, full of joy, and was from that hour made whole, and never again did she walk upon crutches or lean upon a staff (Benjamin Johnson, "Show Us a Sign").

When Seth returned from Zion's Camp, he was quite ill with cholera, which had caused the death of many in the camp. During the winter of 1834-35, he tried to teach school but soon became too ill to continue and returned to his mother's home. In reflecting on Seth's experiences, Benjamin sadly wrote,

> Here all was solicitude—our beloved brother had come home, perhaps to die—a brother beloved by all who knew

> him, of whom no unkind word was ever known to be spoken; by *me* more than beloved, *almost worshipped*! Must he—could he die and leave us? Oh the cruel agony of such bereavement to the young, to whom in such sorrows, life appears so long and lonesome. But after all our anxieties, prayers and tears, in the midst of his testimonies to us and blessings upon us he died February 19, 1835. (*MLR* 18)

Prior to his passing, Seth told the family that a personage had appeared to him and told him that because he had retained his faith, his earthly work would be completed by another and that an even greater work was now awaiting him. This greatly disturbed Benjamin. He felt it was not right that another person should receive blessings that belonged to his faithful and beloved brother. Comfort came, however, under the hands of Joseph Smith Sr. In early 1835 the Patriarch was giving patriarchal blessings to members of the Johnson family and although Benjamin had not yet been baptized, he received a blessing.

> He blessed all according to age until he came to Joseph E. and myself, when he placed his hands first upon my head. My mother told him I was the youngest, but he said that mattered not—to me was the first blessing; and in blessing me, among other great and glorious things, he told me the Lord would call me to do the work of brother Seth, who had been called away by death. In this promise there was to me more joy than ever before I had known; my dear brother was not to be robbed of his blessings, and if I could only live faithfully, his work would be done, and I should do it for him. I felt this was the greatest boon the Lord could bestow upon me. (*MLR* 19)

Baptism and Early Missionary Efforts

With his father living in Mentor, Benjamin, now sixteen years old, overstepped his objections and was baptized by Elder Lyman Johnson in March 1835. He became an active participant in the Kirtland Branch and was a member of the choir, led by Marvil C. Davis (Huntington 7-8).

At this time, Benjamin's brother-in-law Almon W. Babbitt returned from his mission in New York for a brief visit to Kirtland. His work had been very successful, and he invited Benjamin to go back to New York with him. Recalling the taunts and ridicule which had been hurled at his family only two short years before, Benjamin yearned to return as a missionary to his native town. He remembered how all their neighbors had promised to believe in the Gospel if his sister Nancy should ever walk again. She had been healed by the power of God, and he thought that if he could tell them so, all would at once be converted (*MLR* 20-21).

Realizing he would need money for the journey, Benjamin tried to obtain some of the "Kirtland Scrip," which the Saints were using for currency.[2] These were notes signed by the Prophet and issued from the Kirtland Bank. Once Benjamin obtained enough of the "scrip," he had to find a way of exchanging it for coins which could be used outside the Kirtland area. But he was unable to find anyone willing to exchange currency without charging such a discount that it would leave him insufficient funds for his journey. After considerable thought and prayer, Benjamin decided to appeal to the Prophet Joseph Smith. He told the Prophet where he wanted to go, and asked him if he would exchange the money. The Prophet said, "Yes, Bennie, I will. It is right for you to go." He comforted and blessed Benjamin and his words brought greater joy than did the money (*MLR* 21).

In the forepart of October, Benjamin and Elder Babbitt began their journey. They walked the 150 miles through mud and storms. It had been two and one-half years since seventeen-year-old Benjamin had seen his neighbors. His sister's miraculous healing filled him with new confidence, but he soon learned that they were not as anxious to see him as he had been to visit them. When he told them the news of his sister's healing, and that it was by the power of God, all interest seemed dead, and they did not want to talk about the matter. After a few days of disappointment and disgusted at his misplaced confidence in their sincerity, Benjamin boarded a steamboat at Dunkirk and returned home (*MLR* 21).

School of the Prophets

Soon after Benjamin's return to Kirtland, he was privileged to broaden his education and experience by attending the School of the Prophets, which was an organized effort by Joseph Smith to educate the members of the Church. Benjamin noted that his studies inspired within him a thirst for history and reading (*MLR* 22).

> Through childhood and early youth, my advantages, even for primary education, were the most meager. At seventeen I

[2]In 1837 an unchartered bank was established by the sale of stock, principally among the members of the Church. After excessive speculation and problems of misappropriation of funds, the bank collapsed in the financial panic of 1837. During the existence of the bank, notes were issued which were not honored by other banking institutions because the Kirtland Bank was not a chartered bank (Joseph Fielding Smith 196-97; Robert Kent Fielding 162-206).

> attended the winter term of the grammar school taught by Wm. E. McLellin, in Kirtland, and presided over by the Prophet; at the same time attending night lectures in geography. These were my greatest opportunities for schooling, and in them was finished my school education; and if I have acquired in life anything further of worth, it has been as snatched from the wayside while on the run as a missionary, pioneer, or while in Nature's great laboratory with the axe, plow, spade or garden implements. (Benjamin Johnson, Letter to George S. Gibbs)[3]

The Johnson family was once again struck with death. Susan, about twenty-two years of age, suddenly became ill. Family and physicians were unable to improve her condition. After about two weeks of suffering, she called all the members of the family to her bedside, expressed to them her faith in the gospel, bid them all farewell, then quietly passed away 16 March 1836. The Prophet Joseph expressed sympathy to the Johnson family in their time of sorrow so soon after the death of two faithful sons. Two days following Susan's death the Prophet wrote in his diary,

> At ten o'clock went to the school house to attend the funeral of Susan Johnson, daughter of Ezekiel Johnson. She was a member of the Church of Jesus Christ of Latter-day Saints, and remained strong in the faith until her spirit took its departure from time into eternity. May God bless and comfort her afflicted parents, family, connections and friends. President Rigdon delivered a fine discourse on the occasion, and much solemnity prevailed. (*HC* 2:407-9)

Benjamin later lamented, "Such bereavements come with crushing weight. So much sickness and death tended not only to keep us as a family limited in means, but no doubt the more prompted us in humility to seek the Lord" (*MLR* 22).

Kirtland Temple Completed

The Kirtland Temple, begun in 1833, was completed three years later. The cost of the building was estimated at about sixty thousand dollars, which was largely donations of money, materials, and labor (Jensen). As the work on the temple progressed, greater unity prevailed within the Church,

[3]This letter was written in 1903 at the request of the First Presidency and addressed to George S. Gibbs, secretary to the First Presidency. A copy is in the Appendix. Future references to this letter will be listed as "Gibbs Letter."

but the opposition and persecution of the Saints also increased. During the construction of the temple, the Saints had to guard it day and night. Benjamin got involved in protecting the temple by assisting M. C. Davis, who operated a gunsmith shop in the Johnson's basement (*MLR* 24).

As the time for dedication of the temple drew near, Benjamin attended meetings where those who had helped build the temple were given blessings. He felt great joy as he listened to the prophetic words. He longed for the privilege of receiving such a blessing, but thought that because of his age and having not yet been baptized, he would not qualify. Benjamin said,

> When on the last day of blessings, I was standing by the door in the crowded congregation, and oh! how I did yearn for a blessing! And as the last blessing, apparently, was given, the Prophet earnestly looked towards the door where I was standing, and said to his brother Hyrum, "Go and see if there is not one more yet to be blessed." Brother Hyrum came to the door, and seeing me, put his hand upon my shoulder and asked me if I had not worked upon the Temple. I said, "No sir," but it seemed like passing a sentence upon my fondest hopes. He then asked if I had done nothing towards it. I then thought of a new gun I had earned and given as a donation, and of the brick I had helped to make. I said, "I did give often." "I thought," he said, "there was a blessing for you," and he almost carried me to the stand. The Prophet blessed me, with a confirmation of all his father had sealed upon me, and many more also. I felt then that the Lord had respect for my great desire.
>
> Even to be the youngest and last to be blessed seemed to me a high privilege. When the Prophet had looked towards the door, I felt as though he would call for me, though I could not see how I had merited so high a privilege. But so it was, and my joy was full. (*MLR* 22-23)

At the dedication of the temple, Benjamin heard about spiritual experiences received by the elders, and of the ministering of heavenly messengers within the temple (*HC* 2:432). As he had not yet received the priesthood, he was not privileged to participate in the temple ordinances, but he did feel their influence. "Greatly now was the power of God manifested in the gifts of the gospel, and a general joy pervaded the hearts of the Saints" (*MLR* 23).

It was during this time in Kirtland that the Johnson family became acquainted with Doctor Philastus Hurlburt, the originator of the *Manuscript Found* story. Hurlburt claimed a manuscript by Solomon Spaulding to be the real source of the Book of Mormon. Even as a youth Benjamin developed some personal views concerning Hurlburt and his story.

> I then occupied a position through which I could obtain accurate knowledge of all that transpired on both sides; my father being regarded as an opposer, knew all their secrets, none of which did he withhold from me; and as Hurlburt had boarded at my mother's, I had good opportunity as well as reason for watching his course. (*MLR* 26)

> [Dr. P. Hurlburt] was called "doctor" from his being the seventh son of his mother. He was of a conceited, ambitious and ostentatious turn with a degree of education, but of a low moral status. He had been baptized, ordained, and sent eastward with others, to preach the gospel. He labored for a time near Jacksonville, Erie County, Pennsylvania, but was soon for illicit association called back to Kirtland, where he was excommunicated, but afterwards rebaptized. He soon became enamored or greatly in love with Electra, sister of E. R. Sherman, and because she despised him for his immorality and rejected his suit he swore revenge upon the whole community and boastfully declared he would destroy the Church. While preaching about Jacksonville he had learned of Solomon Spaulding, who once lived in that vicinity, and had written a romance called "Manuscript Found," and out of this he hoped to gain notoriety, obtain money, and work his spite upon the Mormons. So he gave notice to our enemies that he had struck a lead to destroy Mormonism, and if they would come together he would tell them where "Joe Smith" got his "Mormon Bible." He soon collected around him the congregations of our enemies, and in pert and pompous style told them the tale he had concocted of the "Manuscript Found," which of course was good enough when they could get nothing better. And so they readily advanced him means to hunt up the manuscript, and were greatly in hopes that now Mormonism would be at an end. But to all of them it was a failure, but not to Hurlburt, for he had their money. (*MLR* 24-25)

Tragedy once again struck the Johnson family. In the early fall of 1836, Nancy became weak with consumption. With another family member so near death only a few months after Susan's passing, a dark cloud of fear fell upon young Benjamin. After their previous bereavements, he wondered how they could endure another severe and crushing blow and whether all the family might die of the same disease (*MLR* 26). Nancy's condition grew worse, until on October 30th, she bid farewell to the family and quietly passed away. With four siblings having died within three years, Benjamin's fears of an early death continued to grow.

> Everything now seemed to confirm the idea of a short life for myself, if not for all my father's children. My muscular powers were small, and though large in vitality I had but small physical endurance. Through close application to my shopwork and long readings at night, I became effeminate and weak, and some influence like the whisper of the Evil One was always saying in my ear, "You are doomed to die young." At times I would remember the promises made by Father Smith in my patriarchal blessing, and the blessing of the Prophet upon my head, and a desire to live and fulfill them, and to preach the Gospel would enthuse my whole being. Then the Evil Power would tell me all these blessings were forfeited, for through wild shopmate associates while away from home, I had been led into temptation, which brought me sorrow and repentance before the Lord. But under no circumstances had I ever failed to stand firm in the defense of our religion. (*MLR* 26-27)

Bereaved after the deaths of her two daughters, Julia felt unable to continue her small business in town, and moved to a farm about a mile from Kirtland.

Apostasy

In 1836 a wave of financial speculation swept across the nation, and Kirtland was caught up in it. The Saints appeared to feel that Kirtland would become and remain a great center of business. The price of property and real estate soared and people rushed into all types of businesses (*MLR* 27). The Saints rode the crest of this wave of speculation with the Kirtland Bank generously issuing large amounts of credit. Suddenly, with the nationwide financial crash, the bottom fell out of the investments, and a general panic resulted. The days and weeks that followed ripped at the very foundation of the Church and proved to be one of the greatest tests the members had faced up to that time.

> Men in high places began to complain of and reproach each other, and brotherly love was found smothered. . . The spirit of charity was not invoked, and brethren who had borne the

> highest priesthood and who had for years labored, traveled, ministered and suffered together, and even placed their lives upon the same alter, now were governed by a feeling of hate and a spirit to accuse each other, and all for the love of *Accursed Mammon*. All their former companionship in the holy anointing in the Temple of the Lord, where filled with the Holy Ghost, the heavens were opened, and in view of the glories before them they had together shouted "Hosanna to God and the Lamb," all was now forgotten by many, who were like Judas, ready to sell or destroy the Prophet Joseph and his followers. And it almost seemed to me that the brightest stars in our firmament had fallen. Many to whom I had in the past most loved to listen, their voices seemed now the most discordant and hateful to me. From the Quorum of the Twelve fell four of the brightest: Wm. E. McLellin, Luke and Lyman Johnson and John Boynton; of the First Presidency, F.G. Williams; the three Witnesses to the Book of Mormon, Oliver Cowdery, David Whitmer and Martin Harris.... I was then nineteen years of age, and as I now look back through more than fifty years of subsequent experience, to that first great Apostasy, I regard it as the greatest sorrow, disappointment and test through which I have ever passed; the first real experience among false brethren, the greatest sorrow and test for the faithful. (*MLR* 28-29)

This shocking experience, where men of great faith and leadership rejected the Prophet and followed the counsel of others, caused Benjamin great concern for his own spiritual security.

> But with all my faults I did not forget the Lord nor His chosen servants. And in this day of great affliction and separation by apostasy, I felt to call mightily upon His name, that He would never leave me to follow these examples, but that He would keep me humble, even though in poverty and affliction, so only that I fail not. This prayer of my youth I have never forgotten, neither do I feel that it is forgotten by Him to whom it was made. (*MLR* 29)

The apostate group made claim to the temple, printing office, and everything regarded as Church property. The Prophet Joseph Smith's life was threatened, and he was sought by those desiring his arrest. Opposition became so intense that the Prophet and his family quietly and quickly left for Missouri in mid-winter. To prevent the printing office and materials from falling into apostate hands to be used against the Church, they were burned and destroyed by Lyman R. Sherman, Benjamin's brother-in-law (*MLR* 29). The faithful Saints, or "lick-skillets" as they were dubbed by the apostates, had to hide to avoid vexatious lawsuits (Huntington). Benjamin did everything he could to help the Church leaders escape to Missouri.

As Church leaders were forced to flee, most members made preparations to follow them to Missouri. It was difficult to sell property because of the financial depression, but after great effort the Johnson brothers were able to sell their mother's farm and obtain teams and wagons for the thousand-mile journey. They planned to leave by July 4th, but Benjamin's health was so poor that he feared he would be unable to go with them. When the departure time arrived, the family needed help driving some of the unmanageable stock, so Benjamin offered to help. As he walked along, he felt a new vitality and he began to feel stronger.

> A new faith and feeling sprang up in my heart, and I felt that the Lord had heard my prayers. I felt sure I was not soon to die, a dark cloud rolled from over me and a great weight from my heart; and to all in camp it was surprising to see how fast I increased in health and ability to assist in our camp life. But to none was it so great a surprise as to me, and I felt in my heart to thank God and to devote myself to doing all the good in my power. (*MLR* 32)

With this new faith and strength, Benjamin continued with his family toward new experiences and the western frontier.

Chapter III

Trials and Tribulations in Missouri

Benjamin and his family were among the last of the Saints to leave Ohio, consequently they joined what was later called the Poor Camp. This company of seventy wagons consisted mostly of Saints who required financial help from other members of the Church to make the trek to Missouri. The group was led by Joseph Young, Elias Smith, Jonathan Hale, and others (Huntington). All resources were combined and shared equally among the group (*MLR* 32-33). Benjamin observed,

> So large a company, poor in appearance, and known to be Mormons, passing through the country where runners [salesmen] with Kirtland money had swindled the people, caused us to be more or less objects of contempt and persecution, and in a number of towns writs were served upon our leaders to compel a redemption of Kirtland bank notes. But the blessing of the Lord was with us, and there was always a way open for escape, and friends always at hand just in time of need. (*MLR* 33)

When their supplies were nearly gone, the group stopped in Dayton, Ohio where the men earned money constructing a road. During the month they were there, Benjamin made two trips to Cincinnati to visit relatives and do business for the Saints. Upon returning from his last trip, he found that sickness had spread throughout the camp, causing some deaths. Benjamin used his knowledge of medicine, gleaned from previous experiences with his family's illnesses, to nurse the sick of the camp. They became his "especial charge," and he did all he could to ease their discomfort, even trading medicine and other articles for much needed food (*MLR* 33). To him this service was a labor of love. "Such was the increase of my health and hopes that I felt that I could do or endure anything to prove my gratitude to the Lord, for His blessings" (*MLR* 33-34). Benjamin's efforts to trade for things he felt would help the sick often brought him into contact with members of other faiths who were curious about the Mormons. He frequently found himself surrounded by religious leaders who asked questions, but Benjamin was never insulted or abused. He felt that such incidents were of great value and realized that the Lord always provided him with sufficient answers and testimony to represent the Church.

While in a large town, Benjamin found himself surrounded by people asking questions. He wrote,

> I...commenced to talk, and as I proceeded the people gathered, and when I ceased and looked around there were hundreds before me and all windows were open on both sides of the street, and crowded with listening women; and all appeared to wonder at the dirty, bare-footed boy. But no one marveled more than myself, and it was near night when I left them and had eleven miles to walk to camp.
>
> The next day being Sunday, a number of carriage loads of people came from town to our meeting in camp, stayed for a time and inquired for the young man who had preached to them in town the day before, of which no one knew anything. I saw them come and go again but was too bashful to attract their notice or speak to them. Such evidences of the favor of the Lord, through which, by the power of His spirit I could bear a faithful testimony to the world was of great worth and comfort to me. (*MLR* 34)

They arrived in Springfield, Illinois in October. Here Brother Samuel Hale became ill and passed away. As his wife was also sick, Benjamin's mother and other family members stayed behind to care for her and her ten-year-old daughter, Mary Ann. After Sister Hale died, Julia adopted her daughter, Mary Ann, who later became Benjamin's second wife (*MLR* 34-35).

In his anxiety to get to Missouri and again see and hear the Prophet Joseph, Benjamin left his family and continued on with the Saints (George Washington Johnson 5-6). On 13 October 1838 they crossed the Mississippi River and entered Missouri. While in Missouri, Benjamin was rebaptized. This was a common practice among the early Saints to show their devotion to the work of the Lord.

The company of Saints had traveled nearly one thousand miles to escape persecution but soon realized they were unlikely to find peace in Missouri. Since 1832 there had been trouble between the Missourians and the Mormons for various reasons. The Missouri settlers were largely southerners strongly in favor of slavery and greatly suspicious of the large numbers of northerners settling among them. The Saints' declaration of their intention to establish Zion in Jackson County "where only the righteous would live," did much to increase distrust toward them. The Mormons also held great political power and could sway an election. This and the tremendous influx of Mormons into Jackson County caused Missourians to believe they would soon be completely outnumbered. Protestant ministers used their influence to excite opposition against the rapidly growing Mormon community (Roberts 321-29).

Rumors of trouble at Far West and threats against them if they stayed, urged the Poor Camp to move on. About 20 October, Benjamin's company camped at Haun's Mill. When the company moved on, Joseph Young and his family chose to stay behind and barely escaped the Haun's Mill massacre of October 30th when an armed mob killed seventeen Mormons and severely wounded twelve others (*MLR* 35). This attack came because of an order issued by Governor Boggs that the Mormons must leave the state of Missouri or be exterminated (*HC* 3:182-87; Roberts 1:480-83).

As the camp approached Far West, the Prophet came out to greet them. Benjamin "felt joy in seeing him again." Although Benjamin had planned to remain in Far West with his two married sisters, Delcena and Julia, the Prophet counseled him to proceed to Diahman to help defend the Saints against mobs from the surrounding counties.

Under the direction of the Prophet, Diahman had been surveyed and divided into lots. Each man was allowed to choose one, beginning with the oldest and married men. As Benjamin was only twenty years old and unmarried, he was one of the last to choose. He was left with an undesirable rocky area which overlooked the Grand River Valley. He said,

> After a few days, the Prophet accompanied us to this spot, and pointed out those rocks as the ones of which Adam built an alter and offered sacrifice upon this spot, where he stood and blessed the multitude of his children, when they called him Michael, and where he will again sit as the Ancient of Days, then I was not envious of anyone's choice for a city lot in Adam-ondi-Ahman. (*MLR* 36)

A Defender of the Saints

Since many of the Saints had their homes and property stolen or destroyed, they made organized efforts to defend what was left. They also made raids among the Missourians "for arms, ammunition and sustenance" (Benjamin Johnson, "A Life Sketch"). Benjamin was assigned to guard duty during the night and was a scout for raiding parties during the day. As persecution increased, many families left their farms and almost all their earthly possessions to seek safety in the Mormon communities. Benjamin observed their pitiful condition and tried to help them in whatever way he could. In addition to enduring cold and snow, these new immigrants faced starvation.

> We were being hemmed in on all sides by our enemies and were without food. All the grain, cattle, hogs, and supplies of every kind were left in the country, or so far from home they could not be obtained except with a strong guard. So our only possible chance was to go out in foraging companies and bring in whatever we could find, without regard to ownership; and in this way corn, beef, cattle, hogs, bee stands, chickens, etc., with anything and everything left in the country that would sustain a thousand people, we took wherever it was found. Thus we did our best to obtain food, dividing it as was needed. (*MLR* 37; Gentry 317-64)

At Diahman, Benjamin was without money, kindred, or home. Except for a few pieces of warm clothing, everything he owned had been used to comfort the sick during the trip from Ohio. Benjamin suffered much from privation and exposure.

> Too proud and bashful to make my wants known, or to accept gratuitous favors offered me, many nights I laid in freezing weather with nothing under or over me but the hay in the loft on which I slept. Many nights did I remain by the guard fire alternating between a roasting and freezing condition, as I changed sides to or from the fire, until mother of President George A. Smith, who was always kind to me, learning my condition, came to the log barn in which I slept and gave me a nice warm quilt, which owing to the circumstances I shall never forget. (*MLR* 36-37)

One morning, after Benjamin had spent the night on guard duty, he was asked to go with Cornelius P. Lott and a company of twenty men to a farm where they suspected their enemies were storing arms and ammunition. As they approached the farm, they noticed two men and a number of women and children running from the house into the cornfield. They gathered up the prisoners and questioned them about weapons. The Missourians claimed to have neither arms nor ammunition on their property. They were assured that if there really was none, they would be left alone, but if arms were found their property would be burned (*MLR* 38-39). After a thorough search of the buildings uncovered nothing, the company looked in the cornfields and found arms and ammunition. As the women gathered up all they could carry from the doomed house, Benjamin's heart went out to them.

> When the horses were brought up for their use, there was one animal with a side saddle, on which the young [very pregnant] woman was to get away; but it was taken away by one Sloan, who had kept the boarding house where I stayed, a man of education and apparently a gentleman. It was too much for me, so I took the animal away from him by force, and put her upon it, and then got from another a roll of homemade cloth and fastened it on behind her. While others were doing the burning and plunder, my mission was of mercy as far as duty would permit. (*MLR* 39)

By noon the company had set fire to the buildings and were headed home.

With much of the day still ahead of them, they decided to separate and scout in different directions. Benjamin went with two of the men in pursuit of a band of horses they had seen earlier. After they had followed the animals for some time, it began to rain. They decided to rejoin their group, but realized they were lost. They searched all night, fearing that at any moment they would be discovered by their enemies. Toward morning they came upon a deserted but secured house. They forced open a window, and Benjamin went through first. As his feet reached toward the floor, he fell straight into the cellar. The floorboards had been used to bar the windows and doors. Benjamin, "weary and faint through want of sleep and food," wet from the rain, and "more dead than alive," told his companions he could not take his watch and laid down to sleep on a pile of deerskins (MLR 41).

About two hours later Benjamin awoke with fear at the sound of men who had surrounded the house and were demanding to know who was inside. They were relieved to learn that the men were not enemies, but some of their brethren of the Church. One of them, John Butler, was even riding the Prophet's black horse, Charley. He volunteered to take Benjamin and his companions back to Diahman. On the way, they came upon a herd of good beef cattle and took nearly forty of them to the hungry people of Diahman. Concerning such actions by the Saints, Benjamin explained,

> Here let me say that it should not be supposed, though we sought to repel mob violence and were compelled to forage for food when hemmed in on all sides by a mob who had driven us from homes they had sold to us and been paid for, robbing us of everything but our lives and the little we could carry away leaving our crops, stock, and household goods to our enemies, that we were common robbers because we took by reprisal that with which to keep from starvation our women and children. Ours was a struggle for our lives and

> homes, and a more conscientious, noble, and patriotic spirit never enthused man than that which animated our leaders in this just defense of our rights. (*MLR* 42-43)

Trials as a Lone Prisoner

When Benjamin returned to Diahman he learned that most of the men had been called away to protect Far West, but he was asked to remain behind. While he was alone on guard duty a few days later, he received word that Far West, the strongest of the Mormon communities, had surrendered. Although Benjamin felt the capture of Diahman was inevitable, he continued in his line of duty.

One day while Benjamin was on guard duty, General Wilson and his militia arrived and demanded to see all the men in Diahman. One of the militia recognized Benjamin and accused him of being involved in the burning of his home. When the colonel asked if this was true, Benjamin admitted that it was. The colonel drew his sword and marched Benjamin with "quick step" to the General's marquee. Here he was at once put under strong guard, a prisoner in General Wilson's camp (*MLR* 44).

O. B. Huntington, a friend who shared many of these experiences with Benjamin, said that when the Mormons surrendered their weapons, "Benjamin laid down probably the most valuable rifle owned by a Mormon at that time. Besides being a true shooting gun it had sixty pieces of gold and silver inlaid upon stock and barrel" (Deseret News, 16 October 1897, 7).

Benjamin had found that where there was culture and refinement, his reticent and somewhat genteel appearance commanded respect. With the rough Missouri frontiersmen, however, he was a hated Yankee, and the object of insult (MLR 44).

Following his arrest, Benjamin was questioned by the state's attorney from St. Louis and Dr. Carr of Gallatin, who had made the first speech in that county to drive out the Mormons. Benjamin earnestly prayed in his heart that his answers would not implicate any of his brethren but also that he could tell the truth. He was blessed with the ability to remember the answers and explanations he had given previously. When he was pressed to tell who led him to the Taylors (the place of the burnings), he told them he was new in that area and had made few acquaintances but had heard the man called Captain Cornelius, meaning Cornelius P. Lott. His inquisitors also questioned the Taylors and learned how Benjamin had treated them as prisoners and assisted the women, even quarrelling with his own companions for their sake. After considerable examination the two men said,

> Now young man, we have questioned you over and again, and you have given us always the same answer, and in no way have you contradicted your statement. We believe you tell the truth, and have been raised an honorable man. We know you are in a very bad fix here, and apparently but little hope for escape from conviction. You are the only prisoner here, and the chances for you are the worse, as there is much expectation in the army here as at Far West of bloody revenge. If you are the only one to answer for all the burnings and raids upon the old settlers then your case is bad indeed. But we are your friends, and unasked will do all in our power to save you. (*MLR* 45)

The day after his arrest on charges of robbery, Benjamin was brought before Justice of the Peace Adam Black, a man whom the Mormons regarded as "a pronounced and bitter mobocrat." In Black's log cabin courthouse, two Missourians came forward and challenged Black's authority to try the case. They claimed this trial should be under military jurisdiction rather than civil. At first Benjamin was fearful of their motives, but he was soon convinced that the Lord had touched their hearts with compassion when he heard them say that he had "sought food for perishing women and children wherever it could be found" (Benjamin Johnson, Handwritten Manuscript of *My Life's Review*). Benjamin's new friends so befuddled Judge Black in various points of law that he jumped up in anger and declared that he would have nothing more to do with the matter, and the military might do whatever they pleased with Benjamin (*MLR* 47). He was released from the charge of robbery because, as he wrote: "That crime would not require my being hung or shot and the mob spirit was hungering for Mormon blood, and being the only prisoner, I must be the scape-goat or sacrifice to appease the wrath and meet the hopes of the people" (Benjamin Johnson, "What I Know of Mormonism").

Considering the possible consequences of his trial, Benjamin felt very alone among these hostile strangers. As he awaited trial, he would have chosen to go with the Prophet, even to certain death, rather than stay there alone (*MLR* 46).

As a military prisoner, Benjamin was often promised his freedom if he would disclose the names of the Mormon leaders. His interrogators constantly reminded him that they planned to kill him in vengeance for all the Mormons had done. Nothing, however, frightened him as much as his guards.

> One relief was composed of Haun's Mill murderers, including the fiend, Rogers, who killed Father McBride with the corn cutter, by cutting off his fingers, hands, arms and then splitting his head. That same corn cutter, still crimson with blood, hardly dry, was swung over my head once and again, with boasting of what it had done and what it would yet do, and with oaths and cursings picturing the fate that awaited me. . . Yet it was not the fear of their killing me, for I could think upon death calmly; but it was a something that grew out of being with and subject to those monsters. (*MLR* 45-46)

Benjamin was kept without shelter or regular food for eight days. His only relief came from meager warmth from the guard's fire and occasional scraps of food which the black cook sneaked to him when possible. Benjamin's captors frequently threatened him, "We'll kill you tomorrow, sure, and in a way to make you yell right smart" (Martineau 337–40). It was reported that one guard even attempted to carry out his threats.

> While sitting upon a log one day a brute came to him [Benjamin] with a rifle in hand, saying, "You give up Mormonism right now, or I'll shoot you." Receiving a decisive refusal he took deliberate aim not 10 feet distance and pulled the trigger. No explosion occurred, and he cursed fearfully, saying he had used the gun 20 years and it had never before missed fire. He examined the lock, put in fresh priming and again essayed to shoot Johnson, but without effect, and a third time with the same result. A bystander told him to fix up his gun a little, and then said he, "You can kill the cuss all right." "Yes," said the would be murderer, "I'll put in a fresh load." He did so and again essayed to kill Johnson. This time the gun bursted [sic] and killed the wretch upon the spot, and a bystander was heard to say, "You'd better not try to kill that man." And thus, day after day, Johnson was continually threatened with death. (Martineau 337–40)

In spite of the circumstances, Benjamin always sought to keep a cheerful face, and whenever possible entered into light conversation with his captors. He often sang to himself and occasionally got his guards to join him in song, hoping they would forget he was a hated Mormon.

To keep the fire blazing during the cold nights, much wood had to be gathered during the day. At first Benjamin volunteered to help, but soon the soldiers began demanding his assistance.

> I was walking slowly, for my load was heavy and the snow deep, when the guard behind me ordered me with an oath to "step faster, or he would stick the bayonet into me." Upon this a terrible revulsion of feeling came over me, and had I been Sampson, I should have felt no stronger. I threw down the load as if it had been a straw, and raised my hand as I turned and confronted him. I shook my fist, and told him I would not carry so much as another chip; that if I had a sword I would split him from end to end. My voice was earnest, and the Colonel just passing came quickly and...with an oath told him that if I was not from that time treated as a prisoner should be that they would all be put under guard. (*MLR* 48)

After Benjamin had been a prisoner for six or seven days with no one to share his sorrows, his integrity was put to the severest test. He was offered release and reward if he would betray his brethren, but death if he would not. Many years later, as Benjamin reflected upon this test of his loyalty, he said, with tears running down his cheeks, "I would rather have been tied to every tree in the woods and shot, than to have forfeited my integrity to my brethren" (Desert News, 16 October 1897, 7).

William D. Huntington was sent by some of the brethren to talk with Benjamin to learn whether he would betray them to save himself. They were allowed to talk only in the presence of the guards. In ambiguous words William conveyed to Benjamin the fears of the people that he would prove a traitor. A sense of injustice came over Benjamin. He had stood alone in the face of death, or worse, and had been true. Now instead of praying for him and giving him their faith, they were prophesying evil, and exercising faith against him. His very soul felt thrust to the center with their suspicions, and the feeling went to Brother William's heart (*MLR* 49).

William was convinced of Benjamin's loyalty and upon returning home, he related his experience to his mother and sister Zina. They all agreed that Benjamin had been neglected, and Zina went to every family in the settlement and persuaded them to meet at the log school house to pray for Benjamin's release. Her efforts were successful. Men and women gathered at the appointed place and, in fervent prayer, asked God that Benjamin might escape or be released. No sooner did one prayer cease than another commenced. Thus, without intermission, a continuous supplication ascended to heaven, hour after hour, all that day and night, some going home when necessary, while others returned to pray (Martineau 337-40).

That night Benjamin felt that the people were praying for him, and all grief, sorrow, fear, and hardness left him. When William came the next morning to bring consoling words to Benjamin, Benjamin felt he had words of comfort for William instead (*MLR* 49).

The following day, Benjamin was turned over to the military to be tried by court martial. He received some unexpected help from a young attorney from St. Louis who, although a stranger to Benjamin, offered him sympathy and friendship. Using his best efforts he plead with General Wilson to release Benjamin. The General excused everyone and privately told Benjamin that "he felt a strange indescribable interest and love for him" and asked many questions about him. He said that if Benjamin would come and live with him, he could be "one of the richest young men of the state" (Deseret News, 16 October 1897). Benjamin gratefully thanked him, but declined. He wrote,

> [The General's] words were tender and kind, softened by a power he did not comprehend; but I told him I had parents back in the east, from whom I had till now never been separated, and that if I was ever free again I must go to them, for I knew my kindred were in great anxiety for my safety, and would fear I was dead until they saw me again. He said he did not blame me, and he would take the responsibility to give me a pass, but I must avail myself of the night time to get away, for old citizens around Diahman would certainly kill me if they found I was set at liberty. (*MLR* 50)

The Long Road to Freedom

About an hour before sunset Benjamin was given a pass and taken to the Huntington home about a half mile from camp. There he hurriedly ate, obtained a few matches and a small amount of corn, and started through the woods toward Far West, twenty-five miles away. Although he had gained his freedom, he could not go to the nearest Mormon village, for the enemy would find him and he would be murdered. It was many miles through snow two feet deep, with no blanket, no weapon to kill game or for self defense, and no food except about two quarts of parched corn (*Deseret News*, 13 December, 1905).

Benjamin watched for a house where he could spend the night. He found one late that night, but it was full of Mormon emigrants fleeing Governor Boggs' extermination order. They directed him to another home. He wandered in the snow and cold until he came to a house, but found it to be the same one he had left an hour or two before. This time he was escorted to the home of Elisha H. Groves where he was kindly received. But the house was cold and the floor icy; lying only on a rug, Benjamin shivered without sleep until dawn.

After a small breakfast, Benjamin resumed his journey. Nearly twenty miles of deep snow and rolling prairie lay between Benjamin and his two sisters in Far West. He began this dreadful journey on what he believed to be "the bitterest cold day of the whole winter." He was already exhausted, and through his light clothing "the searching winds seemed to find the very marrow of his bones" (Deseret News, 16 October 1897). In describing his situation, Benjamin wrote,

> I became so benumbed with cold and exhausted by fatigue that it seemed I could proceed no further, without warmth and rest. I was upon a high, bleak prairie, and not a house, tree or shrub could be seen. It seemed that the angel of death stood before me, for my heart and hope began to fail me. Yet I did not forget to pray in my heart, and as I looked around upon the snowy expanse I saw just at my left, a little from the road a small deep swale, where the grass stood high and thick above the snow. I thought, "Oh that I had saved just one match last night!" At the thought I felt in my vest pocket and found just one match. With it, through the blessing of the Lord I fired the grass. I inhaled the heated air, and soon recovered warmth, and after a rest the wind was somewhat abated. (*MLR* 51-52)

With renewed strength and hope, Benjamin continued his journey and reached his sisters' home before dark.

Benjamin recognized the hand of the Lord during his imprisonment and liberation. The little swale of tall grass and the one match when he supposed all were gone, he regarded as special providence to preserve his life. He felt these experiences were significant in shaping his life.

But Benjamin found no safety in Far West, for the mobocrats of Diahman were hunting him there. With an old friend, Arthur Millican, who was also wanted by the mobs, Benjamin purchased a few supplies and commenced walking toward Fort Leavenworth, in Indian territory, where they hoped to find protection.

Through his experiences of recent months, Benjamin felt he had achieved a degree of maturity to go with his large stature. As they walked, he thought about the can of honey his sister had obtained for his trip. He yearned for some when they stopped for lunch, but when he opened his pack it was not there—it had been left behind. Being overcome by disappointment, his emotions took over, and he sat down and wept (*MLR* 53).

After travelling nearly two hundred miles, Benjamin and Arthur arrived at Fort Leavenworth. Here they found employment and were promised protection. Living on the frontier, Benjamin was thrust into a new environment where he was exposed to the vices of the world: gambling, drunkenness, and prostitution were all bare and open-faced. Yet the men at the fort respected Benjamin and his Mormon friends when they refused to join the gambling and carousing. Benjamin spent the winter driving six yoke of oxen to haul supplies to the fort and reservation.

About the first of March he learned of the death of Lyman R. Sherman, his sister Delcena's husband. Benjamin immediately made preparations to return to Far West so he could help her and her children leave Missouri. During the trip, he needed to cross a river where "much ice was running fearfully." The only transportation available was a canoe being prepared for its final trip. Benjamin made the necessary arrangements but as he stepped into the canoe six others with baggage stepped in also, nearly sinking the vessel. When the canoe was stationary the rim was not more than one inch above the water. The ferryman said it was too dangerous and some had better get out, but all refused. It was terrifying as they made their way through the masses of floating ice, but they finally landed safely on the other shore.

In Far West Benjamin saw to the welfare of Delcena and her children. He then travelled with Almon W. Babbitt to Richmond, to learn what they could about the Prophet and others who were in prison there and to retrieve the guns they had surrendered. When Benjamin requested that his gun be returned to him, he was offered a common gun as a replacement but refused, insisting that he would accept only the gun he had laid down. After he finally located it, he took it against the wishes of the officer in command (*MLR* 56).

While in Richmond, Benjamin inquired about some of the Saints' possessions which had been shipped prior to their departure from Kirtland. He learned that the last shipment was being auctioned to pay the freight charges, for the Saints had no money with which to redeem their belongings.

Upon returning to Far West, Benjamin renewed his association with William D. Huntington, and spent much time in the Huntington home. His spiritual experiences with the Huntington family made a lasting impression upon Benjamin. They often held exceptionally spirited and enjoyable testimony and prayer meetings. Here Benjamin received the gift of tongues, which never left him. To Sister Zina Huntington was given both the gift of tongues and the gift of interpretation of tongues. Before Benjamin left Far West, he and Zina formed a mutual attachment which grew into feelings of reciprocal love.

When the Saints were expelled from Missouri in the winter of 1838–39, there were many poor and sick who needed assistance. Under the leadership of Brigham Young, President of the Quorum of the Twelve Apostles, 214 able bodied men, including Benjamin, entered into a covenant "to stand by and assist each other, in removing from this State, and...never desert the poor who are worthy" (Tullidge 81; HC 3:251–54). Benjamin assisted as many as he could during the Mormon exodus, assuming special care for his widowed sister Delcena and her six small children. Their journey took them over bad roads and through storms and cold weather. The Saints arrived in Illinois in early spring where the people of Quincy, Illinois and adjacent counties received the sick and hungry Mormons with sympathy and succor. Their humanity was a stark contrast to the bitterness, hate and suffering from which they had fled (Benjamin Johnson, Handwritten Manuscript of *My Life's Review*).

After finding a comfortable home for Delcena, Benjamin travelled to Springfield, Illinois to visit his family. Upon his arrival about the first of April, "there was a meeting and greeting, with gratitude to the Lord" for their reunion. As Benjamin recalled all that had transpired since last seeing his family, he wrote,

> I arrived [in Missouri] in October just in time to take part in and become familiar with all that transpired with us as a people. I knew of the onslaught upon DeWitt in [Carroll] County and misery and deaths that accompanied it—knew all of the circumstances attending the murder of Elder David Patten and others on Crooked River—Knew all the details of that most horrible butchery at Haun's Mill, when men, women, and children were indiscriminately shot; and I looked into the well where 20 mangled bodies including small children were thrown together with Father McBride, a Revolutionary veteran, who fought with Washington the battles of Freedom—shot with his own gun and mangled with a scythe blade corn cutter, which I saw myself in the hand of his murderer, smeared with the blood of his victim, which I have great cause to remember. I was the witness of the terrible sufferings of those who were compelled to flee from the homes they had built or bought from our enemies by whom many were robbed of whatever they could not bear upon

> their backs; and as winter with its storms was now upon us, and terrible was the sufferings of women, children and the aged, for they were without tent or covering; and in this condition children were born; while the old and feeble perished both by famine and exposure. For we were hemmed in by the mob who now were in possession of our homes, grain, stock and all our resource for food. Under this condition of famine and exposure, myself with others made forage expeditions outside of our town or camp to procure upon a principle of reprisal corn, beef cattle, hogs or anything with which to sustain life. The cry then went out of plunder and robbing upon citizens by Mormons, and the Government listening to all the vile calumnies heaped upon us by our enemies, gave order to Major General Clark and Atchison to legalize or organize the Mob military into an Army of 5,000 and with it exterminate the Mormons. The awful particulars of what followed in the betrayal of our Leaders—their insurrection with the fiendish insults and abuse to which they were subject, while a Military Mob in all their unbridled [sic] license ravished wives and daughters of now imprisoned or disarmed and defenseless people—shot down that of less value in the streets. While every man of prominence was either in prison or making his way through winter storms to get outside of the State. . . In all these things *I was more than an eye witness.* (Benjamin Johnson, "What I Know of Mormonism")
>
> I was now...with increased health, energy, endurance, and animated with brighter hope than before had ever inspired me, all begotten within me through a travail of tribulation and sacrifice since leaving Kirtland not more than nine months ago.
>
> In looking back over the vicissitudes through which I had passed in that short period it seemed more like a dream than a reality; and when I think of it all as real, I feel a weight of gratitude to God that I find no words to express. (*MLR* 57-58)

O. B. Huntington stated, "The events of that time inducted him [Benjamin] to lessons of experience that created pages of history in his life" (*Deseret News*, 16 October 1897).

It is evident that through his brief but courageous service in Missouri, Benjamin grew in stature in the eyes of the Church leaders and in his confidence before the Lord. On 10 March 1839, Benjamin was ordained an elder by Elder Heber C. Kimball and told that he would soon be called to go with Elder Kimball on a mission to England (*MLR* 57). Although it does not appear in Benjamin's personal writings, the family history records that the Prophet Joseph Smith commended Benjamin for his heroic devotion. Rose A. Openshaw, Benjamin's granddaughter recorded,

> Grandfather had been numbered with the guard protecting through the cold winter, the life of the Prophet Joseph and his home from mob-violence, and as he returned from his beat, half frozen, snow streaking even his hair and beard, tears sprang to the Prophet's eyes. "Benjamin!" he cried in commiseration, and in a moment of prophecy, "to prove to you that your labors are acceptable to the Lord, your hair shall never turn white but shall always be black!"
>
> And so it was, coal black still, even at 87, while lying in his coffin. Yet his long distinguished beard seemed to have caught some of the winter snows of life, for it was streaked with silver. (Openshaw)

Chapter IV

Illinois Period—A Trusted Servant

In Springfield Benjamin found employment with Charles Lamb, a wholesale merchant and banker who placed a great deal of confidence in him. During this time he received a letter from President Heber C. Kimball stating that during the June conference at Quincy, Benjamin had been called to accompany the apostles on their mission to Europe. This appointment is a significant indication of the confidence and esteem which the Lord and the Church leaders placed in Benjamin. He immediately began saving money for the journey.

While preparing to go on his mission, Benjamin became acquainted with a rich young widow, the sister of Mrs. Lamb, his employer's wife. She had been married to Secretary of State Falguar and had one child. Of their association, Benjamin wrote, "My vanity was at least a little flattered even if I was not tempted by the partiality of this young lady. She was reputed very rich—a millionaire, and I felt very sure I could win her hand if I would, especially after I overheard a conversation between her and her sister." In considering these opportunities, Benjamin wrote,

> I pondered the matter prayerfully, and I could not but feel that to marry a woman with wealth would be to bring myself to the world, and would keep me from my mission, and if allured away from my calling in the Gospel, then all the new and bright hopes that had wakened within me would become a failure. I felt it would be a sacrifice too great even for a lovely wife with inheritance of wealth. (*MLR* 59-60)

With the question of matrimony clearly decided, Benjamin's thoughts turned back to his mission. By now Benjamin had saved about one hundred dollars and felt that the time was near to leave for Europe. He learned that Commerce, in Hancock County, Illinois, had been purchased as a gathering place for the Saints and that the Prophet Joseph Smith had escaped from Missouri. Anxious to see the Prophet and other old friends, Benjamin left Springfield by horseback, on his twenty-first birthday, 28 July 1839.

Service in Time of Sickness

Arriving in Commerce, Benjamin found general sickness and death among the Saints. Many had already died and almost all were sick with chills or typhoid malarial fever (Benjamin Johnson, "A Life Sketch"). It was rare to find even one among the Saints able to wait upon and care for another. Every house was a hospital, but without nurses. There were hardly enough healthy persons to bury the dead (Benjamin Johnson, Letter to Deseret News, 15 January 1893).

From his past experiences Benjamin knew what needed to be done, and he was immediately called to help. Don Carlos Smith and George A. Smith were called to administer to and comfort the sick, while Benjamin cared for them. Two medical students, Wiley and Pendleton, were assigned to prescribe medication (Benjamin Johnson, Gibbs Letter).

Since the houses of the Saints were scattered for some distance up and down the river, Benjamin kept his horse saddled and rode from house to house giving medicines and nursing the sick. For six weeks he did not take off his boots or coat for even one night's sleep (*MLR* 61). When someone was too sick to be left alone through the night, Benjamin would ride several miles through the country to bring women to care for them. This enabled him to visit and care for a larger number of the Saints.

After four weeks without a full night's sleep, Benjamin rode out without his coat and was caught in a storm. A fever and chills overtook him, forcing him to rest for a day and a half at Bishop Oliver Granger's home until they could get word to Hyrum Smith who sent food to his sick friend. Several days later, with the help of quinine and the care of the Saints, Benjamin was again on his feet and was well enough to accept an invitation to the Prophet's house. Upon seeing Benjamin's condition, the Prophet asked him to stay with them until he was fully recovered (*MLR* 61).

Within a few days, the Prophet had a violent attack of the same sickness. Because Emma was unable to care for him, they asked Benjamin to be his nurse and companion (Benjamin Johnson, Gibbs Letter; *MLR* 61). Benjamin wrote, "It wholly evolved upon me, and both day and night, through a period of little less than two weeks, I was hardly absent from his room and if any sleep came to me it was while lying upon his bed or sitting in my chair" (Benjamin Johnson, Gibbs letter). Soon after the Prophet's recovery Benjamin "came apparently nigh unto death" through a violent attack of the fever and "was kindly looked after by the Prophet" (*Deseret News*, 16 October 1897).

Benjamin served the Saints selflessly, giving of his strength and means for many weeks. This he did privately and without public acclaim or recognition. As Charles S. Sellers observed, "The Saints are generally well informed, but of the part which Brother Johnson took, none are apprised, a fact undoubtedly arising through Brother Johnson's modesty, and perhaps lack of friends, among those who write history" (545).

Near the first of October 1839, Benjamin received a letter from his family informing him that his mother was very sick. They advised him to come as soon as possible, for it was doubtful she would recover. O. B. Huntington said,

> [Benjamin's] mother was the joy and stay of the family, and Benjamin was ready to undertake almost an impossibility to see his dearly beloved parent once more. His love for her, his faith and his will power, so far overcame the disease that he prepared hastily for the journey of over 100 miles on horseback. (Deseret News, 16 October 1897)

Through the previous two months of caring for the sick, Benjamin had ruined all his best clothes and spent all but ten dollars of the money he had saved for his mission. Feeling feverish and weak, he took double doses of quinine pills, gathered his few belongings, and began his journey. Before leaving Nauvoo, however, he stopped at the home of the Prophet to pay tithing on his remaining ten dollars. Of this parting visit Benjamin wrote,

> Going to the Prophet I told him I was ready to leave and reaching to him the bill, I said, "As this is all I have left, I want to pay a tithe of it." He saw I was weak in body and that my heart was sad in leaving him, so thinking to cheer and arouse me, when putting the nine silver dollars in my hand he playfully knocked my hand upward, and scattering the money all over the room. My heart was full of tears, and my emotion must have vent, so forgetting all but the feeling that we were boy companions playing together, I sprang at and grappled him, as though to teach him a lesson, but the lesson was all to me for on making the one grand effort to throw him, and as my strength was fictitious and my real recovery but an illusion, I collapsed and fainted in his arms. He placed me in repose, and did all necessary for my restoration and comfort. Then gathered up the scattered money, and after a period of delay, weak, trembling and desolate, yet determined to start, I led my horse to the outer gate, and as I was passing through, with the bridle on my arm, his hand detained me, and placing his hands upon my head, he seemed to pour out his soul in blessing me. He told the Lord

> I had been faithful to care for others, that I was now worn and sick, and that on my journey I would need his care, and he asked that a special guardian might go with me that day and stay with me through all my life. (Benjamin Johnson, Gibbs Letter)

This incident served to assure Benjamin that the bond of love and friendship between himself and the Prophet had grown. Throughout his life he reflected fondly upon his close association and friendship with the Prophet Joseph Smith.

With the Prophet's parting blessing to comfort and sustain him, Benjamin commenced his journey. The first night of his trip was spent near Carthage with his brother, Joel. As he was travelling the following day, Benjamin developed a severe chill, followed by a high fever. Overcome by this sickness, he fell unconscious beside the road. The Prophet's brother William, and his wife, who were out picking wild plums, found Benjamin in this condition and took him to their home in Plymouth. William's sister Lucy tenderly cared for him until he was able to resume his journey at ten o'clock the next day. Benjamin travelled that day without suffering a chill, but the fourth day he was stricken even more severely than before. This time a kind stranger picked him up from the roadside and took him home.

In this way, alternately traveling and resting, Benjamin got home and found his mother and sister in better health than himself. He was frightfully ill, his money gone and his clothing worn and ruined. With so much sickness in his family, they were also in poor condition with very limited resources. Considering the circumstances, Benjamin's prospects for fulfilling his mission seemed dim. His condition grew worse and he had the chills every day. The spasms in his stomach became severe, and he began hemorrhaging and suffered from loss of blood. So serious was his condition that the doctor said if the chills came again, he would die.

In pondering the doctor's words, Benjamin decided it would be better for him to die because he was a burden to his friends and had no money for his mission to England. The doctor prescribed another medication to be taken in double doses twice as often. After two days, the chills, paroxysm, and hemorrhaging ceased and life began to look hopeful again (*MLR* 63-64).

On 5 October 1839, Elders Brigham Young and Heber C. Kimball arrived in Springfield on their way to England (*HC* 4:11). Both of them had left Nauvoo extremely ill and were still unfit to travel. Their families were deathly ill as well and in great poverty. Benjamin wrote,

> But when they saw how sick I was, and without money or suitable clothing they did not urge me to go but left it to my

> own faith and desire. I much wished to go but was so diffident, had no missionary experience, and fearing they would feel me a burden I had not faith enough to start. They told me to take a mission east as soon as I was able and this I felt determined to do. (*MLR* 64)

A Mission to Canada

In February 1840, Benjamin's desire to fill a mission increased. Although he was too sick to sit up for very long and unable to walk more than a few yards. Benjamin let it be known that he would leave for his mission if he could obtain one day's ride out of Springfield. Mr. James Standing volunteered to take him in a sleigh as far as the snow would last. Lying on a bed in the back of the sleigh, Benjamin was taken to Paris, Illinois, a distance of 110 miles. Here Mr. Standing left him. Benjamin, recalling his feeling of isolation, said,

> Here I was left, and here now was a test of fortitude and perseverance that may find few equals.
>
> Only twenty-one years of age, I was alone, sick, and among strangers without money, the mud deep, weather stormy, without education or mission experience and bashful beyond the power of words to tell. Yet I did not wish myself back. The Lord had brought me carefully through an experience calculated to teach me that it would not do to depend upon my own wisdom and strength, and as for my own capability, it was really as nothing, and if the Lord had ceased to care for me I was of little worth. I told the Lord I had taken that mission because I was told to by His servants, and if there was anything a poor ignorant boy could do to please Him I was willing to try and do my best, but if He left me alone I was certain I could accomplish nothing. (*MLR* 65-66)

From Paris, Illinois Benjamin walked to Pleasant Garden, Indiana where he met Jonathan Crosby and his family, whom he had known in Kirtland. Soon after arriving he again became sick with chills and fever and was kindly cared for by Sister Crosby. When he had sufficiently recovered, he was invited to preach.

Benjamin had never before attempted preaching in a public meeting. As he stood with his eyes closed and began to speak, the Spirit came upon him and he preached one hour and a half. After the meeting a number of people came forward requesting baptism, and Benjamin baptized his first convert.

Calls to preach came from many directions, and he increased in confidence and began to feel the spirit of his mission (*MLR* 67).

However, Benjamin was once again distracted from his missionary work. He was befriended by Dr. Knights, a prominent physician in the area, who was also a member of the Church. Dr. Knights was very devoted to his wife and two young sons. When his wife became ill and died, he was heartbroken. But adding to his bereavement was her shocking deathbed confession that Dr. Knights' young apprentice had seduced and dishonored her. Immediately following the funeral, Dr. Knights secretly attacked his young protege, beating him with a club and shooting him with a shotgun. The young man miraculously survived, although he was severely injured. Dr. Knights confided in Benjamin the details of the event and of his obsession to complete the young man's execution. But Benjamin was able to persuade him to do otherwise and to travel with him the four hundred miles to Kirtland and then on to Canada. Benjamin preached along the way, in places where the Doctor was known. Dr. Knights returned to Kirtland, but Benjamin stayed in Canada and continued his mission.

In Toronto, Canada, Benjamin found himself alone among strangers, over a thousand miles from home, on foot and penniless. He tried to get back into the spirit of his mission, but after unsuccessful attempts at proselyting, he concluded that "instead of being in a new and fresh field of labor I was in the stubble field, already harvested by older and more experienced elders." So he moved into the rural areas where he preached twice a week to large congregations.

Benjamin began to feel a degree of self-importance which he soon learned was not approved of by the Lord. On one occasion, as he stood to preach, he began with a scripture from Daniel, but the scripture that had seemed so full of light was now dark. He turned to others, but all was dark. The light of the Lord had left him, and he stood before that large congregation alone in his weakness (*MLR* 67–73). When he suddenly became aware of his own pride and ingratitude, he wept openly before the silent onlookers.

> I asked them if they had not often heard me speak to their understanding and edification, and if I had not always told them I was but a plow boy sent out like the apostles of old, to preach by the inspiration of the Holy Ghost, and that without it, I was nothing, as was now proved there before them; that for some cause known to the Lord, His Spirit had left me, and they now saw me in my own strength, in which I could do nothing. I said, "As you have come out today only

> to be disappointed, perhaps you would not be willing to come again." But I saw they believed me honest, and I said, "If you will allow me to have another appointment, rise to your feet." When all the congregation rose, I said I would preach again if the Lord would help me, at the usual time, and dismissed the meeting. A feeling of kindness pervaded all, but oh, how small I felt. (*MLR* 73-74)

As Benjamin continued his labors, many believed what he taught, yet no one requested baptism. He wondered if perhaps he looked too young or feeble to baptize anyone. He was very thin and frequently afflicted with pain in his side. However, he seemed to lose all care for his health or life and would sometimes stand for three hours vehemently speaking to a congregation. So great was his desire to bear his testimony that he felt he could not die in a better cause. He thought that it was the Lord's business to take care of him, if he was of any use to the Lord.

Seeking for a more receptive group of people, Benjamin travelled north to South Gilensburgh, and then on to North Gilensburgh, on the shore of Lake Simcoe. Again he found people who he felt believed his message, but they also seemed to think him too young and feeble to be trusted with their baptism. His health was poor, and he was often told that he would not live to return home. Although Benjamin seemed to be getting weaker, this did not deter him from filling every invitation to preach.

Benjamin recorded an unusual experience which occurred in this locality.

> In this vicinity there were many Indians on an island in Lake Simcoe. . . One morning while taking my walk I came upon a number of Indian families encamped. I found one Indian who could talk very good English and was quite intelligent. I questioned him in relation to their traditions of the past, and of their hopes of the future. At first he did not seem disposed to talk, but seemed willing to listen. I commenced talking to him of their forefathers, when the Spirit came upon me, and I spoke in their own tongue. All the Indians came running to me, to listen with glistening eyes and great attention through all my talk to them. When I ceased, the Indian with whom I had been talking said, "You talk good Mohawk, and we all understand." This was manifest to me, the Spirit of the Lord rested upon them, and they would now tell me anything I wished to know pertaining to their religion. I learned that their hopes of the future were

> almost identical with our own, and they realized that because of wars and wickedness they had been cursed, but that through the ancient fathers it was promised that the power of their enemies should be broken, and a great prophet or prince would be sent to them by the Great Spirit. All of this was in the highest degree joyful to me, for I felt that I had been led to them to bear a great testimony to these Lamanites, that would not by them be forgotten, and that it would live in the hearts of their children. (*MLR* 76)

Leaving Canada about the middle of November 1840, Benjamin walked toward Kirtland. He stopped at Fredonia, his native home and was greeted by old friends. This was his second visit to Fredonia since he had left seven years earlier. This time he wanted to bear a stronger testimony in hopes someone would believe him. He was disappointed once again. His former friends and neighbors could not be awakened to any love for the gospel. Realizing this, he bore his last testimony to them and left (*MLR* 77-78).

While travelling through the snow and cold in Erie County, Pennsylvania, Benjamin felt impressed to visit a family he had been asked to contact. At once, word went out that a Mormon elder had come. Many people appeared anxious to hear him, so Benjamin preached to several large congregations. At last, a wide door for preaching seemed to be opening for him. But the opposition was not asleep. Soon local ministers came and filled the stand, without invitation, fully expecting to overwhelm and embarrass the Mormon boy (*MLR* 79).

Following one of Benjamin's talks, Rev. Jesse E. Church, a talented and renowned preacher in that area, arose and announced that he would preach the next evening. He said that he would put down all this Mormonism and that he had once challenged Sidney Rigdon, who would not meet him in debate. Benjamin visited two of the Reverend's services and held two of his own. In referring to one of his own meetings, Benjamin wrote,

> I invited any present who wished baptism to arise. Seven of his [Rev. Church's] own members arose, and repairing to the creek and cutting through fifteen inches of ice, were baptized by the boy for whom he had shown such contempt... Instead of squelching Mormonism, and the Mormon boy, he had squelched himself, and few were left to follow or honor him. (*MLR* 79-80)

Although Benjamin preached two or three times each day for many weeks, he did not feel very successful. Benjamin felt that it was not really truth the people were seeking, but they were interested only in his novel and exciting ideas. They were bored with what their own ministers taught and were looking for someone else to follow. As the dullness of winter waned and spring brought it's own sensations, his invitations to preach died away (*MLR* 84). Benjamin stayed in Pennsylvania and worked at various jobs through the summer.

During this time Benjamin met the Walker family and Jane Matilda Warren, Mrs. Walker's sister who was living with them. Jane Matilda, in her seventeenth year, was a beautiful young woman with a warm personality and friendly manner. From their first meeting Benjamin was interested in her, and they were in almost constant association. Although Jane Matilda had many admirers, Benjamin felt certain his attentions pleased her the most. Most of their conversations centered around the gospel, and although there was no promise between them, they mutually understood each other's hopes regarding their future together (Benjamin Johnson, Handwritten Manuscript of *My Life's Review*).

Since Benjamin enjoyed the close relationship with Jane Matilda, he decided to stay for a time. He soon learned, however, that Mr. and Mrs. Walker opposed her involvement with Benjamin, for they wanted her to marry Mr. Walker's brother. This, along with the feeling that Jane Matilda seemed to be growing less interested in him and the Church, Benjamin decided to leave. He told her that he would write to her and come back to see her.

Benjamin wrote several letters but never received any in return. However, he kept his promise to see her again. In November, he borrowed a horse and buggy from his father and travelled through deep mud to Pennsylvania, determined to "bring back a wife or sever every tie" that held him to her. Of this meeting with Jane Matilda, Benjamin wrote,

> I felt indignant at her neglect to write me, and when I arrived at Mr. Walker's, and greeted all others, I merely bowed to her. The next day passed in visiting my old friends, but on the afternoon following I gave notice that I should leave the next morning. I saw the crimson flush her face, and she went at once to her own room, where I soon made an errand to follow, and found her weeping. I asked the cause. She said she could not see why I should treat her with such coldness. I told her of the letters I had written—all unanswered—and I had concluded she had changed her mind, and would marry Mr. Walker. She declared she had received no letters; that Mr. Walker and her sister were opposed to me, and had kept my letters from her, and that

> she did not love and could not marry any other man. I put my arm around her, and told her my love for her was unchanged, and that if she really did love me still I was only too glad. But if she was to be my wife she must make up her mind at once, that I would stay another day, and then she should go with me to the Justice of the Peace, be married, and start with me for the West. I felt it was hard for her, but oh! how I hoped she would conclude to do so. She said she could not go so soon, that she must visit her parents in Canada, as she had promised them. But she could never love another, and she felt sure I would not leave her. I told her if I went from there and left her she would probably never see me again, and the only hope I could hold out to her was to go with me, and I earnestly hoped and prayed that the Lord would incline her to do that which would be for the best for us both.
>
> When I gave her the positive assurance that I would start homeward in the spring, she said perhaps she would go and that she would think upon it till morning and let me know. Oh how sorrowful was the thought of leaving her forever!...I waited until morning, yet fearful that we were to part, to meet no more in this life. In early morning I found her alone sobbing and heart broken. I clasped her in my arms, but read her decision without a word. "And must I," I asked, "go and leave you. Must I go alone?" "I cannot go," she said, "but I am sure you will come back again." But I said, "never, never again!" I clasped her in a last embrace and almost wild with emotion of grief I left her alone. Alone in my buggy I whipped up my horse and I drove for miles before I could sufficiently control my emotions. (Benjamin Johnson, Handwritten Manuscript of *My Life's Review*)

Benjamin's sister Julia and her husband Almon W. Babbitt invited him to come live with them in Kirtland. He welcomed the opportunity. After serving about two years as a missionary, he was going home wiser because of his experiences and more courageous in defending his religious beliefs.

Benjamin noted that the spirit of settling and rebuilding Kirtland was growing among some members of the Church, even though the Prophet had counselled them to gather at Nauvoo. It was apparent to Benjamin that all those who were faithful Saints would follow the Prophet, but his brother-in-law was concerned about losing his business if he left Kirtland. Because of

Brother Babbitt's disobedience he was severely reprimanded in a revelation which the Prophet Joseph Smith received on 19 January 1841. The revelation stated in part,

> And with my servant Almon Babbitt, there are many things with which I am not pleased; behold, he aspireth to establish his counsel instead of the counsel which I have ordained, even that of the Presidency of my Church; and he setteth up a golden calf for the worship of my people." (*HC* 4:28; Doctrine and Covenants 124:84)

Benjamin observed that Brother Babbitt was hurt by the rebuke and was "in great temptation to complain and turn his heel upon the Prophet" (MLR 87). Soon after the revelation, action was taken by the Church leaders to disfellowship Almon W. Babbitt (*HC* 4:424). Benjamin continued to have great respect and love for his brother-in-law. He said,

> Almon was a magnificent character; he dared any tribunal to protect his client or his belief, and yet this characteristic ofttimes gave him trouble. He often disagreed with his superior authorities, but his redeeming quality was his honest humility. He always made humble amends when wrong, and would go to any end to right his wrong. He was kind at heart, never arrogant with anyone less fortunate than himself. I was three years younger than he, but he always made me feel much older and was always kind and generous to me. (Almon Whiting Babbitt, "Our Pioneer Heritage")

Benjamin, greatly concerned for Brother Babbitt's spiritual welfare, used every influence he could to induce him to return to Nauvoo. However, Almon had bought many notes and claims against the Prophet and the Church, and Benjamin feared he would use them to injure the Prophet and do great harm to himself. Benjamin's love for his brother-in-law was so great that he was willing to do anything to help strengthen Almon's love for the gospel and fellowship in the Church (*HC* 4:424). At Almon's invitation Benjamin joined him as a partner in obtaining a small law library. Benjamin began to study law with him so that he could be close to him and encourage him in his church activity.

While living in the Babbitt home, Benjamin met a young lady, Melissa Bloomfield LeBaron, who was a student at the Academy in Kirtland. Melissa was an orphan but Benjamin believed that in appearance, education, and ease of manner she had no equal in that vicinity. Because Benjamin was a highly respected and successful returned missionary and Melissa was a comely young heiress beloved by all who knew her, their friends hoped that they would "make a match."

Benjamin felt that the Lord had provided him with a young lady of culture and refinement. She was also a good Latter-day Saint who would be willing to go with him to Nauvoo. When Benjamin proposed to Melissa, he knew before he asked her that she would accept (*MLR* 86).

On Christmas day 1841, the couple was married by Almon W. Babbitt in the house where the Prophet had lived in Kirtland. There were so many friends and well-wishers at the wedding that every room in the house was crowded.

Benjamin was now more determined than ever to follow the Prophet and he anxiously began working to earn sufficient funds to move to Nauvoo, the "home of the Church in the west" (*MLR* 86).

Near the end of January, Benjamin and his new bride travelled to Rochester to collect money from her inheritance. This trip was also to be a mission among her relatives and friends (Benjamin Johnson, "A Life Sketch"). When Benjamin and Melissa inquired about her inheritance, they were disappointed to learn that much of it—about four hundred dollars in interest and some valuable household goods left by her mother—had been "borrowed" by a Bishop Granger. The money had been spent and the household goods scattered. Melissa was never reimbursed although they did recover the principal (*MLR* 73).

Return to Nauvoo

With financial matters in hand, Benjamin and Melissa prepared to move to Nauvoo. In June 1842, they left Kirtland with Benjamin's father, and his sisters, Julia and Esther. Almon W. Babbitt planned to join them later, bringing with him goods to start a merchandise business.

Travelling in beautiful weather and on good roads, they anticipated a safe and pleasant journey. In their eagerness to see their family and friends, they decided to travel on Sunday. About noon as they dismounted from their young and spirited horses, the animals became frightened and broke loose from their handlers. They ran wildly into a wooded area, smashing the wagons and scattering goods behind them. Regarding this costly experience, Benjamin wrote,

> A greater smash up it was never my bad luck to see. At first I looked upon the wreck as impossible to reconstruct, but we gathered up and put the parts together and got all mechanical help possible, labored hard, and by the next Sabbath day we had so far reconstructed our vehicles that by noon we

> hitched up, and feeling again tempted through anxiety we drove fifteen miles to early camp, but when unhitching our horses they again—all but one—took fright, took the back track, and as though spurred by the Evil One ran the whole distance to our former camp. Upon the horse left I followed with utmost speed and found them with legs terribly lacerated by the tug chains, and streaming with blood and sweat. I made no stop, but hurried them back as fast as I could ride, arriving in camp just before sunset, and was up much of the night bathing the bruised legs of the animals, and telling the Lord if He would now forgive me and give us His blessing for the rest of the journey I would promise never to forget the experience of those two Sabbath days. We started early the next morning, and with all the fatigue and bruises, our animals seemed all right, and made us no trouble afterwards. I knew then and I know now that this experience was given to me of the Lord for my profit, and to record as a testimony to my children, that the Lord will not hold in favor those who do not rest upon and hallow the Sabbath day. (*MLR* 89-90)

Benjamin and his group arrived in Ramus, Illinois on 1 July 1842. When they were reunited with their family, they learned of the recent death of Amos, Benjamin's youngest brother.

In contemplating the changes in his life since he had left Nauvoo, Benjamin was moved to write,

> My return after an absence of two and a half years of such varied experience, was a time of glad greeting for all. I had left home when but a boy in experience, the uneducated one—starting while sick and without money; and truly, that promised Angel had been with me, to preserve my life and to open the way for my return in health, not now alone, for a loved and loving wife accompanied me, I was not now so poor, and I felt truly the Lord had given me more than I had earned and repaid all my sacrifices. (*MLR* 91)

Benjamin soon travelled to Nauvoo where he was welcomed by the Prophet Joseph Smith. Among other things, they discussed the business matters between the Prophet and Almon W. Babbitt. Benjamin expressed confidence that with the Prophet's arm around him, Brother Babbitt would remain true to the faith. This was the first time Benjamin had ever spoken to the Prophet to express feelings and opinions of his own. He felt that the bond between himself and Joseph grew as he told the Prophet how much he loved his brother-in-law and how anxious he was to help him. The Prophet told Benjamin to bring Almon to see him as soon as he arrived in Nauvoo.

When Joseph and Almon met to discuss matters relating to the notes Almon had purchased, Brother Joseph said, "Now, Brother Almon, we will not disagree, for here is Brother Benjamin; you have all confidence in him and so have I; and now let us leave all our differences to him and stand by it, and be good friends forevermore," to which Almon agreed (*MLR* 91).

Because of his role as intercessor in this problem, Benjamin was given other positions of trust. He was given power of attorney for the Church's property in Kirtland and Ramus, which responsibility he held until the Prophet's martyrdom.

In Nauvoo Benjamin entered into another business partnership with Brother Babbitt. Prospects looked very good, and he felt that business success might be the road to real usefulness in the Church. But then Brigham Young, President of the Quorum of the Twelve Apostles, called Benjamin to preside over the branches of the Church in Pittsburgh. He felt sorrowful "like the rich young ruler who did not want to leave his wealth." It was with mixed feelings that Benjamin told the Prophet of his call. Joseph told him to "tell Brother Brigham that Brother Joseph said, 'Send some one else.'" Benjamin felt the Prophet had discerned his feelings and decided accordingly (*MLR* 92).

Benjamin and Melissa made their home at Ramus, Illinois, about thirty miles east of Nauvoo. His work involved selling goods, keeping a tavern, and doing all the Church business in Ramus, which was second in size only to Nauvoo. He later confessed that he was beginning to like the idea of getting rich. However, he did not forget his Priesthood responsibilities and frequently preached both in meetings at home and in the surrounding area.

While living in Ramus, Benjamin's friendship with the Prophet Joseph Smith became even more intimate.

> The Prophet often came to our town, but after my arrival, he lodged in no house but mine, and I was proud of his partiality and took great delight in his society and friendship. When with us, there was no lack of amusement; for with jokes, games, etc., he was always ready to provoke merriment, one phase of which was matching couplets in rhyme, by which we were at times in rivalry; and his fraternal feeling, in great degree did away with the disparity of age or greatness of his calling.

> I can now see, as President George A. Smith afterwards said, that I was then really "the bosom friend and companion of the Prophet Joseph." I was as welcome at the Mansion as at my own house, and on one occasion when at a full table of his family and close friends, he placed me at his right hand and introduced me as his "friend, Brother B. F. Johnson, at whose house he sat at a better table than his own." (*MLR* 92-93)

Benjamin felt that such favoritism aroused some jealousy among the local residents. The Johnson family was quite numerous and influential, and some people dubbed them the "Royal Family." When the Prophet heard of this *honor* conferred upon the Johnsons by his neighbors, he said the name was and should be a reality as they were a royal family. Even knowing the intemperance of Benjamin's father, Joseph said that Ezekiel would yet be a great man and stand at the head of a kingdom. On one occasion, the Prophet blessed Benjamin's mother and told her that not one of her children would ever leave the Church (*MLR* 93-94).

Personally Taught by a Prophet

In his daily journal dated Saturday, 4 March 1843 the Prophet Joseph Smith records,

> In council with Brother Benjamin F. Johnson and others from Ramus, on the subject of building a meetinghouse there, out of Church property I told them the property of the Church should be disposed of by the direction of the Trustee-in-Trust, appointed by the voice of the whole Church, and made the following comparison—There is a wheel; Nauvoo is the hub; we will drive the first spoke in Ramus, second in LaHarpe, third Shokoquon, fourth in Lima; that is half the wheel. The other half is over the river: we will let that alone at present. We will call other Saints from Iowa to these spokes, then send elders over and convert the whole people. (*HC* 5:296)

This seems to be the first time Benjamin understood the idea of spokes of a wheel representing stakes in the organization of the Church.

When the Prophet stayed in the Johnson home, Benjamin would take the opportunity to ask him gospel questions pertaining to the past, present, and future. In his journal dated May 1843, the Prophet Joseph Smith recorded, "Tuesday, 16...went to Benjamin F. Johnson's with William Clayton to sleep. Before retiring, I gave Brother and Sister Johnson some instructions on the priesthood" (*HC* 5:391). On that occasion, the Prophet received the revelation contained in the Doctrine and Covenants 131:1-6. Of these experiences, Benjamin wrote,

> On April 2nd and May 16, 1843 the Prophet was at my house with Wm. Clayton as Scribe, at which time was written, in answer to questions asked, all of Sections 130 & 131 Doc. & Cov., and he then gave to us all keys of knowledge contained in Sec 129 & 132...before it was written. (Benjamin Johnson, Letter to President Anthon H. Lund)

On 20 October 1843 the Prophet recorded that, "In the evening I gave instructions to Benjamin F. Johnson and others in relation to the blessings of the everlasting covenant and the sealings of the Priesthood" (*HC* 5:391). Benjamin later testified in an affidavit that on this date President Smith "sealed my first wife to me for time and all eternity" (Benjamin Johnson, Affidavit 4:221-22).

During one of his visits to the Johnson home, the Prophet Joseph Smith said, "The way I know in whom to confide—God tells me in whom I may place confidence" (*HC* 5:392). He had confided in Benjamin on many occasions and found him to be a friend worthy of trust. As time passed, the Prophet's confidence in him increased until, as Benjamin said, "It did seem to me that he had few secrets to keep from me" (Benjamin Johnson, Letter to Deseret News, June 25, 1902; see also *HC* 4:260-63, 267, 341). One night Joseph showed Benjamin his garments and explained their meaning. He also told him about the endowment and explained that free-masonry was the apostate form of the endowment just as sectarian religion was the apostate religion (*MLR* 96).[4]

Introduction to the Law of Plural Marriage

The Prophet privately taught Benjamin one doctrine which would greatly affect the rest of his life. In recalling this experience, Benjamin wrote,

> About the first of April, 1843, the Prophet with some of the Twelve and others came to Macedonia [Ramus] to hold a meeting, which was to convene in a large cabinet shop owned by Brother Joseph E. and myself, and as usual he put up at my house. Early on Sunday morning he said, "Come Brother Bennie, let us have a walk." I took his arm and he led the way into a by-place in the edge of the woods surrounded by tall brush and trees. Here, as we sat down upon a

[4]Masonry was a popular organization in early America and the Prophet and other church leaders were members of a Masonic lodge while living in Nauvoo (Bilderback).

> log he began to tell me that the Lord had revealed to him that plural patriarchal marriage was according to His law; and that the Lord had not only revealed it to him but had commanded him to obey it; that he was required to take other wives; and that he wanted my sister Almira for one of them, and wished me to see and talk to her upon the subject. (*MLR* 94)

Learning of plural marriage was a shocking experience for Benjamin. The whole idea was in strong opposition to his puritan background as well as the accepted standards of American society. However, Benjamin had great faith in Joseph Smith as a prophet of God. In describing his reaction to the Prophet's message, Benjamin said,

> If a thunderbolt had fallen at my feet I could hardly have been more shocked or amazed. He saw the struggle in my mind and went on to explain. But the shock was too great for me to comprehend anything, and in almost an agony of feeling I looked him squarely in the eye, and said, while my heart gushed up before him, "Brother Joseph, this is all new to me; it may all be true—you know, but I do not. To my education it is all wrong, but I am going, with the help of the Lord to do just what you say, with this promise to you—that if ever I know you do this to degrade my sister I will kill you, as the Lord lives." (*MLR* 94-95)

Joseph smiled and, looking into Benjamin's eyes, told him softly that he would never see that day, and that Benjamin himself would not only know of its truth, but would fulfill the law and greatly rejoice in it (Benjamin Johnson, Gibbs Letter; *MLR* 95). Benjamin asked the Prophet how he could teach his sister something he himself did not understand. Joseph told Benjamin that when he opened his mouth to talk to her, light would come to him and he would understand; his mouth would be full and his tongue loosened (Benjamin Johnson, Gibbs Letter). The Prophet added that he would preach a sermon that day which only Benjamin would understand. The sermon focused on the parable of the talents. Benjamin understood that the talents represented wives and children (Benjamin F. Johnson's Testimony, pp. 221–22). However, speaking to Almira about this sensitive matter was a test of Benjamin's faith.

> To me there was a horror in the idea of speaking to my sister upon such a subject, the thought of which made me sick. But I had promised, and it must be done. I did not remember [Joseph's] words, and have faith that light would come, I

> only thought, "How dark it all looks to me." But I must do it, and so told my sister I wished to see her in a room by herself, where I soon found her seated. I stood before her trembling, my knees shaking, but I opened my mouth and my heart opened to the light of the Lord, my tongue was loosened and I was filled with the Holy Ghost. I preached a sermon that forever converted me and her also to the principle, even though her heart was not yet won by the Prophet. And so I had great joy after my tribulation. (*MLR* 95)

Benjamin's and Almira's acceptance of this new doctrine, which was so contrary to their religious background, is evidence of the faith and confidence they had in the Prophet. The subject that had seemed so dark to Benjamin became the most lucid and plain of all gospel principles. Benjamin said that never again did he need evidence to sustain this high and holy principle. Later in his life, he explained the divine origin of the law of plural marriage in a letter to the President of the United States in which he wrote,

> I was taught by [Joseph] in the principle of Plural or Celestial Marriage, as a revelation from the Almighty direct to him, and for his Church, and it was shown, to me plainly, that the whole object and end of matrimony was the procreation of our species and that the command to multiply and replenish the earth fell upon all the children of Adam both in obligation and privilege.
>
> He also unfolded to me the scripture in which I saw that the most honored men of Bible history, those of whom, and by whom, the scriptures were written were polygamists and that so great was the distinction between polygamy and adultery that Moses prepared the tables of stone on which the Lord, with His finger in his presence wrote, "Thou shalt not commit adultery." And while the glory of God so shone from the face of Moses that, Israel could not look upon him. Yet at the same time he was a polygamist. And while the law in Israel was death for adultery, Moses and many of the camp of Israel had a plurality of wives, and so far was this principle honored of God that when His Son Jesus was to be born, He chose for him the royal lineage of Abraham, Isaac, Jacob, Moses, Boaz, David, Solomon and other wise patriarchs and kings, who had honored the law of plural marriage.

> With these teachings, accompanied by the spirit in which they were given, I was able to overcome my Puritanical ideas of monogamic marriage. (Benjamin Johnson, Letter to the President of the United States)

Within a few days, Almira accompanied Benjamin to their sister Delcena's home in Nauvoo where they were met by the Prophet, his brother Hyrum, and William Clayton, the Prophet's private secretary (*MLR* 95). Of their meeting, Benjamin wrote,

> Brother Hyrum at once took me in hand, apparently in fear I was not fully converted, and this was the manner of his talk to me: "Now Benjamin, you must not be afraid of this new doctrine, for it is all right. You know Brother Hyrum doesn't get carried away by worldly things, and he fought this principle until the Lord showed him it was true. I know that Joseph was commanded to take more wives, and he waited until an angel with a drawn sword stood before him and declared that if he longer delayed fulfilling that command that he would slay him." This was the manner of Brother Hyrum's teaching to me, which I then did not need, as I was fully converted. (Benjamin Johnson, Gibbs Letter)

After some instruction, Almira stood by the Prophet's side and Brother Clayton sealed her to Joseph as his wife.[5]

Almira continued to live in the Johnson home but stayed with the Prophet on his visits to Ramus (Benjamin Johnson, Gibbs Letter). Seeking to provide a home for her, Joseph authorized Benjamin to construct a large brick residence at Ramus, which was to be the joint residence for Almira and Benjamin's own family (Benjamin Johnson, Letter to Deseret News, 25 June 1902). Benjamin also became the legal business agent for the Prophet Joseph Smith.

Joseph asked Benjamin for permission to marry his youngest sister, Esther, but when he was told that she was already promised to someone else, he dropped the matter. Benjamin suggested that Joseph marry Mary Ann Hale, the orphan who had been raised by the Johnson family. The Prophet replied, "No, but she is for you. You keep her and take her for your

[5]Following the death of the Prophet, Almira married James Reuben Barton and five daughters were born to them, none of whom married. She later separated from Barton after he apostatized from the Church. Delcena, who had also been sealed to Joseph, remained a widow after his death (Rose A. Openshaw, "Highlights of the Life of Julia and Ezekiel Johnson")

wife and you will be blessed." Benjamin was hesitant and said that he thought this was rushing his blessings too fast. But the spirit of it came to him, and he began to think of her as a wife the Lord had given him.

Benjamin now thought of the doctrine of plural marriage as a law which he would soon embrace, for he accepted plural marriage as a duty which he owed because of his calling as an elder in the true Church (Benjamin Johnson, Letter to the President of the United States).

Because the Prophet realized what the public reaction would be if the doctrine of plural marriage was taught openly, he discussed it only with those in whom he had great confidence. Benjamin recalled, "I do so well remember his declarations in the meetings of the Saints, that the Lord had revealed to him principles, that should he teach and practice them, those who were now his best friends would become his bitterest enemies" (*MLR* 97). Nothing the Prophet Joseph Smith had taught previously, departed so radically from the social norms of the day. As early as 1842, apostates accused him of immoral teachings and practices and this soon led to open opposition.

Benjamin sensed that the Prophet was somewhat depressed on occasion. Of the Prophet Joseph's last visit to Ramus, Benjamin wrote,

> After he had all evening preached with great animation to a large congregation, and had blessed nineteen children, he turned to me and said, "Benjamin, I am tired, let us go home," which only a block distant, we soon reached, and entering we found a warm fire with a large chair in front, and my wife sitting near with her babe, our eldest, upon her lap, and approaching her, I said, "Now, Melissa, see what we have lost by your not going to meeting, Brother Joseph has blessed all the children in the place but ours, and it is left out in the cold." But the Prophet at once said, "You shall lose nothing," and proceeded to bless our first born, and then with a deep drawn breath, as a sigh of weariness, he sank down heavily in his chair. (Benjamin Johnson, Gibbs Letter)
>
> The Prophet said, "Oh! I am so tired—so tired that I often feel to long for my day of rest, for what has there in this life but tribulation for me? From a boy I have been persecuted by my enemies, and now even my friends are beginning to join with them, to hate and persecute me! Why should I not wish for my time of rest?"

> His words to me were ominous, and they brought a shadow as of death over my spirit, and I said, "Oh, Joseph! how could you think of leaving us? How as a people could we do without you?" He saw my feelings were sorrowful and said kindly, "Bennie, if I was on the other side of the veil I could do many times more for my friends than I can do while I am with them here." (*MLR* 97)

> The Prophet continued, "I should not be far away from you, and if on the other side of the veil I should still be working with you, and with a power greatly increased, to roll on this kingdom." And such was the tone, earnestness and pathos of his words to me then, that they can never be fully recalled but with emotion. (Benjamin Johnson, Gibbs Letter)

During these trying times Benjamin became concerned for his father who had not accepted the gospel and had spoken out against the Church. His concern increased when his mother, obedient to the counsel of the Prophet, was sealed to Father John Smith, brother of Joseph Smith Sr. and Patriarch of the Church. Benjamin felt sorrow for he loved his father and knew him to be "a kind and loving parent, a just and noble spirited man." In spite of these feelings, Benjamin was consoled by his mother's sealing and was comforted by the Prophet's words that his father would see a better day (*MLR* 98-99).

On 28 March 1844 Benjamin's sister, Esther Melita, married David Tully LeBaron, Sr. and they lived in the Mansion House. Esther was present at a meeting when the temple garment was presented to some of the Saints in Nauvoo. The Prophet held it up before them and said it was the exact pattern of the one shown to him by an angel. It was to be a protection against all physical and spiritual dangers if they would be faithful to the covenants they made with the Lord. Esther was so impressed that she made "union suits" of the same pattern for her children in hopes they would learn to love the garment as they grew older. Esther and her husband were caretakers of the Nauvoo temple and witnessed it burn at the hands of a mob on 19 November 1848. They brought the key of the Nauvoo temple to Utah with them ("Esther Melita Johnson LeBaron," National Society Daughters of the Utah Pioneers).

The Council of Fifty

On 11 March 1844 the Prophet Joseph Smith held a council meeting to organize the political kingdom of God. This was a separate organization of the Church to function as an "outer wall of government around the inner wall of priesthood" (Benjamin Johnson, Gibbs Letter). As it was composed of about fifty members, including the Twelve Apostles and other most trusted friends of the Prophet, it was called the Council of Fifty (Barrett, 579–80). Some of the Church authorities were not on this council, such as Presidents Rigdon, Law, and Marks; the High Council; and Presidents of Quorums (Benjamin Johnson, Gibbs Letter).

Benjamin and Almon W. Babbitt were called to be members of the Council at its inception. They had the privilege of being taught by the Prophet in private meetings where many new doctrines and practices were explained.

> The keys of the endowments and plural marriage had been given, and some had received their Second Anointing. Baptism for the dead had been taught and the keys committed....These sacred principles were then committed to but few, but not only were they committed to me from the first, but from the first I was authorized by the Prophet to teach them to others, when I was led to do so. (*MLR* 98)

Sitting in meetings with the presiding officers of the Church was an opportunity which Benjamin cherished (*MLR* 83). One of the members said, "Being called into the Council appears to me to be one of the greatest steps in my life" (Minutes of Council of Fifty, 10 April 1880).

As the Prophet feared, some of those who had been intimately associated with him in the leading councils of the Church did not accept the teaching of plural marriage and looked upon it as the corrupt doctrine of a fallen prophet. Having lost confidence in their leader, these men set about secretly to remove the Prophet and establish their own leadership (Neff 28-30). Traitors inside joined with outside enemies and as the Prophet Joseph foresaw, "the days of tribulation were now fast approaching" (*MLR* 98-99). Benjamin recalled,

> As the Prophet so often told us, so it came to pass; and those he had called around him as a cordon of safety and strength were worse than a rope of sand, and were now forging his fetters. William Law was his first counselor, Wilson Law, Major General of the Legion, Wm. Marks, President of the Stake; the Higbys, his confidential attorneys, and Dr. Foster, his financial business agent. All of these and many others entered into secret covenant so much worse than Judas, that they would have the Prophet's life, just in fulfillment of what he had said so often publicly. With all their power, they

> began to make a party strong enough to destroy the Prophet. (*MLR* 99)
>
> I will relate a dream told to us in council by the Prophet but a short time before his death, which was as follows: "I dreamed that by the Laws, Marks, Higbys and Fosters, I was bound, both hand and foot, and cast into a deep well, soon after which I heard screams of terror and cries of "Oh! Brother Joseph, save us, save us." This cry continued until with my elbows and toes I had worked my way to the top, and looking out, I saw all of those who had bound me within the folds of a terrible serpent, that was preparing to swallow them, and I told them thatas they had bound me, I could render them no assistance. (Benjamin Johnson, Gibbs Letter)

The Prophet was powerless to help them, and they were devoured by the serpent (*MLR* 100). Benjamin never forgot this dream for those were the men who later opened the way for the Prophet's assassination (Benjamin Johnson, Gibbs Letter). Speaking of the Prophet Joseph Smith, Benjamin said, "Many great things were given by him, some of which, as with the ancient disciples, we could not comprehend until fulfilled" (*MLR* 101).

In April 1844 the Prophet spent considerable time instructing the Twelve, and Benjamin was present when he made an unusual presentation in one of their last meetings. Having given the Twelve all of the keys of the Kingdom of God, the Prophet Joseph Smith then gave them a charge regarding their responsibilities. Benjamin recorded,

> With great feeling and animation [the Prophet] graphically reviewed his life of persecution, labor and sacrifice for the Church and Kingdom of God, both of which he declared were now organized upon the earth. The burden of which had become too great for him longer to carry, that he was weary and tired with the weight he so long had borne, and he then said, with great vehemence: "And in the name of the Lord, I now shake from my shoulders the responsibilities of bearing off the Kingdom of God to all the world, and here and now I place that responsibility, with all the keys, powers, and privileges pertaining thereto, upon the shoulders of you the Twelve Apostles, in connection with this council; and if you will accept this, to do it, God shall bless you mightily and shall open your way; and if you do it not you will be

> damned. I am henceforth free from this responsibility and I now shake my garments clear and free from the blood of this generation and of all men;" and shaking his skirt with great vehemence he raised himself from the floor, while the spirit that accompanied his words thrilled every heart as with a feeling that boded bereavement and sorrow. (Benjamin Johnson, Gibbs Letter)

Those who were secretly conspiring against the Prophet now openly opposed him, and everything possible was being done by apostates and outside enemies to aggravate the Mormons. Hoping to weaken the Prophet's influence, they began publishing *The Nauvoo Expositor*. The goal of this most foul and slanderous newspaper was to subvert the liberties of the people and inflame public hatred against the Church. It was declared a nuisance by municipal authorities, and the press was destroyed by order of the Nauvoo City Council (Benjamin Johnson, "What I Know of Mormonism"; *HC* 6:430–32). Only one edition of the paper was printed, dated 7 June 1844. This action greatly excited the anti-Mormon population, and they accused the Mormon leaders of denying the people freedom of the press. Writs were issued for the arrest of the Prophet and others who were charged with rioting and destruction of the printing press. When Joseph was released by *habeas corpus*, "all hell now seemed in commotion" (*HC* 6:487). Mobs rose up in all the adjacent counties, with Missouri and Iowa in sympathy with the anti-Mormons. They conspired to destroy the Prophet and Nauvoo with its majestic temple (*MLR* 101).

When the mobs began destroying property, burning homes outside Nauvoo, and threatening the city, the Saints feared a repetition of the Missouri incidents. Governor Ford ordered troops to enforce the law and secure peace, but they were not reliable. On 15 June 1844 all able-bodied men at Ramus were ordered to hasten to Nauvoo. Benjamin was among the group. To avoid attack they travelled all night through rain and mud. The group was met by the Prophet who came out to greet them. Benjamin was there only a few days before he was sent back to guard Ramus. Benjamin did not see the Prophet and his brother Hyrum again (*MLR* 101-102).

The Prophet Joseph prepared to leave Nauvoo when it was revealed to him that his only chance for safety was to flee to the Rocky Mountains (*HC* 6:547). However, through the persuasion and reproaches of his wife Emma and others, he was induced to return to Nauvoo and give himself up to the authorities to be tried for treason. On his way to Carthage, the Prophet stated, "I am going like a lamb to the slaughter; but I am calm as a summer's morning....It shall yet be said of me—he was murdered in cold blood"

(Doctrine and Covenants 135:4; Millennial Star 24:775). The Prophet Joseph Smith was killed on 27 June 1844.

Benjamin heard of the martyrdom the following day. He was incensed when he learned that some of the people close to Joseph had convinced him to return to Nauvoo. He felt that they had used poor judgment and that their persuasion had, in part, led to his beloved prophet's death. Benjamin observed,

> With all the persons who induced him to return I was well acquainted, and I know that fearful has been the hand of the Lord to follow them from the day they sought to steady the Ark of God, which resulted in the martyrdom of his servants. (*MLR* 102)

News of the tragic murder of Joseph and Hyrum struck the Saints with shock and grief. Those who had been closely associated with the Prophet were especially distressed. Benjamin said,

> To attempt to delineate the feelings of woe and unutterable sorrow that swelled every heart too full for tears, I need not attempt. I stood up, dazed with grief, could groan but could not weep. The fountain of tears was dry! "Oh God! What will thy orphan church and people now do!" was the only feeling or thought that now burst out in groans. (*MLR* 102)

Soon after the martyrdom, Benjamin realized his own life was in danger. Mobs began searching for him, claiming he was a refugee from Missouri justice. He was forced to hide in the woods, receiving food and supplies from close friends (*MLR* 103).

Gradually the excitement and persecution seemed to diminish, and the Saints began to hope for a period of peace. But Benjamin lost confidence in Nauvoo as a future home, and although the house he was building in Ramus was enclosed and material was ready for its completion, he had neither the energy nor faith to invest more in it (*MLR* 103).

A Special Witness is Given

With the death of the Prophet there arose the question as to who would now lead the Church. The principle of succession was not understood by the members, and this was the first time in the Church's fourteen-year history that this situation had arisen. To settle the issue a conference was called in Nauvoo on 8 August 1844. Two men were scheduled to speak: Sidney Rigdon, who claimed authority to lead the Church by virtue of his position as counselor to the Prophet Joseph Smith; and President Brigham Young, who was then President of the Quorum of the Twelve Apostles (*HC*, Period

2, 7:231-42). At this conference Benjamin witnessed a miraculous manifestation. Listening to President Rigdon's appeal to the members to recognize and sustain him as "Guardian for the Church," Benjamin felt his remarks were void of all power or influence (*MLR* 103). Benjamin recalled,

> I was perhaps, to a degree, forgetful of what I knew to be the rights and duties of the apostleship, and as he closed his address and sat down, my back was partly-turned to the seats occupied by Apostle Brigham Young and other Apostles. When suddenly, and as from Heaven, I heard the voice of the Prophet Joseph, that thrilled my whole being, and quickly turning around I saw in the transfiguration of Brigham Young, the tall, straight and portly form of the Prophet Joseph Smith, clothed in a sheen of light, covering him to his feet; and I heard the real and perfect voice of the Prophet, even to the whistle, as in years past caused by the loss of a tooth[6] said to have been broken out by the mob at Hyrum. This view, or vision, although but for seconds, was to me as vivid and real as the glare of lightning or the voice of thunder from the heavens, and so deeply was I impressed with what I saw and heard in this transfiguration, that for years I dare not publicly tell what was given me of the Lord to see. But when in later years I did publicly bear this testimony, I found that others could testify to having seen and heard the same. But to what proportion of the congregation who were present, I could never know. But I do know that this, my testimony is true. (Benjamin Johnson, Gibbs Letter)
>
> Then I remembered his saying to the Council, of which Sidney Rigdon was never a member, and I knew for myself who was now the leader of Israel. (*MLR* 104)

As a result of this spiritual experience, Benjamin became foremost in testifying that President Brigham Young was the true successor of the Prophet Joseph Smith. Benjamin declared,

> I will again bear this as a faithful testimony that I do know and bear record that upon the head of Brigham Young as

---

[6] "The Prophet's lost tooth, to which I alluded, was as generally understood, broken out by the mob at Hyrum while trying to pry open his mouth to strangle him with acid, from which time, until the tooth was replaced by a dentist neighbor, a year or so previous to his death, there had been a whistle-like sound to accompany all his public speaking which I again plainly heard at the time of which I write." (Benjamin Johnson, Gibbs Letter)

> chief, with the Apostleship in full, was by the voice of the Prophet Joseph, in my hearing, laid the full responsibility of bearing off the kingdom of God to all the world. (Benjamin Johnson, Gibbs Letter)

Benjamin knew that President Brigham Young was now the leader of the Church and Prophet of the Lord. He was the right man in the right place. Benjamin relates that "new confidence and joy continued to spring up within me, and the subject of our finding a new home in the wilderness of the great west was one that occupied much of my thoughts." (*MLR* 104)

Chapter V

Conflict, Exodus, & Pioneering

In the brief period of peace which followed the martyrdom, the Saints worked night and day to finish the temple so they could receive their temple ordinances before they moved west. Benjamin was called by the Council of Fifty to rent out and manage the Nauvoo Mansion House, home of the late Prophet (*MLR* 104). He did not move to Nauvoo, however, until the spring of 1845. In order to fill this assignment, Benjamin was forced to give up his home and property, worth thousands, for the sum of $250. He went from having a prosperous business and living in good circumstances, to being a renter, with all of his means invested in the furnishing and upkeep of a public house (*MLR* 105).

The law of plural marriage was now being practiced by some of the Church leaders. Wishing to follow the Prophet's counsel Benjamin told President Brigham Young what the Prophet Joseph had counselled him relative to taking Mary Ann Hale as his wife. President Young said it was right and authorized Father John Smith to seal them, which he did on 14 November 1844 (The Historical Record 6:22). Benjamin regarded her as the wife who was given to him by the Prophet Joseph Smith (Benjamin Johnson, Gibbs Letter). The following year Benjamin was sealed to his third wife, Clarinda Gleason on 1 December 1845 (MLR 106).

On 11 June 1845 Benjamin's younger sister, Mary, died while giving birth to her second child. He recorded,

> She dropped away before we could reach her, to receive her last adieus. But she, like the others, died in full assurance of the reward for the pure in heart of womankind. None could approach nearer to angelic character, in childhood, girlhood or womanhood, nor was there ever known from her associates one unkind word or feeling towards her, and she died as she had lived, beloved by all who knew her. (*MLR* 104)

The Conflict

As the temple neared completion, trouble with the mobs began again. Violence drove the Saints from outlying areas into Nauvoo (*MLR* 105).

Five sons of Ezekiel and Julia Hills Johnson

Seated, left to right: George Washington Johnson, Joel Hills Johnson and Benjamin Franklin Johnson

Standing, left to right: Joseph Ellis Johnson and William Derby Johnson.

Seated, left to right: Esther Meita Johnson LeBaron, Joseph Ellis Johnson
Standing, left to right: Benjamin Franklin, William Derby

Benjamin at age forty-eight

Benjamin at age sixty-nine

Photographs taken in the later life of Benjamin F. Johnson

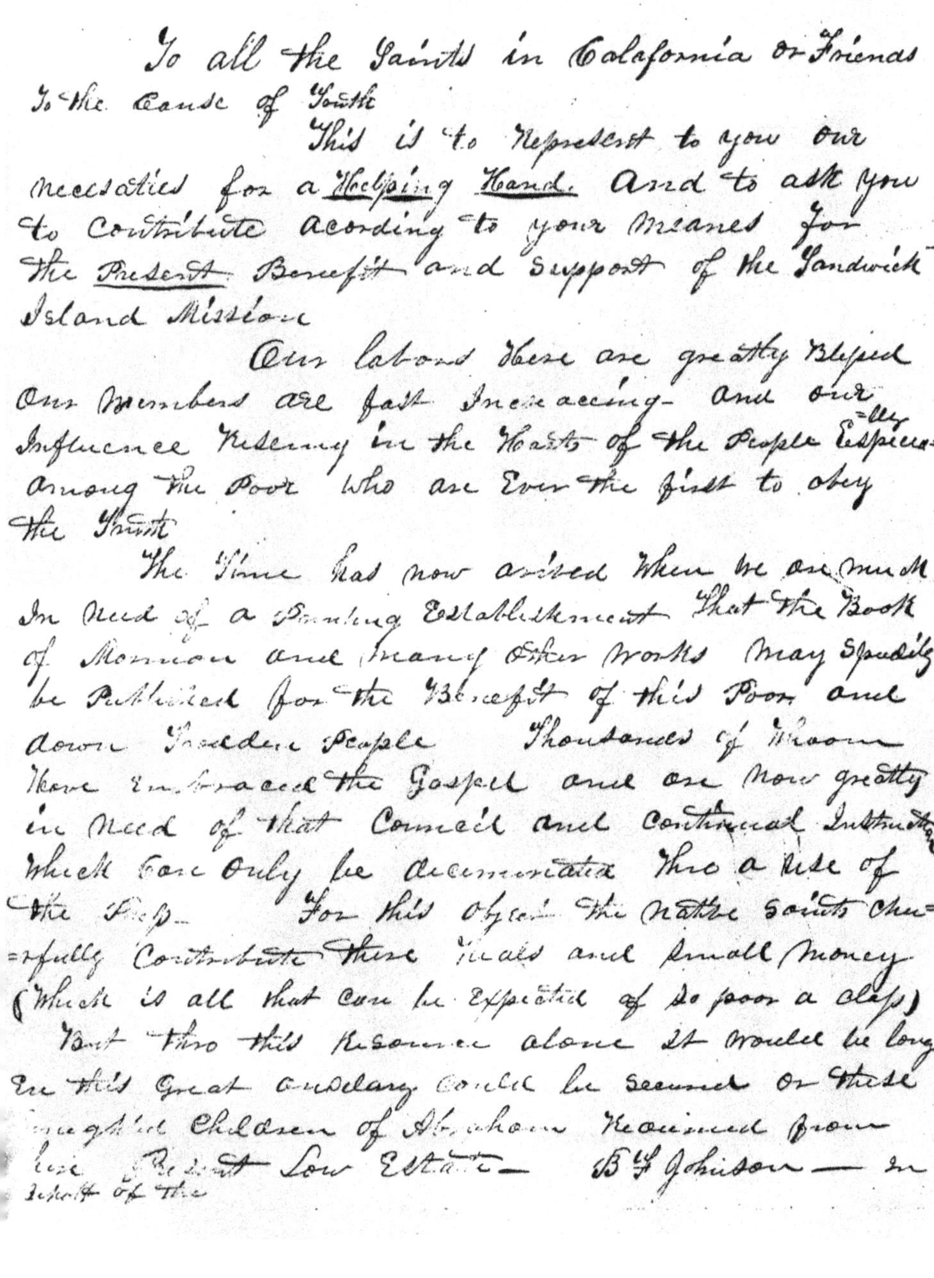

To all the Saints in California or Friends
To the Cause of Truth
This is to Represent to you our
necessities for a Helping Hand. And to ask you
to Contribute acording to your Meanes for
the Present Benefit and Support of the Sandwich
Island Mission
Our labors Here are greatly Blessed
Our Members are fast Increaceing and our
Influence Riseing in the Hearts of the People Especia=lly
among the Poor who are Ever the first to obey
the Truth
The Time has now arived When we are much
In Need of a Printing Establishment That the Book
of Mormon and many Other works may Spedily
be Published for the Benefit of this Poor and
down Trodden People Thousands of whoom
have Embraced the Gospel and are now greatly
in Need of that Council and Continual Instructio[n]
which Can Only be Accomplished Thro a use of
the Press For this Object the Native Saints Chee=
=rfully Contribute their Reals and Small Money
(Which is all that Can be Expected of So poor a class)
But thro this Resource alone It would be long
Ere this Great auxilary Could be Secured or these
Benighted Children of Abraham Redeemed from
their Present Low Estate— B F Johnson — In
behalf of the

Petition for funds written to the saints in California by Benjamin

Benjamin F. Johnson seated with his wife Sarah Melissa Holman Johnson. Next to h mother is Cassandra, and next to her father is Sarah Agness. The other children in th picture are not identified.

Benjamin F. Johnson, and Melissa B. LeBaron family after arrival in Utah.
Left to right: Melissa Almira, Julia Didamia, Delcina (baby) Melissa B. (mother), B.F.J., Jr., B.F. Johnson (father), and Esther Melita.

B. F. Johnson & Sons

Market Gardners, Fruit Packers, and Dealers In

General Merchandise and Garden Seeds

And Keep In Stock

Flowering Bulbs, Shade Trees, Ornamental Shrubbery,

Grape Vines; Choice Spring; Summer; And

Bedding Plants.

Spring Lake, Utah Co. Utah.

The family of Benjamin F. Johnson gathered at a party in celebration of his seventy-second birthday. Photo taken in 1890.

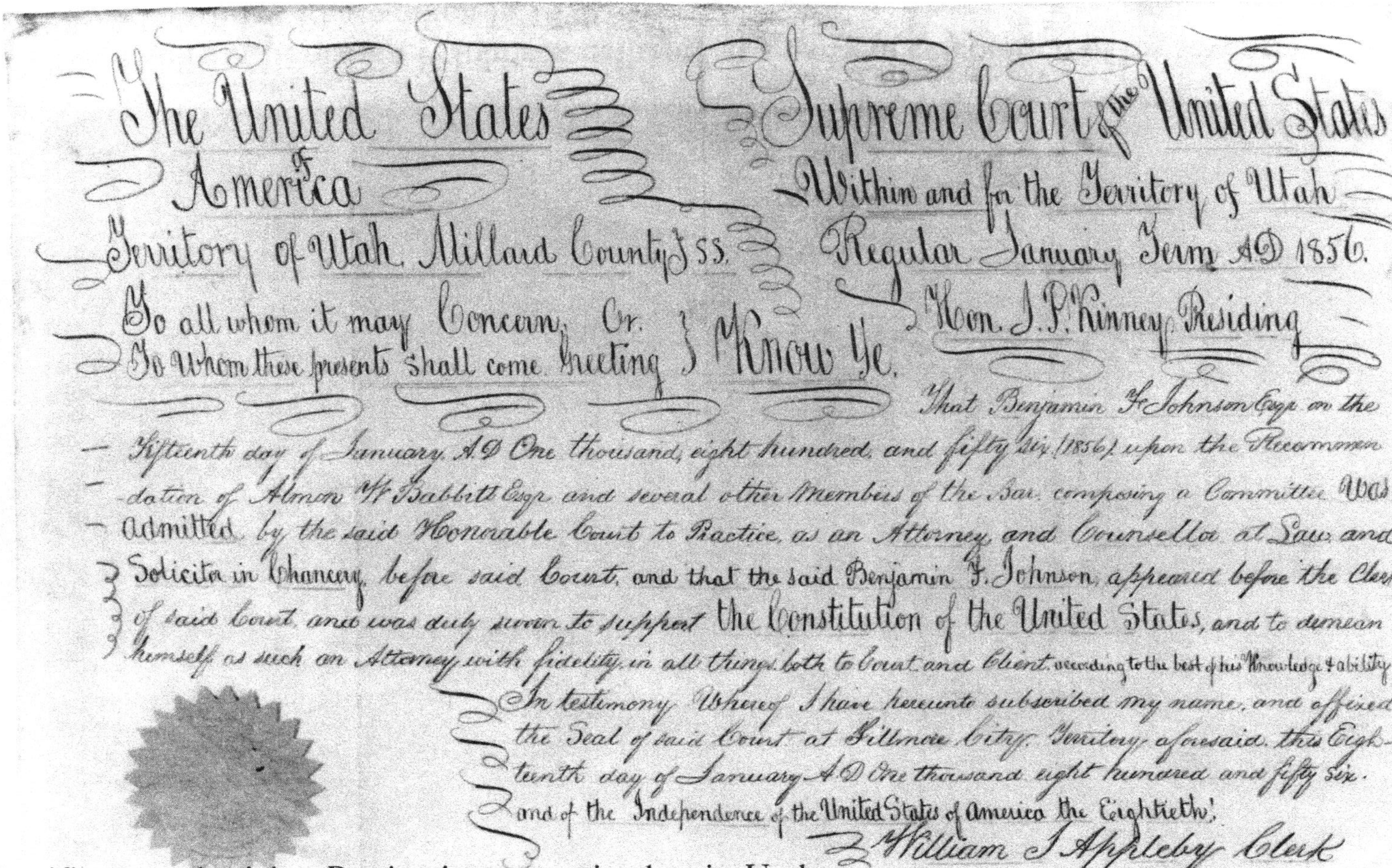
The United States of America
Supreme Court of the United States
Within and for the Territory of Utah
Territory of Utah, Millard County } ss.
Regular January Term A D 1856.
Hon. J. F. Kinney Presiding
To all whom it may Concern, Or. To whom these presents shall come Greeting } Know Ye,
That Benjamin F. Johnson Esqr on the Fifteenth day of January A D One thousand, eight hundred, and fifty six (1856) upon the Recommendation of Almon W Babbitt Esqr and several other Members of the Bar composing a Committee Was admitted by the said Honorable Court to Practice as an Attorney and Counsellor at Law and Solicitor in Chancery before said Court, and that the said Benjamin F. Johnson, appeared before the Clerk of said Court and was duly sworn to support the Constitution of the United States, and to demean himself as such an Attorney with fidelity in all things both to Court and Client according to the best of his Knowledge & ability
In testimony Whereof I have hereunto subscribed my name, and affixed the Seal of said Court at Fillmore City Territory aforesaid this Eighteenth day of January A D One thousand eight hundred and fifty six. and of the Independence of the United States of America the Eightieth.
William I Appleby Clerk

Certificate authorizing Benjamin to practice law in Utah

Anti-Mormon rallies were held in Carthage and Quincy in the fall of 1845 which resulted in the demand for the prompt removal of all Mormons from the State of Illinois. The Latter-day Saints agreed to leave Hancock County in the Spring of 1846, when there was sufficient vegetation to provide food for their animals (*MLR* 106).

There was intense activity among the Saints as they made preparations for their exodus to the West. In October President Young announced that captains of twenty-five companies had been chosen with each company consisting of one hundred families (Nibley, *Exodus to Greatness* 73). Benjamin was appointed as one of these captains (Young 7:481-82). Each captain was to organize his company and supervise preparations for the journey. These preparations included constructing wagons, procuring teams and tents, and arranging for food and supplies. Benjamin's group started making wagons in the basement of the large brick stable near the Mansion House. But this project was not without problems, for some of the group had an eye more on their own profit than the general good of the company. This caused considerable trouble and financial loss to Benjamin (*MLR* 105).

Benjamin also had financial problems in managing the Mansion House. Although public travel was now cut off, the place had to be kept open to receive county and state officials and others who came to inquire into the causes of their troubles. The expenses of operating the Mansion House were nearly the same as before but there was little income. All the money and supplies from Benjamin's house in Ramus were used for rent, furnishings, and supplies to keep the Mansion House in its status of respectability. Among the guests were Judge Stephen A. Douglas, James Arlington Bennett of New York, and military officers sent by Governor Ford from time to time (*MLR* 105).

As if his troubles with finances and anti-Mormon mobs were not enough, Benjamin was also plagued with family problems. He now had three wives and three children to care for. His third wife Clarinda was older and felt she was much more capable than his second wife, Mary Ann. Hence, Clarinda was unwilling to be second to the younger woman and was unsatisfied with her place in the family. During this time, Benjamin was invited to bring his wives to the Nauvoo Temple to receive their second anointing. He could not accept the invitation however, because at that time General Arlington Bennett and his associates were staying at the Mansion House, and it was Benjamin's responsibility to see that they were properly entertained (*MLR* 106-107).

Sheriff Jacob Backenstos, a friend to the Church and "a man of sterling integrity for law and order," was also a boarder at the Mansion House (*MLR*

106). A member of his posse had killed a mob leader named Frank Worrel who was attempting to shoot Sheriff Backenstos. Worrel had been in command of the militia that participated in the murder of Joseph and Hyrum Smith. His death increased hatred for the Saints (Roberts, 2:481).

A false report was spread throughout the region that many anti-Mormons were being murdered in Nauvoo, and the Nauvoo Mansion was cited as the probable location where these alleged crimes were committed. To allay excitement, the Governor sent soldiers to examine the premises and find the bodies said to be secreted there. After their investigation the soldiers were satisfied that nothing was wrong and quietly went away, but the rumors continued (Benjamin Johnson, Letter to *Deseret News*, 15 January 1893).

Although the Saints had been granted permission to remain in Illinois until the spring of 1846, the non-Mormons became impatient. The Latter-day Saints were frequently subjected to mobbing and violence. To convince the non-Mormon citizens that the Church leaders were sincere in their promise and also to protect themselves, an exodus from Nauvoo began in February 1846 which Benjamin hoped to join (Roberts, 2:540-41; *MLR* 106-8).

Just prior to his departure, Benjamin was assigned to go with Newel K. Whitney to visit Emma Smith and try to persuade her to leave Nauvoo with the Saints. She had resisted the law of plural marriage when it was presented by the Prophet, and she resented President Brigham Young and other Church leaders for continuing the practice after her husband's death (Bailey 110). Although she had turned down previous invitations to join the Saints, Benjamin and Newel tried all night to convince her to go west. She finally agreed to go if she could be "the leading spirit." Being unable to change her thinking, they had to leave without her (Benjamin Johnson Handwritten Manuscript of *My Life's Review*).

The Exodus

When the time for leaving Nauvoo drew near, Benjamin lacked the necessary supplies for the journey. President Young advised Benjamin to obtain help from certain men in his company. By selling his beds and other furnishings, Benjamin was able to buy three oxen and acquire a fourth with the help of Brother Bostwick. He got a spring wagon from a Brother Ovid, and beans and feed from William Weatherby. With these newly acquired supplies and his family carriage and camp outfit, Benjamin was now prepared to cross the river.

As conditions in Nauvoo grew worse, Benjamin was grateful that he had prepared early. He wrote,

> One afternoon I think the 6th of February, 1846, I learned of a posse being sent from Carthage to search the manure piles around the Mansion stables for dead bodies, with a warrant for my arrest and others employed about the premises. Tales of great horror had gone about the country, of murders committed at the Mansion. But I left before the arrival of the posse, and with Mary Ann and Clarinda, went to a friend's house near the river and crossed about midnight in a bitter-cold storm. The next day the river was closed with ice from bank to bank. The camp of the Presidency and many others was on Sugar Creek, and on our arrival there we were without even a bit of canvas to cover our heads, but were kindly received by those who had shelter, one of the kindest of whom was the fated John D. Lee, whose generosity there I do not forget. But soon President Young ordered for us canvas for a tent, by which we were made comfortable. But my first wife and children were at Nauvoo, with the wagons, which our friends loaded, and upon the ice brought all over to camp. (*MLR* 108–9)

This sudden change from the comforts of the Nauvoo Mansion to the discomforts and desolation of the snow-covered prairie caused great tribulation for Benjamin and his family. He said,

> Now here we were, started in midwinter without a dollar, on a journey without any knowledge of its length or the time it would occupy, with three wives, the youngest in a delicate condition, three small children, and two spans of animals to care for, with only provisions enough to sustain us for a few weeks at most, and with poor health which for the last year or more had been exceedingly precarious. I often suffered with acute, cutting pain in my stomach, which at times would cause the sweat to start from every pore. This, with constant piles and tendency to dyspepsia, made me very unfit for such arduous labors. The duties alone of caring for the teams and other camp duties looked great indeed to me, and coming from one of the best tables in Nauvoo, with my delicate appetite—now how was I to live! (*MLR* 109)

Hundreds of Saints hastily left their homes during February 1846. About four hundred families crossed the frozen Mississippi River on 11 February

(Roberts, 2:541). Many of them did not have sufficient food and protection from the winter storms. When the poor conditions caused some to complain, President Young told them that anyone who could not live on boiled beans and corn, trust in God and be grateful for what they had, should start back at once, for the camp would be a poor place for them (*MLR* 109). Up to this time Benjamin had been unable to eat cornbread or beans without getting unbearable stomach pains. He was, therefore, greatly concerned, for his family's limited food supply was comprised mainly of these items.

Besides serving as captain over his division, Benjamin was also appointed custodian of all property that was found during their journey (*HC* 2:7:592). He often met in council with the leaders while they were camped at Sugar Creek.

To allow other families to catch up to them, the Saints remained at Sugar Creek until 1 March. In spite of the hardships forced upon them, Benjamin noted an improvement in the attitude of the camp members, as well as his own physical health. He wrote,

> From near the first of February to the first of March we were camped on Sugar Creek amid storms, the mercury at one time recording 20 degrees below zero. Yet there was a warm feeling in our hearts for we felt to trust in God. Even in the midst of tribulation, in a stormy winter's encampment, merry songs and happy voices were heard at every camp fire, and when the weather permitted all ages would join, inspired by sweet music, in the dance. At the signal for prayer, every occupation was suspended, and around the campfire, in wagons and tents, every knee was bowed, and a voice from every circle was raised in gratitude for past and in petition for continued protection. And here I will say that before breaking camp at Sugar Creek, the beans and corn, formerly uneatable by me, I could eat with relish, and from that time the old effect did not return to me on the journey. I had told the Lord what His servant had said, that by His help I would fulfill every requirement, and if it was His will that I should live to be His servant, He must cause my food to assimilate to the condition of my stomach, which I know He did. (*MLR* 110-11)

Moving west from Sugar Creek the Saints experienced inclement weather. Often they had to pitch their tents on ground covered with water and deep mud.

On one occasion while crossing the prairie, Benjamin's team became stuck in mud and were unable to move. The rest of the company passed by leaving them alone on the prairie without sufficient fuel to keep warm. Benjamin was forced to chop up a wooden chest and burn it to keep his family from freezing. The next morning Brother Weatherby travelled one and a half miles to find a green elm pole, which, with a little of the chest, gave them a fire for their breakfast. Soon some of the brethren returned to assist Benjamin and his family, but the ground was now frozen hard enough to bear both wagon and mules. They only needed help to get their wagon wheels out of the deep, frozen mud in which they had been stuck (*MLR* 111).

Besides severe weather, health problems plagued the Saints. Measles spread through the camp, and the wet conditions made it nearly impossible to care for the sick. Several children died, creating a sorrowful scene as parents buried their little ones in graves half full of water. "Yet, with all this, there was hope and cheerfulness in the camp, and perhaps no company of equal size ever journeyed together with less faultfinding or murmuring" (*MLR* 111).

On 25 April 1846 the advance camp arrived at a place they called Garden Grove, 150 miles from Nauvoo (*HC* 2:7:606).

On 26 June 1846, Captain James Allen of the United States Army rode into the Mormon camp at Mount Pisgah. His presence aroused feelings of suspicion and distrust among the Saints, and they resented the order requesting five hundred Mormon volunteers to fight in the war with Mexico. They learned, however, that this recruitment came as a result of President Brigham Young's appeal to the President of the United States, James K. Polk, for financial aid to help the Church emigrate west. As the United States was at war with Mexico, President Polk chose to help the Mormons by providing this opportunity of military service (Roberts, 3:64-74). Members of the Council of Fifty met in Garden Grove to discuss the formation of the Mormon Battalion. According to Benjamin, the Council of Fifty was often called together after the death of the Prophet (*MLR* 107). In describing his perception of this situation, Benjamin wrote,

> To show you that I did know the motive of President Young in sending the Battalion, I will say that as one of that special Council organized by the Prophet, of which I have written, and of which Pres. Young being the head, I still held my seat and still had a voice in all general movements relating to our exodus as a people from Nauvoo. And I was present at the arrival of Colonel Little [Captain Allen] and a company at

> Garden Grove, with the requisition, by Govt. for five hundred volunteers for the American Army, sprung upon the fleeing Mormons as a test to their loyalty and patriotism by Senator Benton of Missouri. It was well understood at the time, as the subject was fully ventilated by the council, and all comprehended it as a great sacrifice and that there was no reward or benefit offered by the government in any degree. (Benjamin Johnson, Gibbs Letter)

A Lesson in Obedience

It was decided to leave some of the families in Garden Grove to plant crops, recruit teams, and be ready for an onward march in the coming spring. Since the Johnson family was asked to remain, Benjamin consented to President Young's request that his span of large, valuable mules "go forward under saddle, for the other pioneers". President Young charged those who were staying at Garden Grove to work together and David Fullmer was appointed to preside over the camp. Benjamin, however, having been guided directly by the Prophet and afterwards by President Young, decided that he "would not be dictated to by anyone there" and found a beautiful spot about a mile from the main camp. He moved his family there and began clearing land (*MLR* 112). After his unsuccessful attempts to raise crops, and after much sickness, Benjamin further disobeyed the counsel of President Young and started back toward Nauvoo. He later realized that whereas previously he "had the favor of both God and man," this move caused him to lose both (*MLR* 115).

After the Saints were driven from Nauvoo, thieves showed up like vultures to feed upon the spoils and rob surrounding towns. One Church member, Brother Gibbs, had been accused of stealing after some stolen objects were found on his property. Being a friend to Gibbs, Benjamin accompanied him to Farmington to help answer the charges. Soon, however, he was convinced of Gibbs' guilt, and aligned with a common thief, Benjamin found himself in precarious circumstances.

> When they learned that I was the Johnson that kept the Nauvoo Mansion, a large crowd gathered around me, inspired by the old rumors to which I have alluded. It was but a few days previous to this, they had hanged Brother Folsom, our temple architect, until he was nearly dead; and apparently they would serve me worse, judging from their savage looks. There seemed little hope for me, but I realized that cowardice would be fatal. So, standing in the center of

> the mob, I placed my thumbs in the armholes of my vest, swelled myself out full size and height, and with hat on the back of my head I looked at them boldly, and asked what kind of a man they wanted, or were hunting for? I said, "If it is an upright, honest, law-abiding man who never in his life willfully or knowingly wronged a fellowman or woman, then they had got just the man they wanted, for I was just that man, and dared all proof to the contrary; the crowd grew less, and soon I found myself free. (*MLR* 116-17)

On 17 September 1846 an armed mob forced most of the remaining Saints to leave Nauvoo. This last group consisted of the elderly, sick, and poor, who were not prepared for the long arduous journey. Benjamin gave the following account of his second departure from Nauvoo,

> In the morning of the third day we started to cross the river; but no sooner was the weight upon the ice than it began to bend and crack for a long distance around. It looked fearful and terrible, but we [could] not [wait] for the river to break up; for that would detain us weeks, and we must risk it. I got out of the carriage with my little five-year-old boy and went ahead, while my wife with the two small children drove the team close behind. It was a terrible ordeal. The bending, cracking ice at every step sounded to me like a death knell of my loved ones. And why were we there? Only through my disobedience to the Word of the Lord. My remorse was great and my repentance full. The promised Angel was there still, and all was safe until passing a large steamboat moored at Montrose, the ice broke under their feet. The whip was applied, the horses sprang, and as the carriage sank deeply into the water the forefeet of the horses struck the bank. They bounded forward, and all came safely on shore. But oh! how small I felt; and how merciful was the Lord! I would never be forgetful and disobedient again! (*MLR* 118-19)

Despite his disobedience, Benjamin was not rejected by the Church leaders. In the spring of 1847, he received a letter from the Twelve, requesting that he and his family join the pioneers at Winter Quarters when they were ready to move west. The Johnson family stayed in the town of Bonaparte, Lee County, Iowa until they were able to go to Winter Quarters. As Benjamin was in poor health much of this time, he became quite discouraged.

> Under these influences [I] dreamed I was alone in a strange place in a great concourse of strangers and enemies. I felt friendless and desolate, and sought to avoid notice by sitting down; and looking up, I saw a man come in with a broad-brimmed, white hat which partly covered his face. He sat down near me. I looked under his hat and saw it was the Prophet Joseph. I clasped him around the legs and wept for joy. He placed his mouth to my ear and told me to be comforted, that he was still my friend and would not forget me. My tears had not ceased, and when I awoke I was still crying for joy; and I felt from that hour a new inspiration that nothing else could have given me. (*MLR* 120)

About the first of January 1848, prior to making the trip to Winter Quarters, Benjamin learned of the death of his father. According to the family record, when Ezekiel learned of the murder of Joseph and Hyrum, his heart was softened toward the Church.

> [His] rebellion melted like running ice from his soul. He was incensed at the brutality and now defended the Mormons as earnestly and spiritedly as he had heretofore contemptuously denounced them.
>
> When an attempt was made by the militia to enter the city of Nauvoo in a treacherous surprise attack before the government date set for expulsion, it found its plans shattered for Ezekiel, entirely alone and without thought of his own danger, was there ahead, carrying his old trusty gun and vehemently commanding a halt.
>
> He poured forth such a bitter tirade of fury and abuse for their treachery, ordering them sternly to retreat or he would blow the head from the captain, that they were taken completely by surprise. Realizing the deadly earnestness of the man, the company hastily withdrew, but only to attempt a later side-street entrance.
>
> But Ezekiel, reading their minds, was again there ahead and implacable as before, threatening with such violence and vindictiveness, the captain again retreated nor offered further disturbance. (Openshaw, "Highlights of the Life of Julia Hills and Ezekiel Johnson")

Ezekiel's display of courage and defiance angered the enemies of the Church and he was beaten by a mob so unmercifully that he soon died from his wounds and was referred to as one of the martyrs of the early Church, even though he had never been baptized. Benjamin observed,

> During the last year of his life he had ceased to use ardent spirits, and had realized the great wrong he had done himself and family by his opposition. He knew the Gospel was true and had asked for baptism, of which his sudden death deprived him, leaving all his work for his children. (*MLR* 120)

By the time Benjamin arrived at Winter Quarters, President Brigham Young and 142 other men had already reached the Salt Lake Valley. President Young and most of the Apostles returned to Winter Quarters on 31 October 1847 (Shumway; Journal History, 31 October 1847). Benjamin realized he had missed out on one of the great epics in the history of the Church. Concerning his reunion with the Church leaders and the rest of the Saints, he wrote,

> At Winter Quarters I was welcomed by the Presidency and old associates, but I had lost blessings and caste, and could not but feel it. The pioneers had gone without me, found the land of our inheritance, and returned; and even now I was not ready to follow, and where was I to obtain the necessary outfit? I felt joy in being again with the Church, but the lessons of the past I must not forget. (*MLR* 120-21)

While eagerly making the necessary preparations to move west, Benjamin had a violent attack of pleurisy. For a time he feared he would die. He sat by the campfire at night bathing his side, taking medicine, and exerting his faith and will to live that he might enter the Salt Lake Valley. His faith and determination prevailed, and on 4 July 1848 Benjamin and his family began their trek across the plains. Travelling with the Willard Richards company, Benjamin's family occupied two wagons. Along the way Benjamin's third wife, Clarinda, left him and joined another family. She later divorced Benjamin and married Abraham Washburn. Of the wearying, toilsome four month' journey he simply wrote, "there were but few prominent incidents pertaining to my own history" (*MLR* 122).

Chapter VI

Struggle in the Valley

The Willard Richards Company arrived in the Salt Lake Valley on 22 October 1848. In gratitude for the mercy and blessing of the Lord, Benjamin felt a desire to dedicate himself to greater service to his Heavenly Father (*MLR* 123).

Being in the valley did not mean that all would now be well. Benjamin and his family had used most of their provisions during the journey west, planning to replenish their supplies when they reached the valley. It was with great disappointment they learned that those who had come the year before had fought myriads of crickets and, after all their toil, had saved but a pittance of their crops. Benjamin said there was "not one pound of bread to be bought even had I money with which to buy. And now, late in the season, winter should be upon us and no house to shelter women and children" (*MLR* 123).

While good weather remained, Benjamin set out to build a house from adobe, but after the walls were built, further work was halted by the deep snows of early winter storms. Benjamin knew that two wagon beds were not suitable protection from the weather. His family was only able to escape this desperate situation when Father John Smith invited them to move into the fort beside him. The room was ten by thirteen feet, built of large poles and covered with corn fodder and chinked with straw. They added a fireplace and moved in (*MLR* 124).

The winter of 1848–49 was severe, with deep snow. Being short of all foodstuffs, the Johnsons did their utmost to be frugal with everything they obtained. They dug thistles, bought beef when it was available, and even cooked the hide and feet of cattle. After the Mormon Battalion arrived in the Salt Lake Valley, bringing with them horses and gold, Benjamin provided for his family by establishing the first harness and saddlery shop in Salt Lake City (Warrum 905). He obtained the necessary leather for his store by trading with the Indians. Although he was paid in gold dust, he soon learned that even gold could not buy a pound of bread.

Along with the harness business, Benjamin began the first drugstore in the valley (Warrum 906). Though occupied with his businesses, he found time to work a few acres of land that someone had started to fence and till but had abandoned. After Benjamin finished fencing and plowing, he planted wheat which he had brought across the plains. When it became apparent that the wheat had rotted in the ground, he plowed again, this time carefully planting the choicest seeds he could obtain. No sooner had all this been done, than a claimant came demanding the land or payment for his improvements, at an inflated price. Benjamin wrote,

> We paid him in full hope of an early, fruitful garden, but as time passed and the sun grew warmer we looked for plants to appear. Here and there a sickly looking pea, bean or spear of corn could be seen, with other plants, all struggling through a white, deadly looking substance forming on the surface. Yet we could not comprehend the possibility of a disappointment, for what could we do if the garden failed, on which we had staked our labor and planted all our seeds. No possibility for another garden in a new place. So we worked, still in hope, fear and desperation to care for a few sickly plants. They *did* grow, but it was less everyday, until by June all hope was gone and our garden abandoned. (*MLR* 127)

Benjamin, now completely discouraged, could see no hope for the future. One Sunday he walked about the settlement too embarrassed to attend church in his bare feet. Meeting Jacob Burnham, he said, "Jacob, there is one consolation to us left—if we starve, the Lord certainly will give us credit for industry, if nothing else. We have worked hard in hunger and weariness, but it does almost seem now that he has forgotten us" (*MLR* 127-28). As they were talking, they heard the news that emigrants were arriving from the east on their way to the California gold fields.

After gold was discovered in California on 19 January 1848 the cry vibrated across the country, but it was not until the summer of 1849 that the gold rush really began. The fortune hunters began to arrive while Benjamin and hundreds of other Saints were struggling with hunger, inadequate clothing, poor housing, and a gross insufficiency of tools and equipment (Arrington 64). Eager to reach the gold fields, they needed supplies, fresh animals, and equipment to continue their hurried trip. The gold seekers readily sold extra clothing and equipment at low prices and purchased whatever they needed to continue their journey. Usually they paid the Mormons high prices for what they bought, as President Brigham Young declared, "What! sell bread to a man who is going to earn his one hundred and fifty dollars a day, at the same price as you do to a poor laborer, who works hard here for one dollar a day? I say, you men who are going to get gold to make golden images. . .pay for your flour!" (*Deseret News*, 20 July 1850). It is believed that about one quarter of a million dollars came into the valley as a result of the gold rush (Arrington 71). The Saints looked upon it as a blessing from the Lord, and Benjamin shared in these blessings by finding a ready market for his products. He said,

> They appeared almost crazy with excitement about California and gold. I traded them a jack and jenny and began the making of pack saddles, rigging them with rawhide. Oh! what a change. I now could get flour, bacon, sugar, rice, soap, tea, powder, lead, tobacco, the finest clothing, with wagons, harness, etc., in exchange for packing outfits, which I could supply in quantity. (*MLR* 128)

With many emigrants settling in the Salt Lake Valley, President Young set up a provisional government to establish law and order. It was called the "Colonial Council" or "Legislature of Deseret" and Benjamin was an elected member of that body (Benjamin Johnson, "A Life Sketch"; Gibbs Letter). He served in the Territorial government for twelve years and felt that this was because of his membership in the Council of Fifty. One of the reasons the Prophet had originally organized the Council was to assist in obtaining constitutional rights for the Latter-day Saints and to help secure a "resting place" in the mountains where the Saints could live in peace (*HC* 6:260-61).

In May 1849, Benjamin served in Utah's first military commission when the Council of Fifty reorganized the Nauvoo Legion. This military body now consisted of two regiments. Benjamin, who was made captain of the first company of cavalry, commanded three lieutenants, four sergeants, four corporals, two buglers, and between twenty-five and fifty-seven privates (Hansen 17–25). President Young ordered Benjamin's company to protect the Saints against possible Indian attacks (Journal History, 26 May 1849). Benjamin held this commission for about three years.

In a meeting of the First Presidency in June 1849, President Young decided to send Benjamin Johnson, Francis Pomeroy, and Charles Rich on missions to California. However, because of the heavy movement of gold seekers at that time, he did not issue the calls (Journal History, 3 June 1849, 10 June 1849). Benjamin also missed other opportunities to serve. He was called to go with President George A. Smith to settle what was then called Little Salt Lake, but an accident prevented Benjamin from traveling. On another occasion the Presidency called Benjamin to be the Bishop of the 16th Ward, but he recommended Brother Shadrach Roundy as an older and better man. Brother Roundy was ordained the Bishop (*MLR* 132-33).

Benjamin married his fourth wife, Harriet Naomi Holman, on 17 March 1850. His brother, Joseph, spent much of that summer visiting them. In August they helped the First Presidency select and survey the Ogden city plot (Jensen, *The Historical Record*, 40). After the Territory was organized in September, a political meeting was held in the Bowery. Benjamin was elected to represent Salt Lake County in the first session of the Utah Legislative Council (*Journal History*, 26 July 1851, 18 September 1851; *MLR* 133). From Legislative Hall he wrote to his wife Harriet:

> There is not much of interest transpiring in the House or City except home manufactory which seems to create some interest, as great credit is publicly given to one member of the House for having a full suit of home spun jeans & also a lady appeared last Sunday at Church in a skin sack—so you will see that home clothing will soon be the rage of the day. (Benjamin Johnson letter to Harriet, 10 January 1851)

Home-made clothing was promoted by President Brigham Young. He realized that survival within the valleys of the mountains depended upon the Saints becoming a self-sustaining people. He was not only determined to survive, but he envisioned a strong nation covering the broad expanse of The Great Basin. Soon after the Saints arrived in the valley President Young sent out exploration parties to study the area, and settlements were established outside the Salt Lake valley within two years (Hunter, *Brigham Young The Colonizer*, 63). Edward W. Tullidge, a historian and contemporary of President Brigham Young, said he was "perhaps the greatest colonizer that the world has ever seen" (Hunter, *Brigham Young The Colonizer*, 6).

A Call to Colonize

In the spring of 1851, President Young invited Benjamin to join him and an exploration party up the Sevier River and over the mountains into what is now Iron County. Benjamin wrote,

> The second night out from Salt Lake City we camped at Summit Creek[7] in Utah County. It was the 1st of May, trees in full foliage, and the grass was like a carpet studded with flowers: the broad smooth lands sloped delightfully away to the west mountain, while here and there were rose and willow patches. The morning sun upon a clear sky, the air fragrant with spring odors, and trees, alive with singing birds. It

[7] Summit Creek was later named Santaquin, after an Indian chief, son of Guffick, both of whom were friends to the Mormon people.

> appeared to me as enchanted ground, and I spoke of it as a place of beauty akin to Paradise. President Young heard me and asked if I would like to settle a colony there, and I said, "Yes, if he wished me to." He said he did, and that I might commence my arrangements as soon as I returned. I felt a little taken back, for I had never thought of leaving the city. I was getting a good run in the saddlery business, had the best drug store in the Territory and was doing well. I owned the half block on which the Utah central depot now stands, besides many other valuable lots in the city and a number of 5-and-10-acre lots in the fields adjoining the city. Yet the call had come, and I could see providence in it. The more I thought upon the subject the more I became enthused with joy and pride, that I had been deemed worthy of so important a call. (*MLR* 134)

They continued their journey up the Sevier and crossed the mountains near Parowan. There they camped for six days exploring for iron and coal deposits. While in the area, Benjamin visited his brother Joel and his family who were building a settlement there. On 24 May 1851 the company arrived back in Salt Lake City (Jenson, *The Historical Record*, 43).

After more than a month travelling with Presidents Brigham Young and Heber C. Kimball and visiting many areas selected for future settlements, Benjamin was beginning to understand what the Church leaders were hoping to accomplish. He realized that this work of colonizing was of paramount importance to President Young. Before returning to Salt Lake City, President Young called Benjamin to colonize Summit Creek, beginning a new era in his life.

To build this inland empire, President Young hand picked experienced leaders who were competent in handling frontier challenges and called them to preside in both a spiritual and temporal capacity (Dastrup 45; Hinckley 113). In some instances the colonizer was allowed to choose the families he wanted to assist him, and Benjamin was given that prerogative. After selecting a group of friends, Benjamin travelled with them to Summit Creek to further explore the area. Some of them were enthusiastic about the assignment, but others did not like what they saw. Benjamin returned to Salt Lake City somewhat disenchanted, but still determined to fulfill his mission, he continued his preparations. Unlike Benjamin, those who were chosen to accompany him did not feel under a direct call of the priesthood, and there were delays and problems. There were not enough of his group ready the first season to establish a safe colony, and the move was postponed (*MLR* 134–36).

During 1850 and 1851, Benjamin tried to grow apple trees from seeds he had brought across the plains. The seeds were planted in his garden, but since there was no sign of growth that year, Benjamin assumed they were dead and allowed a woman to use that area for a garden the following year. One day he noticed the ground was full of young apple trees just coming up. Ignoring all his appeals to save the plants, the "miserable specimen of a woman" intentionally hoed up the young trees. Benjamin estimated the saplings to be valued at more than a thousand dollars since he believed they were the first apple trees west of the Mississippi River. The seeds he gave his brother Joel, produced the first fruit in southern Utah, some of which was later brought to Salt Lake City (*MLR* 136-37).

Benjamin felt a duty to fill the assignment to colonize Summit Creek, although his enthusiasm waned. He now had a harness and saddlery shop, the only drug store in Salt Lake City, plenty of choice farm land, and other valuable property. Despite his obligations, Benjamin sold his Salt Lake City home to Almon Babbitt for $700 and began constructing adobe buildings at Summit Creek. A few months later he sent his first report as a colonizer to the Deseret News.

> Dear Sirs:
>
> I noticed in your columns a wish to hear from all the new settlements, for the benefit of your readers. In response, I would say, that our numbers though small are comfortably provided with houses and supplies for the winter. Seven houses and ten or twelve men compose the present strength of our little town, which we call Summit City. It is situated on the summit between Utah and Juab valleys, about seventy miles from G.S.L. [Great Salt Lake] City. Its situation is picturesque and beautiful, with an entire view of Utah Lake and Valley. Adjoining our town plat is a large tract of the best quality of farming lands. Our range for stock is the most superior, and so situated it can never become scarce. We have not yet explored sufficiently to know what our resources will be for sawing timber, but fire wood, fence poles, and cabin logs are abundant—the water in our creek, we have never known less than would be needed for sawing or grinding purposes, and would be sufficient for from twenty to forty families for all farming purposes.

> We have no disposition to urge our brethren to settle with us; yet we would be highly pleased with a few more neighbors. Such favors, together with the blessing of health, make us feel much at home in our truly romantic place. I remain yours, truly. (Benjamin Johnson, Letter to Deseret News, 24 January 1852)

During the summer of 1851 Benjamin's brother Joseph obtained a contract from the US government for what he believed was the first mail delivery within Utah.[8] He contracted with Benjamin to carry the mail between Salt Lake City and Manti, with stations at Summit Creek and Salt Creek.[9] Although Benjamin employed men to assist with the mail delivery, he spent a lot of time on horseback, sometimes riding seventy-five miles a day. With the settlement already under way at Summit Creek, Benjamin built a comfortable two-room house for his wife Harriet (*MLR* 137).

Wishing also to build a colony at Salt Creek, Benjamin found some families to assist in gathering supplies and materials to begin work in the spring. During the first winter, he and seventy-four others built up the settlement and constructed a house for his wife Mary Ann (*MLR* 137; Nephi Ward History). At a general conference, President Brigham Young paid a special tribute to the settlers at Salt Creek when he said, "The inhabitants there are number one and when I was in that valley I prayed to God that he never would suffer an unrighteous man to live there" (*Journal History*, 6 September 1850).

Along with his many responsibilities, Benjamin continued to be politically active. On 22 September 1851 the territorial government began to function, and Benjamin was among the first to present a bill to the Legislature. His first bill was for the creation of Summit Creek County, which he presented on 23 January 1852. Although it passed three readings in the House, it did not clear the Legislative Council the following day. The Council felt that it was not expedient to divide Utah County at that time and the bill was tabled (Journals of the House of Representatives, 37-39).

---

[8] Benjamin may have been referring to the first mail contract issued for delivery solely within the Territory of Utah. Previous mail delivery under the first official mail service contract began in July 1850. Under this contract which was awarded to Samuel H. Woodson of Independence, Missouri, mail was delivered between Salt Lake City and Independence, Missouri. In April, 1851, another contract was issued to George Chorpening and Absolom Woodward for mail delivery between Salt Lake City and Sacramento, California (McBride 15, 19).

[9] Salt Creek was later named Johnsonville and then changed to Nephi.

Besides the mail contract and his duties in Salt Lake City, in the spring of 1852 Benjamin took time to plant crops in the new settlements. With the help of hired hands, he planted about sixty acres of wheat at Summit Creek and about twenty acres at Salt Creek (*MLR* 137). With hired men and plenty of livestock at each location, Benjamin was beginning to prosper.

Although a busy man, Benjamin was conscious of the needs of others. Upon receiving word from his wife Harriet that her father, James S. Holman, was injured, Benjamin wrote,

> If he is not able to work I want the boys to devote part of their time to watering his wheat even if they neglect mine. He will need a crop as much as myself & he has worked too hard to lose it for want of water. If anyone can be got from Payson to help him I will pay them if he cannot attend to his crops. (Benjamin Johnson, Letter to Harriet)

In 1852, Benjamin was elected to the Legislature as a Representative from Juab County (Deseret News, 21 August 1852). He was well liked and respected as a legislator and was often invited to important social functions (Deseret News, 11 December 1852). With a touch of humor he wrote that: "They brag up some of my speeches when I did not half try. I have lots of invitations to parties but have been so much occupied on Committees of the House I have not attended any" (Benjamin Johnson, Letter to Harriet, 25 January 1852).

Benjamin found that his business responsibilities increased so much that when a "Special Conference of Elders of the Church" assembled in the tabernacle on 28 August 1852 he felt he was too busy to attend (Millennial Star 15:13). The purpose of the conference was to declare publicly the doctrine of plural marriage. During the meeting brethren were called to leave their homes and take this message to the far parts of the earth: Europe, Asia, Africa, Australia, and the Isles of the Pacific. This was the first group of missionaries ever called for this purpose (Benjamin Johnson, "A Life Sketch"). Benjamin's was the last of the ninety-eight names read in the conference. He and eight other elders were called to serve as missionaries to the Sandwich Islands, now called the Hawaiian Islands.

Benjamin did not learn of his call until some time later and by then he had only ten days in which to prepare to leave. With thriving farms, new political responsibilities, and business obligations from Salt Lake City to Manti, Benjamin could not fathom how, in ten days, he could just pick up and go. What would become of his three wives and eight small children? How could he make adequate provisions for them in such a short time? The task seemed too great, and the sacrifice unjust.

> "But what shall I do?" I asked myself; and Faith answered by asking, "From whom did you receive wives and children, farms and houses, goods and cattle? Who redeemed you when you were hopeless of life and name upon the earth? To whom do you owe all you are, all you possess, and all you hope for, but to God? Then why hesitate when you have professed to be willing even to die for the truth of the Gospel?" I could see but little choice between the grave and my mission. But in gratitude to God I said, "With the Lord's help I will go; and the cord that holds me from my duty I will cut loose from; for go I will with the Lord's help." I told the Lord I would now commence, and wanted His help. (*MLR* 139-40)

Although Benjamin was very concerned about the sacrifice his mission would require, he had learned from experience the need to be obedient to the leaders of the Church, and he was determined to serve in whatever capacity he was called.

Benjamin started for the city to settle business, find someone to take his farm at Salt Creek, and dispose of the mail contract, saddlery, and drug store. Faith and hope grew in his heart as things fell into place. In Salt Lake City those he needed to see were readily available. Those who lived some distance away and who he did not have time to visit, he met on the street. When looking for renters for his Salt Creek farm, the first men he met were Brother Vickers and Brother Udell, who immediately agreed to take his farm during his absence (*MLR* 140). All dues owed to him were paid, and those men to whom he owed money and could not pay were willing to wait. Thus Benjamin prepared for his second mission.

While in Salt Lake City, he received a blessing from Elder Jedediah M. Grant which stated in part, "Through you, succor and sustenance shall come to the mission to which you are called, and your brethren shall be fed, clothed and sustained by the blessings of the Lord through your ministrations" (*MLR* 140). He also received private counsel from President Willard Richards. Benjamin recorded,

> Our mission was to carry to the world the revelation on plural marriage, to advocate and defend it. We were told to go without purse or scrip, and on arrival in California to sell our teams and send the money home. (*MLR* 140-41)

Benjamin moved his wife Melissa to Summit Creek and took Brothers Vickers and Udell to Salt Creek. He was released as the presiding elder and by his recommendation Brother Holman was ordained in his place and assigned to watch over Benjamin's family and property. Benjamin estimated that after all his debts were paid, he left over $7,000 in land, houses, grain, cattle, and other property for the welfare of his family. On 22 October he was ready and waiting for the other missionaries. They left from Salt Creek on 24 October 1852 (*MLR* 141).

Chapter VII

A Mission to the Islands

Benjamin and his companions travelled what was then known as the "southern route," holding meetings in some of the settlements along the way (Benjamin Johnson, "A Prophecy Fulfilled"). The group consisted of over forty elders who were on their way to China, Australia, Ceylon, Hindustan, Africa, and the nine called to the Sandwich Islands (*MLR* 142).

On Sunday the company stopped at Parowan where Benjamin was asked to be the final speaker at church. During his talk he prophesied that through mission labors the "Elders of Israel would grow wiser and leaders of nations would look towards Zion for counselors and statesmen" (Benjamin Johnson, "A Prophecy Fulfilled"). Two weeks after his departure, Benjamin wrote a letter to his wife Harriet, in which he expressed his feelings about his mission.

> I'm greatly blessed on the road & the Powers & Spirit of our mission is felt in a marvelous degree. There never was a company that enjoyed a greater amount of its influence. We rejoice in the sacrifice we have made of an omission of social relations in bidding Adieu to our dear wives & children & severing those ties which entwine themselves so closely in every feeling of our natures & caused our Hearts to yearn & our prayers to ascend to our Father in Heaven for the Health, happiness and well being of those we love—knowing that those alone who are willing to make a similar sacrifice can expect to inherit the great blessings of Exaltation and Eternal Lives—for which alone could I have been induced to make so great an offering. This present world is only a small matter when compared to the great field of enjoyment in the worlds that are to come & I had rather lose my present life in some far off clime in the field of usefulness & prove myself worthy of those that I love than to enjoy all the pleasures of life without a prospect of happy associations in the world that is to come. Where if I am faithful to my trust I may hope to enjoy the society of every loved

> object where our honor & exaltation will be according to our integrity and willingness to sacrifice our earthly pleasures for those of a more exalted nature. (Benjamin Johnson, Letter to Harriet, 5 November 1852)

As the company was travelling through hostile Indian territory, they came upon three German gentlemen who were stranded. Although it was understood that these men would be killed if they were found by the Indians, the group decided not to take them along. Benjamin was disturbed when they passed by "without the Spirit of the Good Samaritan," but was unable to convince his companions to help the men. Early the next morning he was greatly relieved when two of the men walked into their camp. As one of them could speak a little English, he pleaded with the missionaries not to leave them again. Benjamin proposed that they take the men with them, but others disagreed. They held a meeting, in which Benjamin acted as advocate for the men.

> The camp was divided, and I said, "You brethren who are willing may help me to take these men, or with the help of the Lord I will do it alone."
>
> I told them to put their things in my wagon, and from Beaver Dam the men remained with me through the whole journey. They traveled mostly on foot, did all my night guarding, brought firewood, and showed great gratitude to me and I believe the Lord was pleased. (*MLR* 143)

Along the way many of their animals, including two of Benjamin's horses, were poisoned. One of Benjamin's horses was so ill that he expected to find it dead in the morning. Realizing he would have to walk if the horse died, Benjamin sought divine aid.

> I had been merciful to two of His unfortunate children, and I asked Him now to have mercy upon me and heal my horse. And I commanded the disease to depart. I wept before the Lord and asked Him how I could go on without my horse. I got up feeling that I had done all I could, and would now leave it in the hands of the Lord. I left the horse lying upon his side, as I supposed to die; but early the next morning I found him standing up, eating and apparently well, put him in the harness, and he was sick no more. To me it was like raising a horse from the dead, and I know the Lord is just as able to heal a horse, ox, cow, or any other animal as he is to heal us, his children, and will do it if we do our duty. (*MLR* 144)

The company arrived at San Bernardino, California on 3 December 1852. As Benjamin's two German friends prepared to leave him, they embraced him in tears of gratitude for saving their lives. They each laid a blanket, pistol, and bowie knife at his feet and insisted he accept them. Benjamin later learned that the third member of their group, an elderly gentleman, was found by an ox train who cared for him and took him to San Bernardino where he was reunited with his companions (MLR 144).

From San Bernardino the missionaries travelled about eighty miles to San Pedro, a coastal port. Because Benjamin was riding in an open wagon, the December rain made the three day journey extremely uncomfortable. At San Pedro, he and another elder were assigned to arrange the missionaries' passage to San Francisco.

While waiting for travel arrangements to be completed, they stayed at a ranch owned and operated by a Spanish family. That night Benjamin had a shocking encounter in which he felt that "the Lord, as well as the devil" had an interest in his experience. He recorded,

> I sought in my natural way to make myself pleasant, both to parents and children. There were three daughters, the most perfect type of Spanish beauty, the eldest married, and the two younger not over fourteen and sixteen years of age. It seemed to me that one could hardly imagine a more perfect brunette beauty. I went to bed but was soon told the landlord wished to see me. I dressed and went below to his room in which was spread a table with wine and dainties. He greeted me cordially and bade me help myself, and turning to his daughters smilingly, told me they were to await my pleasure and bidding. Of all the sly tricks of the devil I felt this to be his arch attempt to destroy me. I thought of Joseph, in Potiphar's house, I looked upon them with love and pity and my very heart wept for such fallen loveliness. I made my excuse and adieus as gracefully as I could, and went to my own couch, carrying almost an anguish of sorrow, pity and regret that such lovely daughters of Eve could be to virtue and purity so insensible and ignorant. (*MLR* 146-47)

Passage was finally arranged aboard the ship *Frémont*, and after ten long and difficult days, they reached their destination (*MLR* 148-49). Since San Francisco was the common port of departure for all the missionaries, they decided to work together to raise the six thousand dollars they needed for their journey. They rented a house large enough to accommodate all forty of them and then met to devise a plan for raising the necessary funds.

It was customary at that time for missionaries to travel without purse or scrip (money or extra food and clothing) as the ancient apostles had done, relying on the people for their needs. The missionaries believed that this would provide a greater opportunity to share their important message with those who assisted them. Benjamin wrote a circular petitioning donations from the people of San Francisco. It read,

> To all to whom they may come, greeting: We the undersigned, missionaries of the Church of Jesus Christ of Latter-day Saints from Salt Lake City, Utah, to the different nations of the earth, respectfully represent to the honorable people of San Francisco, that we, like the Apostles of old have left our homes "without purse or scrip," and are now in your midst awaiting passage to our respective fields of labor. We therefore humbly ask you, in the name of our Master, to assist us with means to defray expenses incidental to our journey, and the God whom we serve shall reward you a hundred fold. (*MLR* 150)

For several days the missionaries went about the city with their petition, but only received meager donations of two and five dollars. At that rate they would never reach their goal. Having been a member of the Utah legislature, Benjamin was invited to visit the California legislature in Sacramento to present his case and ask for help. He was about to speak when John M. Horner, a wealthy Church member living in San Francisco, told him to stop seeking donations and offered to provide the six thousand dollars when it was time to sail. During their remaining two weeks in San Francisco, the missionaries held meetings to discuss the revelation on plural marriage.

Benjamin and his eight companions sailed to the Sandwich Islands on the *Huntress*. During their voyage, Captain James Lambert treated them with extreme kindness (*MLR* 151).

On 17 February 1853 they arrived in Honolulu where they were met by Philip B. Lewis, President of the Sandwich Island Mission (Roberts, 4:68-69; Jensen, *Encyclopedia*, 210). During the previous two years there had been about fifteen missionaries on the islands, but five of them had become discouraged after a brief stay and returned to California. During those years the elders had baptized over six hundred converts and successfully established a church organization (Benjamin Johnson, Letter to S.W. Richards, Deseret News, 23 March 1853). However, the Protestant churches had been established on the islands for decades and had considerable power over the people.

Shortly after their arrival, Benjamin evaluated the mission and the people in a report to Salt Lake City.

> There are on all these islands, about eighty thousand natives, and a few thousand foreigners. There are about twelve hundred native Saints, with a few among the foreign population. We have much priestcraft to contend with, it bears almost universal sway here, and even the king seems disgracefully controlled by its influence, and the natives generally are enslaved by a fear of offending the [Protestant] missionaries. In fact, the present structure of government, although they [non-Mormon churches] may be worth their hundreds of thousand in lands and palaces, is exempt from taxation, while the poor man who has not even a barren patch to raise food for his destitute family, is made to pay a heavy tax, and to work upon the highways, to beautify and embellish the streets leading to the magnificent residences of the [Protestant] missionaries, etc.
>
> The [Protestant] missionaries upon these lands, with all their home revenue, and near forty years' operation, have done not as much as honest men could have done in ten years, without one dollar of foreign revenue to assist them... The natives might have been taught English language, and have been advanced in agriculture, manufacture, and science. But they are now debased by every degrading, immoral, and degenerating principle. And if I am not much mistaken, this people have decreased at least fifty thousand since missionary influence became established among them. These fertile islands, which are capable of producing all the tropical fruits, and the finest wheat, with every comfort to gladden the heart of man, are producing comparatively nothing; and instead of virtue, wealth, and independence, which might have been realized, almost universal vice, poverty, and slavery are the fruits of this great missionary expense... We feel sanguine that this people are of the Covenant blood, and that a great work is to be done among them. Many of them are quick of apprehension, and are apt to believe the truth. They are naturally an honest, and kind-hearted people, and were it not for that unnatural fear of the [Protestant] missionaries, thousands would believe and soon embrace the truth.

> But we look for this yoke soon to be broken off, a revolution in the government is bound soon to take place.
>
> The eyes of the priests are upon us, and they are reading their own downfall in our success. The hand writing begins to appear upon the wall, and they are beginning to tremble; and may their fears be realized, is our earnest prayer. I will not tell you all that we hope and expect upon those subjects, but let time show what the Lord has designed to effect here. (Benjamin Johnson, Letter to S.W. Richards; History of Hawaiian Mission)

In a letter to Joseph Cain, Benjamin reported that "there is but one feeling in our midst, and that is to honor our Priesthood and do the work where unto we are called" (Benjamin Johnson, letter to Joseph Cain, 19 March 1853).

Benjamin enjoyed working and associating with the people and was often invited into their homes. It was the custom among the natives to give nicknames to the missionaries, and they called him Loe Hee Mormonia, which meant "the tall Mormon with black whiskers" (Benjamin Johnson, Diary book A, 1 March 1853). Being away from home and in such a strange environment was a considerable adjustment for Benjamin. Homesickness and the native food were his greatest challenges. Shortly after his arrival, he recorded in his diary,

> I found it [poi] almost impossible to swallow even one mouthful of it as my stomach would not consent to receive it. I, however, hope soon to be able to eat of it, as without, I shall no doubt many times go hungry for food. In going among the natives to see their manners and customs I begin to think the prospect bids fair for me to soon be cured of my fastidiousness in cooking, etc. The poorest meal that I ever eat in my own house would relish better now than the best that I can expect among the Natives. (Benjamin Johnson, Diary Book A, 28 February 1853)

When Benjamin did not hear from his family for some time, he fell into a depression which made him physically ill. After receiving a blessing, he realized the cause of his sickness and rededicated himself to the work which he had come to perform (Benjamin Johnson, Diary Book A, 12 March 1853). He could see more clearly his own limitations as well as the immense task of trying to lift a people above their environment. In anticipating the challenge before him, he said, "I never in my life felt more the force of my weakness and the necessity of calling on the Lord in mighty prayer" (Benjamin Johnson, Diary Book A, 17 March 1853).

Benjamin found that the mission was in poor financial condition, and although he felt that this could be improved, his optimism was not shared by others. He wrote,

> The blessings, predictions and counsels to me by the Presidency, relating to this mission, all tended to inspire a faith that the results or fruits of my labors would be in temporal as well as spiritual good to the people, and to the mission. But in speaking in relation to an improved temporal condition of the mission it seemed to inspire jealously among the brethren, especially in one brother, whose experience and standing should have inspired greater wisdom and discernment. (*MLR* 152-53)

When Benjamin became sick with a fever the night before a missionary conference, he had his cot carried into the meeting room. He was greatly disturbed by what transpired in the meeting and he wrote,

> While lying sick the things I had said growing out of my faith in the future of the mission were unsparingly criticized and inflated by some of the Brethren. To all appearance I was in disgrace for having faith in the words of the Prophets to me. Prejudice against me resulted in [another brother] being chosen first counselor to President Lewis, and in assigning me to take alone, as my field of labor the poorest and most helpless. I listened to it all and wept and prayed for humility, and power to trust in God, that I was there to do His will, and that all might be overruled for His glory and my good. (*MLR* 153)

While endeavoring to learn the native language, Benjamin's mind was on the social and financial troubles of the mission and he felt something must be done. He was pleased when his assignment was changed and he was assigned to serve in Honolulu, for he would now have the opportunity to work on these problems (*MLR* 154-55). Early in 1853 a branch of the Church, "consisting of white people," was organized at Honolulu, and Benjamin was called to be the branch president (History of Hawaiian Mission, 26 April 1853). In a report to the First Presidency, President Lewis wrote,

> We thought it advisable that brother Johnson remain here for the present, to see what can be done among the foreign population, and act as a watchman in the English language, as this is the capital of the kingdom, and the head of all civil

> and religious liberties. He takes charge of the foreign branch here, composed of fifteen or twenty members. (*Millennial Star* 16:62-63)

During the next few months, between three and four hundred converts were baptized within the vicinity of Honolulu (Benjamin Johnson, Letter to J. Horner, 4 June 1853). Concerning the Church at this time, Benjamin wrote,

> I felt an inspiration to urge the ordination of natives to the priesthood, to assist the foreign elders in preaching the gospel. In this, President Lewis and Brother Cannon and others were with me, while others opposed; but no sooner were a few ordained and sent than all objections vanished, for they proved far more efficient than we had hoped. Through them the work spread mightily, and many of the best educated were baptized and soon became efficient auxiliaries.
>
> About the first of May at Honolulu, after a Sabbath meeting, invitation was given to all who wished baptism, and a hundred or more came forward, followed by a multitude to see the ordinance administered. And now the native Saints, as in the days of Jesus, brought out their sick or sent for the Elders to administer to them, and the power of God was greatly manifest in our administrations. Some are healed who for months had been afflicted. Some even for years, and they go forth joyfully into the waters of baptism.
>
> Native elders now in the field were exerting a powerful influence, and it almost seemed as though all the Hawaiian people would become members of the Church. (*MLR* 155-56)

Benjamin described five or six of the natives who were ordained to the priesthood, as being powerful in preaching and called them "Sons of Thunder" (Benjamin Johnson, Letter to J. Horner, 4 June 1853).

On one occasion the mission president and one of his counselors entered into a dispute which lead to threatening words. Overhearing the argument from an adjacent room, Benjamin felt he must reprimand the counselor and defend the President.

> I told them that being a High Priest it became my duty to rebuke his language and spirit; and although not interested in their quarrel, I was interested in seeing that the President of the Mission was not dishonored or outraged in his calling. (*MLR* 153-54)

Through such experiences and success, the mission president's confidence in Benjamin was strengthened.

With permission from President Lewis, Benjamin wrote a letter to King Kamahamaha III, ruler over the Hawaiian kingdom. Over the years the missionaries had encountered difficulties with the government, but shortly before Benjamin's arrival, they had given full consent for missionary work to continue. Benjamin wrote to the King to receive further assurance that they were free to continue proselyting. In the letter, he explained why the missionaries had come to the Sandwich Islands, explained the principles of the Gospel, and told about the Book of Mormon. The letter was translated into Hawaiian, then presented to a member of the King's cabinet, who in turn presented it to the King. After reading it, the King asked his Privy Council to explain it to him. The letter was then entered in the two court journals and printed for publication in both Hawaiian and English (MLR 154-55).

A Ministering Servant

In mid June 1853, a severe smallpox epidemic swept the island. Benjamin said that when the Catholic and Protestant missionaries learned of the disease, they "left their flocks and fled." Many of the physicians were also too frightened to remain, and the natives were filled with terror. Although Benjamin had not been vaccinated for smallpox, he stayed with President Lewis and Elder Farrar to help in whatever way he could. He realized the danger involved if he remained but he said, "my trust is in God as I only seek to benefit my fellow man" (Benjamin Johnson, Diary book B).

When some of the natives died, others were filled with panic, and at the appearance of fever they fled to the sea and plunged to almost certain death (*MLR* 156). Because of his previous experience in caring for the sick and suffering, Benjamin was able to give relief to the people. The epidemic lasted for weeks, claimed hundreds of lives, and was so terrible that President Lewis wrote, "Such scenes of wretchedness and misery, my eyes never before beheld" (*Millennial Star* 16:62-63).

Besides being severely tested physically, Benjamin found this was also a great spiritual trial. He saw good people dying all around him and could not understand why the Lord allowed such things to happen. He said,

> I was in great affliction, and marveled that the Lord would permit all his most faithful servants to die, so dear to us, and whose help we so much needed. I pondered the subject prayerfully until the light of the Lord shone upon my understanding, and I saw multitudes of their race in the spirit world who had lived before them, and there was not one

> there with the priesthood to teach them the gospel. The voice of the Spirit said to me, "Sorrow not, for they are now doing that greater work for which they were ordained, and it is all of the Lord." So I was comforted, knowing that through the Spirit of Elijah, the hearts of the children were now being turned to the fathers in the Spirit land. (*MLR* 157-58)

Experience as a Lawyer

Because of the good the missionaries were accomplishing, the Protestant ministers became jealous and hateful. Some of them influenced the city officials into preventing the Mormon missionaries from visiting their people. The city marshal threatened the elders with charges of violating quarantine regulations if they dared to enter any of the village homes. When they paid no attention to the threats, the city marshal instructed a noted boxer and bully named Turner, to assault the Mormon elders. Turner attacked Elders Lewis and Farrar and "fell upon them like a fiend, beat and bruised them and tore their coats from their backs" (*MLR* 158). Benjamin insisted that justice be done.

The three missionaries went to the officials and filed charges against the assailant. A trial was held the following day. Since the elders did not have an attorney, the court allowed the defense attorney free reign to prosecute Lewis and Farrar for violating quarantine. On the second day of the trial, Benjamin was called forward as a witness.

> On taking the stand I told what I knew of the assault, and then asked His Honor the privilege of acting as attorney for the prosecution, to review the proceedings of the previous day to see that the case was kept properly before the court; for it now appeared reversed from served process, and being somewhat familiar with law terms and proceedings, the court seemed convinced at once as to my qualifications as an attorney-at-law, and permitted me any privileges I asked. I then said I stood before the court as a practical physician, and that as such the plaintiffs in this case had been my assistants, carrying out my instructions in nursing and ministering to the sick; and if the court had doubts as to my capacity and qualifications, I wished him to summon before his court, Doctors Rook and Lathrop, physicians of the Board of Health and Quarantine of the city. Medical phrases as well as law terms were familiar to me, and a few only were necessary to convince the judge of my eminence in medicine as well as law.

> I now had the case all in my own hands, and my evidence being last, the case rested. Lawyer Blair, the leading attorney in the kingdom, made a short plea for the defense, yet honoring me in all the professional eminence claimed, after which I reviewed the case, showing how we had left our homes, coming to these lands without fee or revenue, even without purse or scrip; and as good Samaritans, when their shepherds had deserted them and fled in fear, we had, at the risk of our lives, remained with them to minister comfort and blessing in their hour of suffering and death, and that the assault made upon us was the fruit of jealousy and hate of those by whom they had been deserted and left to die uncared for and alone. I said I did not blame the poor ignorant man employed to do this dirty work, and asked lenience for him. (*MLR* 159-61; *Deseret News*, 15 December 1853)

Benjamin felt confident that he had effectively presented the case. He then used this opportunity to explain to the people why the missionaries had come to their land. He pointed out that they had left their families and homes in pursuit of a "higher and holier calling." He felt moved by the Spirit as he spoke, and the listeners were so stirred by his remarks that even the bully, Turner, wept. The court found the assailant guilty, fined him twelve dollars and let him go (*MLR* 159-61).

In reporting the trial to the First Presidency, the Mission President wrote, "Benjamin F. Johnson acted as attorney in the case, and brought it through triumphantly, by the assistance of the Holy Spirit" (Millennial Star 16:61-63).

So that Benjamin's talents as a lawyer could be used whenever needed, he was appointed as the attorney for the mission and was given money to purchase the whole code of Hawaiian laws. From this incident sprang a new career through which Benjamin was to continue to render service and gain distinction.

A Counselor to a King

At this time the political situation on the island was very unstable (History of Hawaiian Mission, 29 December 1853; *Millennial Star* 15:429). Dr. Judd, the Prime Minister, who was a former Protestant missionary among the natives, was the real power behind the throne. He had great wealth and influence, and it was believed that he even held a mortgage on the royal palace. As Judd's power and influence grew, he became hated by many people and was also opposed by the dominant church to which many of the cabinet officers belonged. Mass meetings were held, and inflammatory speeches were made against him. The people chose a committee of thirteen to present petitions to the King. The committee demanded the removal of Dr. Judd, but the King did not act immediately, and after a month of waiting the citizens became angry. The committee tried to find out the King's plans, but he would not see them (*MLR* 161-62). The courthouse and other large halls became crowded with people indignantly protesting against Dr. Judd.

One night, after observing one of these meetings Benjamin had a dream.

> I dreamed that I stood upon the side of a mountain and near it ran a large river of beautiful water. As I looked down upon the river I saw a large building apparently designed for a mill, of plain and rude workmanship, built of coarse and unseasoned timber. As I looked I saw a smoke arise from the building, heard the cry of "fire" and saw people running and shouting "fire." (*MLR* 162)

> It seemed that the wind blew strong from the mountain towards the building. The people came up on the opposite side of the building, to put out the fire, and they were blinded by the smoke which blew in their faces. I thought how foolish they were to thus stay on the opposite side from the wind, to be blinded with the smoke. Looking, I saw a bucket with a rope attached on a flume through which the water ran. I quickly took it up, drew it full of water, looked for the center of the fire, dashed it in, and, all at once the flame was extinguished.
>
> I saw a multitude of people came crowding into the building, wondering by whom the fire had been extinguished. Although I was with them, they appeared to comprehend nothing of my agency in the matter. I thought they were almost wild with joy, that the building, although somewhat charred and damaged, had been saved. They calculated that the damage the building had sustained was about fifty thousand dollars. (Benjamin Johnson, "A Prophecy Fulfilled")

When he awoke, Benjamin was strongly impressed by the dream but did not understand what it meant. After relating it to one of his fellow missionaries, Benjamin said that he believed the interpretation was near.

Soon Benjamin was notified that, at the King's request, Prince Leholeho and Chief Halalia, a member of the Privy Council and friend and counselor to the King, would visit Benjamin the following night (*MLR* 162). The King wanted them to explain his great political trouble and ask for Benjamin's advice. Benjamin was convinced that this was the meaning of his dream (Benjamin Johnson, "A Prophecy Fulfilled"). So "as Nicodemus came by night, so did Halalia and the Prince come to obtain counsel from a humble Mormon elder" (MLR 163). Benjamin prayed that he would have the wisdom to counsel these men in matters of government.

> Halalia said the King was now in great trouble; that nearly all of his foreign subjects had become enemies to Dr. Judd and had demanded his removal. While he, and most of his native subjects, felt that he had been a friend and benefactor to the Hawaiian people, the King himself was under great personal obligation to him for money loaned, and he had been for some time considering to whom he should apply for advice. He had thought of the American Minister, but the Americans wished to obtain his kingdom by annexation, and the English, French, and all other governments had some selfish end in view, relating to his government so that he had no confidence in their friendship; but he felt that the counsel we would give him would be disinterested and wise; that he had read our words and seen our acts, and knew of our faithful friendship to his people in their distress. And now he wished to learn our thoughts in regard to his present political trouble. (*MLR* 163)

This situation presented a tremendous challenge to Benjamin for never before in his thirty-five years, had he been called upon to give counsel to a head of state.

Benjamin explained to his guests that he had not been sent to Hawaii to give counsel to the government, but rather to teach the gospel of Christ. But seeing that they were in a dire situation, he consented to give what counsel came into his heart by the Spirit. He told them that if Dr. Judd was a good man desiring the welfare of the kingdom, he would abdicate his position for the sake of peace. As he was not willing to do so, he evidently had motives other than the good of the people and the kingdom. Benjamin said,

> We feel that the present great political trouble and mourning is owing to Dr. Judd not being a good man, but wickedly holding a grasp upon the government office against the wishes of the people, for which there is no necessity, as the King has many true subjects of more than equal ability, any one of whom he could appoint as Dr. Judd's successor. (Benjamin Johnson, "A Prophecy Fulfilled")

The King's messengers seemed pleased with this advice, stating that they had not previously considered such facts. The next morning, Dr. Judd was dismissed as prime minister, which caused great rejoicing among the people (Benjamin Johnson, "A Prophecy Fulfilled"). Benjamin said,

> When the Committee of Thirteen called a meeting for mutual congratulations, I sat in their midst, full of contemplation as to the small and unperceived means by which the Lord brings to pass his purposes. Just as I dreamed, so it all came to pass, and no one but myself could realize that the Lord had used the humble efforts of His elders to accomplish what the wisdom and wealth of the multitude could not accomplish. When the auditing committee examined Dr. Judd's ministerial records and accounts it was said he had swindled the government to the amount of $50,000, as I had dreamed. (*MLR* 164)
>
> Thus my prophecy (that "the Elders of Israel would grow wiser; that the nations of the earth would begin to look toward Zion for counselors and statesmen," and that some of the Elders in that company "would be called upon to give counsel to some of the rulers of the lands to which they were sent,") and my dreams were fulfilled and peace returned to the people. Joy came to our hearts that the Lord, through the inspiration of His Holy Spirit, had made us, His humble Elders, the means of giving saving counsel to his princes. (Benjamin Johnson, "A Prophecy Fulfilled")

This experience strengthened Benjamin's faith in dreams and increased his confidence before the Lord.

Added Responsibility

At the semi-annual conference of the Hawaiian Mission on 6 October 1853 Benjamin was singled out for his commendable achievements during the brief time he had been in the mission. The clerk of the conference recorded that "the conference highly approved of the labors of Elder Benjamin F. Johnson during the past six months in Honolulu." Throughout his mission Benjamin continued to serve in the Honolulu area whenever he was not doing mission business elsewhere (History of Hawaiian Mission, 6 October 1853).

During this conference the mission presidency outlined three mission objectives and organized committees to achieve them. These objectives were to have the Book of Mormon and other Church literature printed in the Hawaiian language, to find a suitable gathering place on the islands for the native Saints, and to work out a solution to the problem between the Church and the government regarding schools.

Benjamin was asked to serve on each of these committees (Benjamin Johnson, "A Prophecy Fulfilled"; MLR 164). To strengthen him in fulfilling this new responsibility, he received a wonderful blessing under the hands of Elder George Q. Cannon. Benjamin wrote,

> Brother Cannon prophesied upon my head many comforting things. He said I should be a counselor to my Brethren; that I should be called to counsel Kings and Princes, and be blessed in all the responsibilities and callings, and be able to preach to the natives, and return to my home in honor. (Benjamin Johnson, Diary Book C, 12 October 1853)

There was great need to have the Book of Mormon and other Church literature printed in the Hawaiian language. Elder Cannon had been working on the translation of the Book of Mormon for nearly two years, but to complete the project they needed supplies and money for a printing press (Jenson, *The Historical Record*, 4). Benjamin was assigned to help President Lewis and Elder Cannon raise the necessary funds and purchase the press (History of Hawaiian Mission, 29 March 1853, 6 October 1853; Benjamin Johnson, Letter to "An old friend," 19 November 1853; Benjamin Johnson, Letter to S.W. Richards). Although the cost would be considerable and the members of the Church were poor, Benjamin approached this assignment with determination and optimism.

> Heretofore the mission had been very poor, and it appeared a great undertaking, especially to raise the money necessary to buy a press and material sufficient for the work before us. But with me it was a principle of faith, and according to prediction that means should come into my hands through the blessing of the Lord, to sustain and comfort my brethren, and to accomplish every purpose pertaining to my mission. Thus far the way had been marvelously opened, and I felt strong faith that we would succeed. (*MLR* 164-65)

The mission's objective for gathering the native Saints in the islands was unusual. As people were converted by the missionaries, they were generally instructed to leave their homes and join the Saints in Utah. This gathering was essential to President Brigham Young's plan to build a strong central location where Zion could be established. It also allowed the new converts to freely practice their religion, including plural marriage, in the isolated Mormon settlements. However, most of the members in the Sandwich Islands were comparatively poor and unskilled. There were also laws preventing the natives from emigrating from the islands. Therefore, President Young sent word that these converts should not be called upon to gather to the Salt Lake Valley, but that a suitable place should be located and established somewhere within the mission (History of Hawaiian Mission, 6 October 1853). Benjamin was selected to help achieve that directive.

To find a suitable location for the gathering of the native Saints, the committee travelled to the various islands. Benjamin said that he viewed terrain and plant life that was more beautiful than anything he had ever seen before.

The night before they left for Lahaini a storm arose causing rough seas in the channel. After getting through the choppy waters, they were caught in "a dead and sultry calm of tropical heat." The oarsmen made little progress through this, and the passengers became seasick. Benjamin and others were so ill that they passed out. He awoke in time to hear Elder Cannon ask a native member to pray. Standing on the bow of the boat, Brother Napela asked the Lord to send wind so they would not perish. Suddenly, the wind began to blow, and they continued their journey safely (*MLR* 169).

A site for gathering was not found at this time, because of a disagreement between Benjamin and another member of the committee. Initially, the dispute was over the location for gathering, but soon developed into a personal conflict. One elder accused Benjamin of seeking to control the mission, but Benjamin felt that jealousy was at the root of the problem. A meeting was called the following day to discuss the charge against Benjamin. After full consideration, President Lewis and the whole council decided that this brother had no cause for accusation, and should apologize (Benjamin Johnson, Handwritten Manuscript of *My Life's Review*). The brother said he was sorry and did not wish to hurt Benjamin. To this Benjamin wrote, "although we may try we can do each other no lasting harm, but we can easily hurt ourselves" (Benjamin Johnson, Handwritten Manuscript of *My Life's Review*). The committee decided to postpone looking for a gathering place.

About this time Benjamin received a sad letter from his sister, Julia, in which she said,

> I suppose you have heard of our dear mother's death before this. She is gone and we are left to mourn her loss, no not her loss but ours. We know she cannot meet with loss; she has gone to receive the crown that was prepared for her, which must be glorious. Oh if I had but one short hour to see you,

> how much more could I say than with this slow pen of mine.
> (Julia Johnson Babbitt)

His mother had died in Council Bluffs while waiting to cross the plains. Benjamin was further bereaved to learn that his sister Delcena, one of his daughters, and a son whom he had adopted some years before, had all died within the past year (Benjamin Johnson, Letter to "An Old Friend" 19 November 1853). To his sorrow was added the news of an Indian attack on the settlement of Summit Creek. His family had been driven from their home, their home was burned, livestock and other property were destroyed, some men were killed, and others wounded.[10] As Benjamin thought about his losses, he was moved to write,

> From a property valued at nearly $7,000, I am again reduced to poverty. But there also came tiding of one great happiness to balance against these disasters: there had been born to me two sons—a great gain—for others are not lost, only gone before, to meet again. And so while I am sorrowful I am yet glad—grateful to the Lord in my heart (*MLR* 170).

Benjamin continued his labors in Honolulu where he presided over the foreign branch of the Church and took care of much of the business of the mission. Elder George Q. Cannon remained there to preach to the natives, and Benjamin took great pleasure in their companionship. (*MLR* 170-71; Cannon, Deseret News, 2 March 1854)

Concerned with finding land for a gathering place for the Hawaiian members and raising money for the printing press, Benjamin was elated when Halalia, the friend and counselor to the King, offered to help with both projects. This wealthy native offered to give any of his lands on the island of Lanai to the Church, and also loan five hundred dollars toward the purchase of the press. Benjamin felt that this unusual demonstration of generosity was due to the close bond between them. Regarding their friendship, Benjamin wrote,

> He regards me as his *hai carne*—meaning a friendship greater than that for a brother, a friendship of perfect reciprocity in everything, not excepting money, wardrobe, grown daughters, young children, and not even his bed and wife. Such was their ancient and still is their present custom.(*MLR* 170)

[10] Benjamin later entered a claim for ten thousand dollars against the US Government for his losses from the Indian attack but never collected anything (*Deseret News*, 6 December 1905).

Brother Dennis, a native member of the Church, also agreed to loan them one thousand dollars for the printing press. Brother Dennis had been a true friend from the first and had sometimes provided Benjamin with shelter, money for clothing, and travelling expenses (*MLR* 171, 175). On one occasion, after selling some property, Brother Dennis was anxious to put his money in safe-keeping. He went to Benjamin's room with a sack containing $7000 in gold and told Benjamin he could use any amount of it as if it were his own and could give any to his friends if they were in need (*MLR* 175).

Besides these two generous loans, the missionaries had collected a large amount of money. Benjamin and Elder Cannon recommended to President Lewis that arrangements be made for procuring a press from Boston. It was decided that when Elder Cannon returned home he should make those arrangements (*MLR* 173). To supplement the funds already received, Benjamin drafted a petition soliciting more funds from members of the Church and friends in California.

In January 1854, Brother Dennis, who planned to emigrate to California, offered his tin and coppersmith business to Benjamin on credit. As President Lewis was a master of the smith business, it seemed that this could prove to be profitable for the mission. Benjamin immediately wrote to President Lewis, recommending that the mission purchase the business, which he did (Benjamin Johnson, Letter to Harriet, 28 January 1854; *MLR* 174). To assure the success of the newly acquired industry, President Lewis devoted most of his time to it. He assigned Benjamin to take over the spiritual duties of the mission and gave him a blessing to this end (*MLR* 174).

Benjamin found that his added responsibilities left him no spare time. He took over all the Church business in Honolulu, visited with officers of government, attended to the legal matters of the mission, and helped Sister Lewis care for the home in which the missionaries lived (Benjamin Johnson, Letter to Harriet, 28 January 1854). Benjamin was also responsible to report the progress and needs of the mission to the First Presidency (Benjamin Johnson Handwritten Manuscript for *My Life's Review*).

Defender of Plural Marriage

It had now been about eighteen months since Church leaders had begun to teach the law of plural marriage publicly. As was the case in other Christian nations, the missionaries in the Sandwich Islands were experiencing intense opposition from the Protestant churches. In April 1854 the largest island newspaper published a scathing article entitled "Mormon Polygamy," which condemned the Church and portrayed President Brigham Young as "a seducer, adulterer, a fiend of lust—a man of all wickedness and corruption" (Benjamin Johnson, Letter to Harriet, 22 April 1854). Using Biblical quotations, the writer sought "to prove all ancient polygamy reprobate to virtue." Benjamin was incensed by this attack and felt that something should immediately be done to vindicate the Church and the Prophet. He tried to persuade President Lewis and Elder Cannon to write a response, but although both men were very able writers, they declined (*MLR* 176-77). Benjamin felt a personal responsibility to teach and defend plural marriage for he had been given this special charge by the First Presidency when he was called as a missionary. Both President Lewis and Elder Cannon had gone on their missions at a time when the doctrine was not publicly preached, and they may have felt it was wiser to keep silent in the matter. However Benjamin favored a direct approach to the problem.

> To me this attack upon our religion and beloved President was more than I could bear, and a desire to repel it was like a smoldering fire within me. Without regard for weakness of body I must attempt what to others stronger seemed too great an undertaking. I realized that if I was able to do anything according to my desire it must be through the inspiration of the Spirit of God.
>
> I closed my door, and bowed weeping before the Lord, told Him our enemies were exulting over us through the falsehoods published against His servants and the Gospel we were sent to preach, and asked Him to make me able to vindicate the truth to His own glory. In this feeling, I poured out my soul in earnest prayer, dedicating myself to the guidance of His Spirit.
>
> I then sat down with my pen, trembling under the great and new duty of writing for publication our defense; and so I wrote, and if fear, doubt, or self glory brought darkness I at once prayed for the light; and thus I continued for two days and nights to write and search the scriptures for the proofs needed in the reply. And when I had finished the manuscript and read it to Brother Lewis he was full of joy, and said the Lord had been with me. Brother Cannon with all the brethren were called in to hear it, and all appeared to feel as President Lewis had expressed. (*MLR* 176-77)

Although Benjamin thought that his twenty-six page article was good, he could not find a newspaper willing to publish it. The missionaries decided to send the article to San Francisco to be published in pamphlet form, and donations were collected to finance the project (Benjamin Johnson, Letter to Harriet, 22 April 1854). The mission received four hundred of these pamphlets which were immediately distributed throughout the islands. Benjamin wrote,

> We at once sent copies to the King, and to each member of his cabinet; his Privy Council, and to each foreign minister; also to the Board of Foreign Missions and to every prominent officer in the government. For many days there was general excitement throughout the city, and had a thunderbolt fallen at the feet of our enemies, it would not have made a greater sensation. To me it was instructive and amusing to hear the comments and remarks by the people.... While men who thought for themselves seemed anxious to make my acquaintance. Even General Miller, the pompous British Minister, made repeated calls and brought the French Minister and others, taking copies to send to his friends, assuring us that one copy should go in a report to his Government. In all of this I saw how honorable the Lord could make His unlearned servants, if humble, when at heart they desire to honor Him in a defense of the truth. (*MLR* 179)

The success of this pamphlet gave Benjamin confidence and experience to write other articles on plural marriage. Benjamin's defense of plural marriage brought his literary skills to the attention of the Church leaders in Utah. In 1854 the First Presidency issued an "Eleventh General Epistle" to the Church in which they reported the growth of the Church throughout the world. In it they said, "In the Sandwich Islands, under the superintendence of Elders Phillip B. Lewis, George Q. Cannon, B. F. Johnson, and others, the work has been eminently successful."

At a mission conference in July 1854, Benjamin was sustained as "Counselor *pro tem*" to President Lewis in the absence of Elder Tanner, who had travelled to California (History of Hawaiian Mission, 25 July 1854). According to the minutes of the three-day conference, the final day was spent in fasting and prayer. This proved to be a day of rejoicing with a rich outpouring of the Spirit. Elder George Q. Cannon wrote,

> We had a long meeting, everyone speaking their feelings freely. Brothers Woodbury and Johnson spoke in tongues and the interpretation was also given; all felt the importance of hearkening more diligently than heretofore to the counsel of the presidency here.

> We adjourned until evening when we held a blessing meeting. Brother Lewis was anointed and blessed first, under the hands of his counselors and the other brethren, Brother Johnson being mouth. Brothers Johnson and Karen were then blessed, Brother Lewis being mouth. I was mouth several times and afterwards by the request of Brother Lewis I blessed him and also Brother Johnson. (History of Hawaiian Mission, 27 July 1854)

Forty years later, Benjamin noted that the blessing he received at this mission conference under the hands of President Lewis and Elder Cannon was still being fulfilled (*MLR* 180).

Soon after the conference, Elder Cannon and other missionaries left for the United States. Benjamin helped provide money for their passage (Cannon 142). He was sad to see Elder Cannon leave, not only because of their pleasant association, but also because Benjamin knew of no other missionary who was qualified to take charge of the press (*MLR* 180).

With more urgent matters taken care of, Benjamin again turned his attention to locating a gathering place. One of the main reasons for gathering was to isolate the Saints and protect them from the corrupt influences of their environment. Benjamin wrote,

> You can hardly imagine the low and drunken conditions of this Priest enslaved people. These Isles are truly the Brothers of the Pacific. And it seems that virtue here was never known or that it has taken to flight. Foreigners are but little different from the natives and thousands are aging with the curse, that nature designed should follow licentiousness. And under the present condition of things, this people would become wholly extinct in a few years but it seems that the providence of God has interposed to preserve a remnant .(Benjamin Johnson, Letter to J. Horner)

Although President Brigham Young had counseled that a location be found in the islands, one of the missionaries believed that it would be better for them to emigrate to California and so he travelled there to obtain a ship for this purpose (Benjamin Johnson, Letter to Heber C. Kimball, 28 March 1854). In the summer of 1854, President Young again sent specific instructions that the place for gathering should be established on one of the islands and that the gathering should commence as soon as possible.

As a member of the original committee and now as a member of the mission presidency, Benjamin was given a special charge to find a suitable place. President Lewis gave Benjamin a blessing and told him he would know the area the Lord had chosen (Hammond). After obtaining farm implements, seeds, and the necessary outfit the missionaries sailed for Lanai in August 1854.

One morning, after several days of searching, Benjamin and Brother Green were walking with little attention to their direction or destination (*MLR* 181).

> We came to a tree, and stopped to look around. But when we did, it was with an admiration and an inspiration that filled us both, and I exclaimed, "This is the spot we have been looking for!" to which he bore testimony. It was a plot of some hundreds of acres of excellent mesa or table lands, sufficiently elevated to overlook the whole beautiful valley. (*MLR* 182)

When the other missionaries saw the valley they all agreed that this was the place. Benjamin dedicated the area as a gathering place for the native saints, naming "the plot 'Joseph' and the valley 'Ephraim.'" He blessed the spot saying that "through the faithfulness of the elders from this spot salvation should begin to go forth to the children of Joseph upon these lands" (*MLR* 182). The native members were enthused about their new gathering place, and through hard work and divine help they prospered (Benjamin Johnson, Letter to George Q. Cannon, 15 October 1854).

When a new group of missionaries arrived in September, Benjamin helped President Lewis instruct and direct them in their various assignments. The group included fifteen-year-old Elder Joseph F. Smith, and they all appeared anxious to learn the language and cheerfully adapted themselves to the task (History of Hawaiian Mission, 29 November 1854). Benjamin's nephew Sixtus E. Johnson was also one of the new missionaries.

Benjamin was asked by the First Presidency to set Sixtus apart upon his arrival in the islands. Benjamin said this was in fulfillment of a dream he had a few nights before in which President Heber C. Kimball told him that his nephew was on his way and that Benjamin was to set him apart for his mission (*MLR* 184).

Since Benjamin had been away from home for more than two years and some of the elders who had come into the mission with him had already returned to Utah, he thought that his mission was also drawing to a close. In writing to President Brigham Young, Benjamin considered the experiences of the previous two years:

> I have ever felt to rejoice in my mission to these lands, and to be thankful for the many mercies and blessings I have enjoyed since leaving the home of the Saints; and humbly

> trust that the experiences I have gained may never be lost upon myself.
>
> I pray that I may ever be humble and that I may live to become a blessing to my fellow man, and to manifest that love which is due to the cause of virtue and truth. (History of Hawaiian Mission, 20 November 1854)

Benjamin found himself growing physically weaker because of a terrible cough and pains in his side so President Lewis advised him to return home (Benjamin Johnson, Letter to his brother, 19 October 1854). But the printing press arrived at the same time, and money was needed to pay the freight bill and other expenses. Feeling a sense of responsibility, Benjamin worked two more months helping to raise the necessary funds. In December the mission presidency received a letter from Elder Parley P. Pratt advising them to ship the printing press and materials back to San Francisco in order to reduce the cost of publishing. (Benjamin Johnson, Diary Book D, 30 December 1854). Since there was now sufficient money to meet all the mission's expenses, Benjamin felt worthy of a full and honorable release from his missionary service (*MLR* 183-84).

Although his two year mission had been primarily a pleasant and rewarding experience, thoughts of returning to his home and family filled him with excitement. His roots had sunk deep into the valleys of Utah and his love and longing for his home in the mountains prompted Benjamin to express his feelings through poetry.

MY MOUNTAIN HOME
Yea beauteous vales of Deseret,
My peaceful, happy Mountain Home;
The lovely scenes I'll ne'er forget
Though far away from Thee I roam.

Thy rock-bound mountains lofty-bold,
With snow-crest tops that tower so high,
Have been prepared from days of old
Thy proud oppressors to defy.

Thy scented chambers are designed
A safe retreat for all the just,
Who peace shall in thy bosom find
When war and pestilence sweep the earth.

There midst Mount Ephraim's tops shall rise
The hand of God by His command,
And catch the wondering nations' eyes,
The joy of Saints from every land.

Then shall the sons of God rejoice,
And there the words of life be known,
And there be heard our Prophet's voice,
And there again his face be shown.

And then from those we've bid adieu,
Who're sleeping now beneath the sod,
We'll learn what we for them shall do
That they, too, may be heirs of God.

Then may I ever faithful prove
Till I return, no more to roam,
To dwell in peace with those I love,
In thee My virtuous Mountain Home.

(Benjamin Johnson, Diary Book C, 1 September 1853)

As Benjamin prepared to return home, he realized he did not have the fifty dollars needed for his passage to California. President Lewis said he would evaluate the financial condition of the mission and use any surplus money for the ticket. Benjamin decided that if there was sufficient money it would be a sign that he should return home, otherwise he would remain until the Lord opened the way. He knew that he had been called on his mission by the Lord and that when the Lord was ready to release him He would make it known. Anticipating a reunion with his family, Benjamin could not help feeling disappointed when President Lewis balanced the mission finances and found no surplus. He tried to suppress a feeling to ask President Lewis to recalculate it, but he finally asked, indicating that he felt prompted to do so. The money was carefully counted again and when every debt had been accounted for, there was exactly fifty dollars left.

> President Lewis was astonished and my heart was full for I then remembered a prophecy to my mother, when in my youth, that while some of her sons were in foreign lands the Angel of the Lord should provide for them and with their own hands should minister to their wants. (*MLR* 186)

Benjamin had developed a love for missionary work and the people of the Sandwich Islands, and he found it difficult to leave. He said,

> The native Saints, learning I was soon to leave them, came with their small offerings in money—large considering their poverty—and with tears and sobs said, "Goodbye." I found about $20 in these small sums. I was glad in the hope of seeing again my family, but had not realized how my heart was entwined with these poor people, and it required an effort to subdue my own grief at parting with them. (*MLR* 187)

This gift from the native Saints was a token of their love and respect for Benjamin. The twenty dollars represented a considerable sacrifice when one considers their poverty. Elder George Q. Cannon explained, "The islanders had but little money. A dollar with them was a very large sum. A ten cent piece was a much larger sum with them generally, and more difficult to procure, than a dollar was to Americans" (Cannon, 142).

At his last meeting before leaving the islands, Benjamin asked President Lewis for a blessing. In the blessing, President Lewis prophesied many joyful things for Benjamin and said that although the voyage home would be prolonged, the angel of the Lord would be with him and he would arrive safely. He also told Benjamin that he would return to his families in health and peace and that he would labor in the Holy Temples of the Lord and become a Savior on Mt. Zion (*MLR* 188).

The Return Home

Benjamin sailed for home on 16 January 1855. During the journey there was a terrible storm and a fire on board the ship. One morning while on deck Benjamin was thrown by the motion of the ship and would have gone overboard had his arm not caught on an iron rod. He knew he was being divinely protected, but he was grateful when his twenty-two day voyage ended (*MLR* 190).

While in San Francisco Benjamin visited with Elder Parley P. Pratt who complimented Benjamin for his service in the islands. Elder Pratt said that nothing had been published on plural marriage that was better than Benjamin's pamphlet (*MLR* 188-92).

From San Francisco the missionaries sailed to San Pedro, encountering a terrible storm at sea.

Needing to secure safe travel to Utah, Benjamin joined a company of men who were leaving the following week. With some of the money he was taking to President Young and others, he purchased horses and supplies for the trip. He was told that the only saddle horse left was a colt which was wild and had thrown everyone who had tried to ride it. He was afraid of being hurt by the animal, but as time was running out, he had no other choice. Deciding to trust in the Lord, he nervously prepared to mount it.

> I saddled my colt, thinking of what Holladay had told me. The feeling I can never forget as I raised my foot to the stirrup, and my heart to the Lord, for I had no hope but in Him. I left the colt to himself; he stood for a moment as if surprised, then awkwardly followed. I patted him and talked to him as if he were a child, and soon saw that my talking and fondling pleased him. I will only say that through the blessing of the Lord in answer to prayer, one of the most vicious colts in Southern California became a faithful servant, friend and companion, gentle, obedient, and true; and proved the hardiest and most desirable saddle horse in the whole company. (*MLR* 194)

While travelling through some thick timber and brush, the company was surprised by a band of about one hundred Indians. Benjamin had just dismounted his horse when several of them jumped up in front of him. When the men tried to drive their pack animals into the open plain the Indians formed lines on either side, with their bows ready. Seeing no chance for escape, they attempted to talk with the Indians. Then Benjamin had an idea.

> I remembered that Nephi—my nephew—had been among the Piutes and spoke his name to them. They at once turned to me, and we made them understand that he was my brother's son; and so they knew we were Mormons, which was what they were trying to find out. Had they learned otherwise we would have been doomed. We gave them biscuits and tobacco and told them of a horse we had left behind they might have, so they hurried away to find it. We hastened forward feeling we had been delivered from the jaws of death. (*MLR* 195)

Arriving home on 26 March 1855, Benjamin found his family was still destitute from the Indian wars (Benjamin Johnson, "A Life Sketch").

> I returned in debt, having used money of others in the purchase of my outfit, to the amount of $150, and I had promised myself I would not go to Salt Lake City to see the Presidency until I could take the money with me and repay it. In the depleted condition of our means this might be difficult to do at once, and it caused some weight upon my mind,

ey told me they had just
for a mule. So I was in no
l been before me. (*MLR*

City and received a cordial wel-
tion for his missionary labors.
the arm and said, "Bennie, I
ead your defense of polygamy,
).
and counseled him to rebuild
uin.[11] Happy to be called to
neet the immense challenge

devastating financial
is mission were gone.
destroyed by locusts.
hich to purchase any.
orely distressed (*MLR*
ke City for $120, and

Santaquin), Benjamin
cted a cabin, and start-
eal inviting families to

build a fort and
ummit Creek, in
s, to invite to our
ho are looking for
who purpose to
are looking for a
s by which we are
the present

Chapter VIII

Return to Colonizing

After returning from his mission, Benjamin faced
difficulties. All the buildings he had erected before h
and shortly after his return, forty acres of wheat were
There was no grain in storage and no money with w
With thirty people to provide for, Benjamin was s
197). In desperation, he sold a choice lot in Salt La
with the money was able to feed his family for a time.

Determined to succeed at Summit Creek (
replanted his crops, built corrals, put up hay, constru
ed building a stone fort. He sent the following app
join him in rebuilding the settlement.

SUMMIT CITY.
Oct. 5th, 1855
EDITOR OF DESERT NEWS:
Dear Sir:

As I am directed by proper authority to
replace the settlement formerly made at S
Utah County, I wish, through your column
assistance, some of the new immigration w
a desirable location, or those of your city
leave for a country residence. Those who
good situation, and understand the facilitie
surrounded will, it appears to us, require
welcome to determine them to become ou

Standing upon the site for our fort we
the Utah Lake and adjacent country, of
miles distant, and of Springville, Palmyr
er being about six miles to the north of
have supposed, from the altitude
ore subject to frost than our n
for frost visits us from fou
wer lands, consequent

> and vines we fancy it will not be excelled by any spot in the mountains.
>
> The plan for our fort was furnished by architect T. O. Angel, as designed by President B. Young, who pointed out the site for its location. It is to be two stories in height; the first story is to be built of stone, and must be put up this fall, in order to be our protection through the winter and cropping season in the spring. It will not be difficult to accomplish this, when each section finds a claimant with willing hands, as materials are easy of access, and some are already on the ground.
>
> Men and teams are needed; also a number of stone masons, a good carpenter, and blacksmith, all of whom it is hoped will soon be ready to lend a hand before the present season is too far advanced. We trust that all who may desire to associate with us, will feel to cheerfully comply with the instructions given, viz: "that our families remain in other settlements until our own is provided with safe and ample protection." Such are the conditions on which we should be happy to see some fifteen or twenty more of our brethren ready and earnest to engaged in developing the facilities of and in beautifying the already delightful situation for the future "Summit City." (Deseret News, 17 October 1855)

That fall, when Benjamin's crops were again destroyed by crickets and an early frost, he decided to postpone the settlement until the following year (*MLR* 197-98).

Benjamin was re-elected to the Legislative Council where he associated with many friends, resulting in an "unusually pleasant" winter in Fillmore.[12] Among those he worked with were his brother Joel, who was Chaplain of the House, and his brother-in-law Almon W. Babbitt, who was Secretary of State. The following fall, Brother Babbitt was killed by Cheyene Indians while returning from Washington, D.C. (*MLR* 198–202).

Wishing to become an authorized attorney, Benjamin wrote and passed the State bar exam and was admitted as a member of the Utah Bar. His certificate, or "Sheep Skin," was presented to him by the clerk of the Supreme

---

[12]The fifth annual session of the Legislature of Utah convened in Fillmore 10 December 1855. This was, however, the only session of the Legislature ever held in Fillmore. Although the site for Fillmore had been selected specifically for the purpose of building the capital city, it was evident that Salt Lake City was industrially and socially the real center.

Court on 15 January 1856 (Benjamin Johnson, Letter to Harriet, 22 March 1856). Because of his political position, experience, and talents, Benjamin was called as a delegate to the Constitutional Convention for the State of Deseret where he played a significant role in preparing Utah for statehood (Hunter, *Utah—The Story of Her People*, 284; *MLR* 198).

On 3 February 1856 Benjamin was married to his fifth wife, Sarah Melissa Holman, by President Young (*MLR* 199). That spring, Benjamin turned his attention to rebuilding Summit Creek. With his other families comfortably settled in Payson, Benjamin took Sarah Melissa with him to establish their new home (*MLR* 199). Benjamin induced more than twenty other families to go with them (Santaquin Ward History).

For the third year in a row their crops were destroyed by crickets. With a severe shortage of food, Benjamin divided what they had among his families and with determination and faith in God, prepared for a year of famine (*MLR* 199). They put their flour and corn meal into two sacks and dedicated them to the Lord. Benjamin and Sarah Melissa agreed that as long as they had flour no one would go away from their door hungry. Benjamin explained,

> As president of the settlement we had many calls from friends and travelers and all were supplied. And whenever we heard that any of our neighbors were without bread a share was taken to them and there stood our two sacks side by side in the one and only room we occupied. How often our eyes turned, wondering to see that they were not yet nearly empty until a conviction strong as knowledge itself, assured us that the Lord had accepted our offering and that our bread was like the widow's meal and cruse of oil. (Openshaw)

As the end of the famine drew near their hearts lifted.

> Realizing that so many were in scarcity while we had felt no lack, I did not wish to pass through the approaching harvest without realizing a little of that scarcity of which others had felt so much. I said to my wife in a partly thoughtless way, that as we have as yet seen no scarcity I hoped our bread would be out a week or two, that we might more fully realize what others had suffered. Our assurance of bread had become to us a principle of faith without fear, so we kept on going as we had and took no further thought even, to look at the sacks, until about 10 days before a new supply would come, my wife said, "Benjamin, our bread is all gone." At

> first I felt a little surprise and chagrin, but in a moment I remembered what I had said, and I knew the Lord had taken me at my word. (*MLR* 200)

When the harvest came it was neither sufficient to replenish depleted supplies nor to provide enough for their immediate needs. Years later Benjamin looked upon those times of comparative poverty as one of the happiest periods in his life (*MLR* 200). Although the crops were sparse, much progress was made in building the colony. After visiting the settlement, Elders Joseph Young and Albert P. Rockwood, said,

> We accepted the polite invitation of President Johnson to remain all day at Santa Quin [sic]. This settlement is only a year old, yet it exhibits a wonderful development for its age.
>
> A big field of 1000 acres has been taken in, and the fence is nearly completed. The crops look well and there is every reason to believe that this will be a flourishing settlement. (Santaquin Ward History; Deseret News 7:96)

Benjamin was re-elected to the legislature in the fall of 1856. Since the legislature had moved to Salt Lake City, he took Harriet and two children with him. While travelling between American Fork and Lehi they encountered a fierce storm. They nearly perished in the blizzard which dumped so much hail and snow that they could not see where they were going. Not knowing where to turn or what to do, and knowing they would freeze if they stayed where they were, Benjamin trusted in his guardian angel and "let the horses take their own course" (*MLR* 202).

> As [the horses] started I could just see my little dog "Ring" forward under the neckyoke in the lead. The horses kept their pace and the dog kept his place through that blinding, terrific storm, in which we could know nothing of our course or whereabouts, until we found ourselves going through the Lehi city gate. I have encountered many fearful mountain storms, but none equal to this in its terrors, or in the marked providence by which we were delivered. And as for our little "Ring" who like a guiding angel led us to safety, he remained always with me until he died of old age and was buried in the garden near one of our children. (MLR 202)

In the winter of 1857 Church leaders inaugurated a general reformation. The Saints were moved to repent and rededicate themselves to obedience and serving the Lord. Benjamin recalled, "In my own heart, when lit by the candle of the Lord, I found more of evil than I wished to carry, and I laid all down at the feet of the Lord and His servants, and in the waters of baptism and repentance sought to live a higher and more perfect life" (*MLR* 204). Benjamin reported to President Young that, "The spirit of the people here has much improved since the reform commenced" (Benjamin Johnson, Letter to Brigham Young, 25 February 1857). The elders were strongly reminded of their duty to increase their families according to the revelation on marriage and Benjamin was counseled to take another wife. After fasting and prayer, Benjamin married Susan Holman and then Sarah Jane Spooner a few months later (*MLR* 204-206).

At General Conference in April, while the Saints were still struggling with poverty, Benjamin's faith was tested.

> President [Heber C.] Kimball said a certain sum of money was needed and must be raised at once—by donation—and he wanted all the elders that were present to empty their pockets of the last dollar for that purpose, before they left the house. If they would do so, trusting in the Lord, on his promise, they should have more instead of less; their way should be opened, and they should lack for nothing while in the city nor on their return.
>
> I felt of the few dollars in my pocket, and remembered that I had not bought even a small present for my new wife, had expenses to meet, and oh! so many things we needed to buy. But I hurriedly emptied my purse, to the last dime, and went out. I did not feel that I had done it in faith, but in obedience, and I wondered how I could get home, and how [I could] get money to pay my present expenses. I thought, too, how I must leave without getting a present for a wife or even for the little children at home.
>
> But when passing through the south gate a man from the north, with whom I had dealt years before, whom I never expected to see again, caught me by the arm and said, "Brother Johnson, I am glad I have found you for I want to pay what I owe you." And he paid me four times more than I had given. And I felt ashamed that I had been so unbelieving; and before I was ready to go home, so many ways had opened to me that I was able to meet every present need and to supply all the real wants of my family at home, so many times this experience admonishes me to trust in and claim all blessings promised by authority of the priesthood that I have learned by obedience. (*MLR* 206)

The Coming of Johnston's Army

In July of 1857 the members of the Church were alarmed to learn that the United States Army was approaching under the command of General Albert S. Johnston. The Army was sent by President James Buchanan "to squelch or destroy the Mormons." He evidently had accepted as fact, charges made by William W. Drummond, Judge George P. Stiles, and others, that all the people of Utah were in open rebellion against the laws and government of the United States. Without thoroughly investigating the charges of insurrection, scandalous behavior, and immorality, President Buchanan sent twenty-five hundred soldiers to put down the supposed rebellion. Benjamin said that "the injustice of such a move upon an innocent people aroused every patriotic feeling and every arm to repel the invasion (*MLR* 207). Many of them had previously experienced oppression by military forces, and the news brought back terrible memories of abuse and persecution.

But the Church had grown during the previous ten years and was like a young man who refused to take another whipping from a mean stepfather. Brigham Young said, "Our enemies have kicked us and cuffed us about so much that I have got used to it. I say now to my enemies, you have got to fire long shots, unless you come much nearer to us than you are" (*Journal of Discourses* 5:5).

President Brigham Young called together the leading men in the territory. They decided to resist the entrance of troops into the valley and formulated a plan of defence. He said,

> Liars have reported that this people have committed treason, and upon their representations the President has ordered out troops to assist in officering the territory. We have transgressed no law, neither do we intend to do so; but as for any nation coming to destroy this people, God Almighty being my helper, it shall not be. (Smith, Joseph Fielding, 500)

> If there is any man or woman who is not willing to destroy anything and everything of their property that would be of use to the enemy if left, I want them to go out of the Territory. Before I will suffer what I have in times gone by, there shall not be one building, nor one foot of lumber, nor stick, nor a tree, nor a particle of grass and hay that will burn, left in reach of our enemies. I am sworn if driven to extremity, to utterly lay waste this land, in the name of Israel's God, and

> our enemies shall find it as barren as when we came here. (*Journal of Discourses* 5:232)

Although the Saints did not want to leave their homes, the settlers of Summit Creek, which had now grown to thirty-one families, called a meeting in the small rock school house to draft a formal statement in support of President Young's policy. They wrote,

> Resolved, that we, as a people have suffered enough from the violence of mobs and soldiery, stimulated by corrupt priests, lying editors and disappointed politicians and that we will no longer bear such injustice and oppression.
>
> Resolved, that our lives, property and all our influence is pledged to repel all further aggression of the approach of an armed soldiery into our midst.
>
> Resolved, that before our peaceful homes and our possessions shall be desecrated by our enemies, our houses shall be burned and our pleasant homes desolated and we, with our families, will show to the world, by our patriotism and struggle for liberty, that their blood flows in our veins.
>
> Resolved, that we consider the present administration totally corrupt and that President Buchanan, by his official movements towards Utah, has forfeited the confidence and respect of every patriotic citizen and that we do not hesitate to give to the world our disapprobation and protest to his feelings and designs towards us. (Benjamin Johnson, Letter to Brigham Young, 22 September 1857; *Santaquin Ward History* 1858)

But support required more than writing a letter. A Mormon army, called the Nauvoo militia, was organized to defend the territory against a possible invasion. Seven men from the Santaquin Ward were called to join the army. Those who were not called to active duty were asked to help in other ways. Although there had not been a good harvest for three consecutive years, Benjamin was required to meet his share of the expense and labor. He borrowed money to purchase supplies for the militia, and provided outfits to carry supplies to the front (MLR 208). He said,

> To me, with a large family, weak in body, and no one old enough to carry responsibility, it was a giant's load. But I called upon the Lord, who had promised to bless and sustain those who were faithful and obedient, and the Lord raised up to me a help in the time of my greatest need. (*MLR* 207)

This help came as a result of Benjamin's willingness to assist others. While returning from Salt Lake City with his sister Julia, he came upon Reece and Ann Llewellyn from Wales, who had just arrived in Utah with a handcart company. They had no particular settlement in mind but were searching for a home. Benjamin took them to Santaquin and invited them to stay with his family through the winter. Reece and his wife lived with the Johnsons for the next four years and Benjamin grew to love him as a son. Reece became fluent in English, was a hard worker, and was trusted with the management of Benjamin's businesses.

In 1858, the threat of invasion increased, and the Saints in the settlements north of Provo were advised to evacuate their homes.

> Every team and vehicle was called into use to assist the people to move: horses, cows, and even dogs were loaded to their capacity, and families marched without even these helps, carrying what they could in their hands. The people of Ogden as a Ward, with many from Salt Lake City and elsewhere came to our little town for shelter, and to await coming events. We divided with them our lands, which they accepted with no apparent expectation of ever again returning to the homes they had left. The entire people felt determined that if the U. S. troops should attempt to quarter themselves in our cities or to arrest our leading men, every city of the north should be reduced to ashes and the country again be made a desert. With this determination all of the cities and elegant houses of the north, with their beautiful furniture, etc., were abandoned, and their owners now lived in tents, dugouts and brush houses. (*MLR* 209-10)

The Army was now camped just thirty-five miles from Santaquin, and Benjamin feared that their large herds of cattle would graze on his land. To prevent this, he hastily moved his own cattle and sheep into that area. Taking part of his family with him, they spent the summer living in tents and booths made of poles and tall cane. As it turned out, Benjamin benefited financially from the army's presence.

> It was now July and the cane was just in proper condition to cut for feed, and as there was no other hay to cut, I began at once to cut and stack all the cane possible. I had faith that the Lord would bless our labors, and we did not cease to call upon His name. One large stack after another arose, as the result of our toil, and my wives, who shared this labor with me, were patient, faithful and true; and their cheerful and

> loving help made the time of our isolation and labors appear quickly to pass. For over three months, we had continued our labors, not knowing what might be the result, yet hoping the army commissary would buy, at some figure, the cane we had stacked.
>
> About the middle of September, I found that a large number of oxen had been driven upon my ranges, and learned they were sent by the army quartermaster. If they were to remain, we would be obliged to move our stock and ourselves, and all our stacks would soon be destroyed. But I arose equal to the occasion, and wrote Gen. Albert Sidney Johnston, the commander of the army, a letter both dignified and persuasive. (*MLR* 215-16)

In response to his letter, Benjamin obtained an audience with the General. He was informed that the army wished to buy his stacks of cane and would give him a contract to deliver it to the army post. Benjamin was surprised when he received more in payment than the amount he had asked.

From this venture, Benjamin was able to pay $200 tithing, clear all his debts, and have one thousand dollars left over. He used the extra money to open a road through the canyon and build a sawmill. He sold lumber to the Army at Camp Floyd (*MLR* 216).

Johnston's army had brought many things into the valleys which the Saints needed: rope, nails, woolen clothing, blankets, boots, money, etc. It seemed more than poetic justice that those who were sent to destroy them should be the means by which the settlers prospered. It was reported that the army sold four million dollars worth of provisions and supplies to local merchants and citizens for only one hundred thousand dollars (Whitney 1:726).

In 1858 a "coarse and profane" woman came to live near the Johnson family who was "subject to fits" and "possessed of the devil." During one of her seizures the elders were called in to help calm her. Three of Benjamin's wives—Sarah Melissa, Susan, and Sarah Jane—and Benjamin's daughter, Esther, also went to assist. When the elders cast out the evil spirits from her, Benjamin's wives and daughter were suddenly seized by the same convulsions the woman had exhibited. Sarah Melissa sank into a state near death in which she conversed with dead relatives. Benjamin wrote,

> Through her whispered converse with my mother, brother Seth, and sister Mary, while lying before us apparently lifeless, were marvelously portrayed the beauteous landscapes with palaces, gardens and flowers awaiting us, if faithful. She

> vividly described the labors of our kindred there, who are preparing for our coming while we complete their work on earth—all seemed made plain; as also their teachings and earnest instruction relating to a family union in the law of obedience, and while expressing the greatest confidence of love for me of those behind the veil, it was most earnestly enjoined upon the family to accept my counsels as the word of the Lord to them; and in doing so none of their children should depart from the truth.
>
> Such was the influence of the heavenly views opened to her, and of the approbation and love of those behind the veil towards me, that on her recovery to consciousness, she appeared dissatisfied, and wished to return to the society of those who had ministered to her.
>
> Through their teachings she had become so deeply impressed that for a season, at least, her feeling of confidence and love towards me was a worship. My wife Sarah Jane, in a large degree partook of the same experience, received the same admonitions, obtained the same views, and bore the same testimony as to the love towards me of those behind the veil, and of their joy in the works that I would do for them and our kindred dead, and with the same exhortation that all, as a family cleave to my counsel as the word of the Lord, and thereby cement a union which could not be broken by the evil one. (*MLR* 211-12)

Benjamin discussed this unusual event with President Brigham Young. President Young expressed concern that Benjamin's wives would "not retain the same influence, but be led away by evil power to the opposite extreme to make a breach in my family union, to destroy my influence, and diminish my power for doing good" (MLR 212). It caused Benjamin to examine his own life more closely. He wondered if the whole event was not a trick of the devil to play upon his vanity and fill him with pride. Benjamin felt a greater desire for the Lord to grant him the humility and strength to live up to the expectations of his family (*MLR* 212-13).

Problems Over Rights

Benjamin was one of the most prominent and influential men in the state, and a close personal friend of President Brigham Young and the other Church leaders (*MLR* 198; Warrum). Following his mission, he and two counselors had been assigned to preside over the Saints at Santaquin (Summit Creek), while the bishop handled the tithing (*Santaquin Ward History* 1856). With these divided and overlapping responsibilities, problems were inevitable. Benjamin noticed that certain men in the settlement manifested a spirit of jealousy and prejudice toward him.

The Territorial Legislature had granted Benjamin control of all timber and range land from Spring Creek north, including a strip of Juab County on the south, and extending west to Salt Creek, and east to the summit of the mountains (*MLR* 198). He said that this large area was under his control for the purpose of establishing herd grounds, building mills,[13] opening canyon roads, and cutting the timber. Granting such rites to the early colonizers was intended to help assure the success of building and strengthening the colonies.

Since there were few fences, and boundaries were not always known, some of the settlers from neighboring communities allowed their cattle to graze on Benjamin's land.

Some of the settlers felt that Benjamin was given unfair privileges, and seeing that much of the timber and range land was not being used, helped themselves to it. Sometimes they even took over resources which Benjamin had already started to develop (Benjamin Johnson, Letter to Brigham Young, 4 July 1859).

Benjamin was also the victim of maliciousness. He had little patience with the offenders and expressed his anger in a letter to his wife, Harriet.

> Don't fail to get your pig fattening fast as there is no chance for beef. Somebody killed that big fat ox out of spite over Payson Springs and the Damned thieves have stolen too good wagon covers from the old house, one was borrowed from [Joseph E.]. I wish they were all in Hell. They think to choke me from saying anything by skinning me but I'll show their mistake as opportunity offers and if some of them don't get out of here it will get hot for them one of these days or they'll get cold with their faces in the dust. I am getting an unutterable hatred for some who I once thought friends and comparatively honest but now know them to be damned villains and they'd better keep out of my way. (Benjamin Johnson, Letter to Harriet, 30 September 1862)

---

[13]Although in 1853 Benjamin and James S. Holman were jointly granted exclusive rights for the establishment of a sawmill in Summit Creek Canyon, the first mill was built by George Wilson in 1856 (Huff, 475-77).

Although his temper may have created challenges in his life, he said there was only one time when he ever used physical force. On that occasion Benjamin was carrying a fence post across a bridge when a man grabbed the post and attempted to knock him into the creek. Reece Llewellyn kept Benjamin from going off the bridge. Benjamin said he went at the man with his fists, "to stamp my brand upon his face." This was the first and only time he ever used his fists upon a human being (*MLR* 208-209).

Benjamin feared that the men who were violating his rights would try to destroy his influence at home and in the community (*MLR* 200-201). As the presiding Church authority in the settlement, he found it necessary to call disciplinary councils and try these men for their fellowship in the Church. They often "professed repentance, but without reformation" (Benjamin Johnson, Diary Book D, 1 March 1859). When the problems increased, matters were brought to the attention of Church leaders. Benjamin related,

> They had become my enemies without cause; our troubles had been investigated by the stake presidency and the presiding bishop, and by them my accusers were rebuked and required speedily to repent, which at the time they professed to, which proved only a regret that they had done so little to injure me. (*MLR* 210)

The problems became so great that President Young sent Elders Hyde and Richards of the Council of Twelve Apostles to investigate.

During a church service, the apostles called a vote to sustain Benjamin as branch president. Fourteen people raised their hands in opposition. The rest of the meeting and that evening were spent hearing their grievances. The next day, the Apostles met to hear testimonies from Benjamin's friends and to hear his side of the issues. They scrutinized Benjamin's life as a colonizer. After hearing all the facts, Elder Hyde stood and rebuked Benjamin's accusers, giving them but a few minutes to repent or be cut off from the Church.

> In the afternoon, Elder Hyde summed up the merits of the investigation and said that it was always grievous to chastise or reprove presiding authorities but in this case it must be done, for they found Brother Johnson in one grave fault and only one, which is, that he did not long before cut from the Church all who have been his accusers; that Brother Johnson had carried their public burdens and was now deeply in debt thereby; he had tried to do them good and they had repaid him with injustice; and being a better man than they

> deserved he should be released from his thankless calling, and another be appointed to preside over them. (*MLR* 214)

Both Benjamin and Bishop Holman were released from their respective positions.

The Church leaders asked Benjamin for a recommendation regarding a new bishop for the ward. William McBride was ordained as bishop, and the position of branch president was discontinued. In his ordination, Bishop McBride was charged to see that the spirit to find fault with and accuse Benjamin have no further place among the people (*MLR* 214). But Benjamin's troubles were not over.

Hoping to take advantage of the inflated price of lumber a group of men from Santaquin constructed a sawmill on the same spot Benjamin had selected for himself. Benjamin was disturbed by the disregard for his canyon rights, especially because Bishop McBride, with whom Benjamin had once enjoyed the fullest confidence and fellowship, had participated in this trespass (*MLR* 174). When Benjamin's protests went unheeded, he hired help to build a mill higher up the canyon.

When trespasses on Benjamin's property continued, he again sought advice from Church leaders. Elders Hyde and Richards were sent to settle the problem. After Benjamin explained the violation of his rights and Bishop McBride's part in it, Elder Hyde reviewed the evidence. He reminded Bishop McBride of his responsibility to protect Benjamin's rights.

> He told him to go home and see to it that he got my forgiveness, and to see that every other one in the ward, who had again imbibed the old spirit, came to confess their sins and ask again to be forgiven: and that until I forgave them they should not be forgiven. But they had so whipped themselves that I felt they were entitled to my pity, and I gave them more for their mill than it was ever worth to me. What was required of the people was but partly fulfilled, but I have forgiven them. (*MLR* 217-18)

Elder Hyde counseled Benjamin to move away from Santaquin to prevent further problems (Orson Hyde, Letter to Benjamin Johnson, 4 December 1858). Obedient to this counsel, Benjamin purchased houses in Goshen Valley, just six miles away, and moved there with his wives Harriet and Susan.

In his new home, relations improved between Benjamin and his neighbors, and prejudice was replaced by confidence and friendship (Benjamin Johnson, Diary Book D, 1 March 1859).

Benjamin continued to work toward the completion and development of his sawmills. All the profits from the lower mill were needed to construct the upper mill. Because of the steep, rugged canyon, with its almost vertical walls, finishing the second mill appeared to be an impossible task. After a winter of hard work, the road was opened, and the mill completed (*MLR* 217).

During this difficult time Benjamin's wife, Sarah Jane was a great support and strength. Benjamin said, "She was a constant companion and help, patiently making her home in the mountain cave or under the shelter of forest trees, as conditions would require" (*MLR* 219).

Adversity and Financial Setbacks

In the spring of 1859 a spirit of jealousy began to destroy the confidence, union, and love within his family. He became concerned that murmuring, disobedience and strife were becoming prevalent. If these negative patterns continued, Benjamin felt that their prosperity would soon end, and he warned his family about the consequences of their behavior. Benjamin said,

> While I knew the Lord was willing to entrust me with riches, I could see plainly that a want of gratitude to God, and a proper family union would necessitate a further experience in poverty; and while yet in comparative prosperity, I told my wives by prophecy, that a day of poverty and great want was again to be upon us. (*MLR* 218-19)

When the Civil War commenced in April 1861 Johnston's army left Utah to become part of the Union Army. With their departure the demand for lumber dwindled and prices fell. At the time Benjamin owned nearly one hundred head of cattle, over one hundred sheep, a large number of town and garden lots, farming lands and equipment, and two sawmills. Within two years all of his stock, with the exception of a few cows, had been killed or stolen, and both mills were nearly destroyed by floods. Benjamin saw that a tide of adversity was again upon them (*MLR* 221-23).

Benjamin was unaware that during this time of adversity he was considered for a high and sacred calling. In a meeting of the First Presidency and the Council of the Twelve Apostles, President Brigham Young asked for recommendations of brethren to fill a vacancy in the Quorum of the Twelve Apostles. Elder Erastus Snow put forth Benjamin's name. Elder George Q. Cannon, the other name submitted, was chosen to fill that position (Journal History, Church Historian's Office, 23 October 1859).

On 4 September 1860 Benjamin suffered a greater loss than material wealth. While giving birth to her ninth child, Melissa passed away. He recalled,

> I saw she was going soon, and called the family, but they had hardly assembled before she drew her last breath. She passed as one falling asleep while in my arms, her head upon my breast. The dear loving wife of my youth had left us; our home and our hearts were desolate and in mourning, with a more perfect knowledge of her value to us, now that she is gone. (*MLR* 222)

Soon after her death the newborn infant died also. His recent trials and sorrows caused Benjamin to became weak and discouraged, until at times he cared little for life (*MLR* 223).

Benjamin felt that it would be to Reece Llewellyn's advantage to leave and establish himself independently. He wrote,

> I felt it my duty to counsel him to leave me, and provide for himself a separate home. This to me was a trial indeed, and I had learned to lean upon him for strength, and I loved him almost more than a son; for he was also a companion and friend.
>
> When I told him the time had come for him to leave me and to go himself, he looked at me as though I had struck him and seemed grieved at the idea of going by himself, and asked if I really wished to get rid of him. I told him he was now able to do better for himself than I could hope to do for him. That he had but a small family; that mine was large and fast-increasing, and it would be unjust to him to stay and share but equally with us; that as a son he should now share equally, according to his number, in what we then possessed. I gave him two yoke of oxen, with wagon, cows, and general outfit; and in addition to the one child born with us, Sarah Jane gave them Viret, a small Pah-erd girl she bought; which the Indians according to their custom were about to kill. (*MLR* 220)

Life as a colonizer was hard. Both nature and people were unpredictable, and both could be unmerciful. Hoping to better his situation, Benjamin sold his property at Santaquin for a small price and in 1862 he purchased land at Spring Lake. This was an undeveloped area located midway between Santaquin and Payson, but it was still part of the Santaquin

Ward. Benjamin was the first elder to preside over that settlement (History of the Spring Lake Ward).

Although Benjamin hoped that the move to Spring Lake would improve the family's circumstances, it was not so. Locusts destroyed their crops, thieves stole their cattle, and Benjamin's health continued to fail. The Johnson family suffered greatly from their poverty. Along with his many other responsibilities, Benjamin made shoes for his six wives, all of his children, and others who were living with the Johnsons, totalling more than thirty persons (Benjamin Johnson, Letter to Brigham Young, 17 February 1859). Due to the high price and scarcity of leather, many shoes were made from military shoes and boots which had been discarded by the soldiers (*MLR* 219).

In an attempt to provide for his family, Benjamin began to manufacture syrup. He was one of the first in the territory to produce syrup from sorghum, a tall cane indigenous to that area. The manufacture of the syrup required his care and labor both day and night. In October 1863, through over-exertion, Benjamin developed inflammation of the lungs and was near death for six weeks. Under the care of his family and through the ministrations of Presidents Young and Smith, Apostle Snow, and others, Benjamin slowly regained his strength (*MLR* 224-25).

While Benjamin was sick, the family's financial condition worsened. Wheat was scarce, and the price increased from one to six dollars a bushel. The family was in debt and destitute. He lamented, "Our prospects for food and common comforts were as dark as death, and only the remembrance of the Angel, who so many times had opened the way for relief, kept me from despair" (*MLR* 225). Their prayers for help were answered when some old friends gave them a wagonload of wheat and other provisions.

Hoping to benefit financially, Benjamin agreed to feed two hundred sheep in return for a share of the profit when they were sold. He had one hundred tons of hay which was more than that number of sheep would need. The winter was very wet and the sheep became ill. The Johnsons desperately tried to save them and even took some into their house and fed them from their scanty supply of milk, but to no avail. Benjamin's own animals also became sick from the same disease. Before spring, almost all of the sheep and all but one of his oxen and cows had died (*MLR* 225-26). Benjamin found himself in deep poverty, and his family did not have even basic necessities. He said,

> Near our dwelling gushed up large springs of the coolest and clearest waters, where many would stop to refresh. One day an acquaintance with strange ladies drove up in a carriage and asked for a cup with which to dip water. My

> daughter, Julia, then approaching womanhood, went to obtain one, but finding nothing she thought respectable, and ashamed of the best, a worn tin cup—she sent it by the Indian girl, Elva. But they chose to do without it, and in a few days there was sent to us by someone unknown, two new tin cups, an offering perhaps of pity or contempt—if pity, we may perhaps return it; if contempt, we will pity them the more. (*MLR* 226-27)

Through continued efforts and by selling some property, Benjamin provided food for his family. His wages as a Representative in the Legislature helped some.

Experiences with the Indians

Benjamin loved the Indians and in return was admired by them. Since boyhood Benjamin had "been enthused with a love and care for the remnants of Jacob." The Prophet Joseph Smith taught Benjamin about the Church's mission to the Lamanites, and had great hopes for them (*MLR* 268). Benjamin's love for them grew during his mission to the Sandwich Islands.

The Johnson family adopted five Indian children and loved them as their own (*MLR* 220). Some of them Benjamin had bought and raised to adulthood.[14] His daughter, Harriet Naomi, recalled,

> One day my father heard a small Indian boy screaming loudly. On investigating, he discovered it to be a child they [the Indians] had stolen from another tribe and it was their intention to torture it to death with hot irons or rocks and flint. He tried to get them to cease torturing the boy and let him go but they refused and after some persuasion they sold him to father for a horse and some flour. Kemo, the Indian boy, remained with our family until he reached manhood. (Harriet Naomi Johnson LeBaron, Biographical Sketch)

This boy was not only cared for but was given every opportunity to learn. He became so skilled as a violinist that he sometimes travelled hundreds of miles to perform (*MLR* 220).

Benjamin had many warm friendships with the Indians. One of them was an Indian named Guffick, who refused to harm the settlers.

---

[14]It was a common practice among the Indians to sell children. This practice was one thing that led to the Walker War of 1865-1868 (Neff 370-96).

> In the year 1855 Chief Guffick had listened to his tribesmen plot to attack the white settlers who were in Santaquin. They were camped on the bench southeast of town. During the night the chief came down to town and warned them. He told Benjamin F. Johnson about their plans, and so the whites fled to Payson for safety. The next morning Chief Guffick accompanied the Indians to make their attack, and when they got there, they found the place deserted. He then told them that the Great Spirit had warned the settlers to flee. Thereafter, the Indians believed that the white settlers of Santaquin were being divinely protected. ("Chief Guffick," *Chronicals of Courage: Indian Tribes and the Utah Pioneers*)

Rather than stay with his tribe, Guffick went into the mountains and hid. Happening upon him one morning, Benjamin offered him the protection of his home but Guffick declined, saying that both the Mormons and the Indians would try to kill him if he accepted. In parting, Guffick hugged Benjamin and wept, as one who had few friends (*MLR* 229-30). Benjamin's daughter, Harriet Naomi said,

> Guffick will always be remembered by us all for being so friendly and true to our people. His stalwart warrior son, Santaquin, was not so friendly or kind, but he had a strong character and became a wonderful Latter-day Saint. (Harriet Naomi Johnson LeBaron, Biographical Sketch)

The Indians trusted Benjamin and often came to him for help. He said,

> They always came to me in their trouble or sickness, for counsel or ministrations, or for food if they were hungry; such was their faith, that when they were sick, if I would only—as they would say—talk to the Lord for them, or give them a letter to recommend them as good Indians, they would become well at once. For years my counsel or requirements was a law to them, my influence growing out of honest, generous dealing with them. (*MLR* 228)

On one occasion, an Indian had not been honest in his dealings with Benjamin. Trying to explain that friendship and honor were of greater value to him than was a buckskin, Benjamin gave the Indian the buckskin, hoping to teach these values to him. The Indian appeared to be overcome with guilt and shame. He dragged the skin behind him, got on his horse and rode away (*MLR* 231-32). Later that day, Benjamin was informed that the Indian had gone home to die.

> He had told the Indians that Johnson was a great and good captain, that all his words were good, and his medicine was good, while he, himself was small and mean; that he had not done right, and my words had killed him, and he would soon die; but that they should have ears to hear what Johnson told them. I did not think it possible that he could die, but soon learned he had disposed of all he possessed, had taken to his bed; and his squaw and friends were already in mourning for him. His home was nearly ten miles away in Goshen Valley, and although Sunday, and a stormy, cold time, I sent for Dr. Simonds, and taking everything for his comfort, we went to see and minister to him. We found him alive, but all our efforts to arouse him were vain, and he died the next day. We felt sorrow. (*MLR* 232)

Because of the circumstances surrounding the Indian's death, Benjamin feared that the tribe would hold him responsible and seek revenge. He was surprised when he learned that they had even greater respect for him as a result of this experience (*MLR* 232-33).

During 1865-1868, the Mormons experienced the most serious and disastrous of all their Indian troubles. The conflict was called the Blackhawk War after the Utah Indian Chief who was foremost in carrying out the attacks (Neff 399–407).

For some time the Indians had resented the settlers for bringing them smallpox and taking their grazing lands. The conflict began over an incident which occurred in Manti, Utah on 9 April 1865. A man named John Lowry, angry because of a threat made against him, thrashed a young Indian chieftain. As word of the attack on the young chief spread, the Indians became incensed and Indian attacks spread across much of the territory.

The Mormon settlers suffered considerably at the hands of the Indians. Benjamin lost a fine mare and some of his stock, however he felt that Blackhawk was unaware that the animals belonged to him, for they had been friends. Despite Benjamin's relationship with the Indians, the settlement had to always be on guard in case of attack. But at times their fears may have bordered on paranoia.

> One night we were startled to see hundreds of lights on the hillside over the meadows. Kemo [an adopted Indian son] gave a loud yell thinking it was Indians. Everyone became very frightened and a council meeting was held immediately. It was decided that Kemo and three other men would go out and investigate to see whether the Indians were on the

> warpath or friendly. The men investigated and returned laughing, to give us the good news that the cause of our great alarm was only swarms of lightning bugs. (Harriet Naomi Johnson LeBaron, Biographical Sketch)

Benjamin was not intimidated by the Indians and did not condone their acts of violence or dishonesty. One afternoon in the fall of 1865, Blackhawk rode up to the Johnson home with his squaw and, holding a tomahawk, demanded melons from the garden. Benjamin stood before Blackhawk and told him the Johnsons had no melons to give him because he was a bad Indian and had stolen Benjamin's mare and shot his cattle. Benjamin said that the good Indians, as well as the Mormons, knew Blackhawk was bad. Turning to Blackhawk's squaw Benjamin told her she looked like a good squaw, and she could have as many melons as she wanted. He then proceeded to fill her blanket with the best of them. Taking the melons, Blackhawk told Benjamin he was a "big and wise captain, and that all the Indians like Johnson." Blackhawk never caused any more trouble in that area (*MLR* 228-29). The Indian hostility continued in surrounding areas however, and many settlements were evacuated.

At Spring Lake Benjamin constructed a fort with a lookout tower to protect his family and others (Deseret News, 2 August 1866). To make the fort he disassembled all the log houses, and using these logs plus others, he erected two hundred feet of heavy stockade on the south side of his buildings. He gathered a good supply of arms and ammunition and twelve to fifteen men for protection (Benjamin Johnson, Letter to Brigham Young, 4 January 1867).

Describing their fort, Benjamin's daughter Harriet Naomi said,

> Our new home was within an enclosure of three walls about fifty feet high, constructed of slabs and lumber with four tiers of bunks for the men to sleep on, and thus be in position to keep a lookout for Indians. There was a large gate to drive through on the west side. However, the danger from Indians was almost over by this time, as Father was beginning to hire them to work for him. He paid them in bright colored beads which they preferred to money, the value of which they did not understand. (Biographical Sketch)

Although neither Benjamin nor his family were harmed by hostile Indians, he saw the results of some of their raids. Early one morning, Blackhawk and some of his friends came to the Johnson home and demanded breakfast. After eating, the Indians produced a short pole or staff from which dangled a number of human scalps, and they boasted of the murders they had committed (*MLR* 229).

In September 1870, Chief Blackhawk died. Benjamin learned of the Indian's death when some of Blackhawk's friends brought his body to Spring Lake to be buried at the place of his birth, near Benjamin's home (History of Spring Lake Ward 1870; *Deseret News* 19:405).

During 1865 and 1866, most of Benjamin's neighbors had moved to Santaquin for protection against the Indians. Because he had chosen to remain at Spring Lake, jealousy once again arose among his neighbors. The Church authorities counseled him to move his family back to Santaquin. This came as disturbing news to Benjamin, as he wrote:

> This, to me, was a test of my obedience. I had colonized Santaquin, and through many years of famine by crickets and Indians had become poor and deeply in debt while living there; and to get away from there had almost given away my possessions, the most valuable in the place, now worth many times the price I had received for them. At Spring Lake we had good homes, excellent land and other great advantages; and to be forced to return to the place of my former experience of injustice and poverty, was to me very irksome and cruel.
>
> But I could not afford to disobey counsel, for I desired to do my duty and be obedient, and I prayed that I might be humble. (*MLR* 233)

Benjamin believed that a cardinal principle of the gospel is obedience to the counsel and calls of presiding authorities, and that failure to obey can actually place a man's salvation in jeopardy (D&C 1:14, 38; 21:4–6; 68:2–4). He was greatly relieved when President George A. Smith told him he could move to southern Utah instead of Santaquin. When Benjamin was unable to sell his property, President Brigham Young advised him to remain there and released him from his call to southern Utah. Benjamin was also promised that by staying in Spring Lake he would be blessed with increased prosperity. Benjamin said that this was what he most desired, and he believed that his obedience had brought this great blessing (*MLR* 235).

Peace and Prosperity

To increase the family's income, Benjamin began making brooms and liquor. He purchased and operated a distillery for one season. He also continued to manufacture excellent syrup and develop gardens and orchards. In the summer of 1866, the Johnson family cultivated 125 acres of various crops and harvested one hundred acres of grass. They also enjoyed an abundance of strawberries, gooseberries, currents, and other small fruits. Utah Lake and the surrounding area provided fishing, hunting, and trapping, and they marketed catfish, carp, ducks, geese, and muskrats. The Johnsons built row boats which they used and rented for pleasurable outings on the lake (Letter by Vera LeBaron Finch). In referring to Spring Lake, the editor of the Deseret News said, "For the number of inhabitants, it will be readily conceded that they are very industrious, and we are glad they have so good a prospect for reward of their praiseworthy labors" (*Deseret News*, 2 August 1866). Benjamin's granddaughter noted,

> Grandfather was a hustler, industrious and ever on the alert to master new trades and professions to widen his knowledge and earning capacity. At different periods until each served its time, he successfully owned an apiary, a nursery, broom-factory, a fruit cannery, a drug store, made syrup, harnesses, saddles, shoes and raised flowers for seed, shipping them over the country, and in addition raised live-stock, vegetables and fruits for home use. He was a wizard with plants and wrought magic in his gardens. (Openshaw, "Grandfather had a Birthday") [See Appendix for more on Spring Lake.]

Benjamin was not only creative and industrious in his colonizing efforts, but he also assisted the less fortunate. John Henry Spainhower was a convert to the Church from North Carolina. When he brought his family to Utah, he was unsuccessful in finding any way of providing for them. His history relates,

> John Henry got work mowing grass with a scythe and cutting grain with a cradle. What he made provided meager fare for his hungry family of eight. For six weeks Utah did not seem much like Zion to the homesick, impoverished family. Then a change of fortune came. B. F. Johnson, a prosperous farmer and businessman came from Spring Lake, a small town south of Payson, looking for a family of workers—the man, a carpenter with a wife who could spin and weave; children who were able to work. He found in the Spainhowers such a family and sent for them the next morning.
>
> John Henry was soon busy. He built a loom, repaired a flax wheel and spinning wheel. His wife went to carding and spinning wool, weaving denim and linsey. The girls were taught to quilt and spin and worked at it regularly. Jacob worked in the broom factory and young William was sent

> into the foothills to herd Johnson's two hundred head of sheep. It was a wonderful opportunity for the Spainhowers. They were given a place to live with plenty to eat and wood for the fireplace. In a few years they were able to buy land of their own. (Carter, VIII, 379)

During the legislative term of 1861-1862, Benjamin served on the House Committee over education and became acquainted with some of the educational problems in the area. The education of his family, one of the largest in the Church, was a great concern to him. Benjamin believed a good education was crucial to the proper development of his children. Just as it was necessary to hire people to help provide food for them, he was prepared to hire someone to educate them. Since there were no other families close by, Benjamin hired a teacher and bore the cost himself.

In the beginning, a large room in the Johnson home was used as the classroom (Benjamin Farland Johnson, *Memories That Live* 473). In January 1867, Benjamin wrote to President Young, "We have a good school, and Mary Ann, my wife, is with us and all my unmarried children have now good school privileges" (Benjamin Johnson, Letter to Brigham Young, 4 January 1867).

To provide improved facilities, a separate school building was constructed in 1874. Besides being used as a school, this building served the community as a Church meeting house and social hall. In a report to the *Deseret News* in 1876, Benjamin wrote,

> We have been able to construct a school-house of comfort and credibility, which is now occupied by a week day school, taught by Brother A. W. Babbitt Jr., and our Sabbath meetings are well attended. Every one here seems manifesting a feeling to wake up to the renewal of their covenants and to a more perfect conformity to the pattern of the gospel. Our young people are so far alive to a desire for self improvement, that each night in the week our schoolhouse is occupied by their classes, lectures, or by public meetings, and our Sabbath school would prove at least that here "the first great command"' is not ignored or forgotten. Our singing class, taught by Brother Thomas Broadbent, appears to be doing credit both to their teacher and to themselves. (Deseret News, 5 March 1876)

To better meet the needs of his large family, Benjamin purchased a house and property from his brother Joseph, who was moving to southern

Utah (*MLR* 235). Benjamin's granddaughter described the home and family life:

> The big house running east and west, with its three large sections connected to the main building over a huge cellar, and with spacious upstairs bedrooms... In the spacious cellar were the storage bins and shelves for food from season to season. There were barrels of pickles, catsup, apple juice, pork and corned beef; bins of apples, vegetables, and dried fruit. Each wife had to prepare a hog for winter—making hams, lard, sausage and head-cheese.
>
> There was one big central dining room where the entire family gathered each night and morning for supper and breakfast, to get instructions for the day's work and to kneel in family prayer. Aunt Melissa usually had charge of the breakfast, and for such a large family, the preparations must have been almost continuous. So it is not surprising that, as grandfather called his flock around him in prayer at the beginning of each new day, Aunt Liss would always kneel at the kitchen door, close enough to the big range to keep an eye on the boiling porridge, and stir the gravy lest it burn. Grandfather's prayers were always lengthy petitions. (Nix)

This home, referred to as the "adobe mansion" or the "Castle," became the cultural, social, educational, and religious center for the family. Until the new schoolhouse was built, it was also used for ward meetings and social gatherings.

Family Troubles

Benjamin had the unique opportunity of being invited by the First Presidency to bring his wives to the temple to receive "further blessings in the second anointing" (*Journal History*, 20 January 1867). Although this was a special privilege, only two of his wives were willing to accompany him. It seemed to him that as they grew in material blessings, they dwindled in humility, harmony, and obedience to the Lord.

Over the years, Benjamin's wives distanced themselves from him which caused him great unhappiness and deep sorrow. In 1864, Mary Ann had left him and moved to Sanpete to live with some of her children. Two years later she signed a bill for a divorce (Benjamin Johnson, Diary Book D, 5 February 1866). A reconciliation was made and Mary Ann returned to live with Benjamin in 1869 (Benjamin Johnson, Diary Book D, 6 Feb 1870).

Benjamin recognized that his "fretful and over-sensitive temper" contributed to much of his family troubles (Benjamin Johnson, Diary Book D, 28 July 1861). Because Benjamin expected his family members to comply with the teachings of the Church and honor the patriarch of the family, he was sometimes impatient with those who disobeyed. While on his mission, he wrote,

> My sensitive temperament has sometimes led me to [be]...so reproving or unkind [but] I have ever loved you faithfully & honorably. I feel you cannot for a moment doubt I have loved all my family but too fondly for my own good, my anxiety for their welfare has often [caused me to be] nervous & irritable, when I have spoken things that have afterwards grieved me to the heart & often brought the tear of sorrow to my eyes. But of this you are well aware. I have my weaknesses, one is to love with too much fondness, another is to speak from the impulse of the moment, words of unkindness & severity, all those subjects have occupied many, many a lonely & solitary hour. I have thought of my severity with my children & my want of that amount of patience which should characterize a Father as well as a Husband & I must honestly confess that I have felt much grieved & ashamed. (Benjamin Johnson, Letter to Harriet, 17 March 1853)

Although while away from home, Benjamin could see his weaknesses as a father and husband, he found it difficult to effect a change when he was involved in the day to day problems of rearing and providing for a large family. A few months after his mission, when he observed his good intentions slipping away, he wrote in his diary,

> And I with the most earnest hopes trusted that I might be enabled so fully to appreciate the blessing of being with this family that its influence might be salutary in governing all my acts and feelings in time to come.
>
> But alas, how disappointed may be the human mind in regard to the powers and ability to govern and control the action with the impulses of the human heart. May it suffice to say that with the experience of the past few months I have learned that I am the same, possessing my former habits and unhappy spirit, which has often tended to render my home unhappy and to bring a cloud upon that spot that I have so

> earnestly desired should become a heaven. (Benjamin Johnson, Diary Book D, 22 December 1855)

About two weeks later, Benjamin expressed his frustrations in a letter to his wife, Harriet, "No man living loves peace more than me, or has much less of its enjoyments...I must grow in patience and self control" (Benjamin Johnson, Letter to Harriet Naomi Johnson, 6 January 1856).

As a husband and father, Benjamin had a strict, uncompromising nature. One of Benjamin's sons wrote,

> Father's word was law to his wives and children and as he listened to the counsel of those who were over him in authority so he expected those whom the Lord had given him to listen to his counsel and obey him. Which made it unpleasant to some of our mothers and they would rebel, whereas if they had discerned what was for the best they would have listened to what he had to say for he had the whole burden to carry of them all; the responsibility of providing for the whole family. (Benjamin Farland Johnson)

A granddaughter recalled the struggle Benjamin had:

> Although grandfather was usually mild and his smile winsome and engaging, the glance from his large expressive eyes could be sharp and piercing, for grandfather was lassoed to a temper—a temper that he himself confessed had the ugly horns of austerity and self-importance. His caustic remarks at such times were far from conducive to the peace and contentment he earnestly sought and longed for. Yet were imperfections removed, how could individuals be anchored and tethered to earth and where would be the challenge to overcome? Aware of and fully recognizing his failings, grandfather's heroic attempts to thrust them into a hermetically sealed container, was in the end crowned with more than a measure of success. (Openshaw, "Grandfather Johnson had a Birthday")

One Sunday two of his daughters decided not to attend Sunday School because they did not have clean dresses to wear. They hid in a field all morning and then snuck back to their rooms, "with fear and trembling" as to what severe punishment they would receive for their rebellion. Benjamin called them downstairs where, instead of the expected "licking," he gave them each a bouquet of his most prized flowers.

In remembering her grandfather, a granddaughter said,

> [He] was a deeply religious man, sometimes stern and austere, oftentimes misunderstood, oftentimes failing to understand those whom he loved most dearly.... I could not imagine my grandfather with a sense of humor, but my mother says, often he was full of fun and play. He was fair and just. He was patient and kind, and there were many evenings, especially in Spring Lake, Utah spent in social amusement, fun and laughter. (Nix)

Although his children seemed to grow up with a love for their father, Benjamin's wives tended to withdraw from him. Disillusioned and discouraged, Benjamin reflected,

> Excessive labors, to which I was not equal, with infirmities for years, and increasing disobedience, unhappiness, and disunion in my family did at times almost dethrone my better judgement, leaving me without the wisdom of "soft words to turn away wrath," as due to the high and holy calling of husband and father. Worn with cares and infirmities and disappointment in my life's ideal of a happy home, I became somewhat austere, perhaps morose, even towards those without whom I couldn't be happy. All this discouraged my ambition, mortified my pride, made me unsocial, and inspired a feeling to withdraw from public callings and positions of honor. (*MLR* 236)

Desire for Isolation

Because of his despondency, Benjamin refused to seek re-election to the Legislature in 1867. After serving for fourteen years, this was a difficult decision. His experiences as a public servant had been rewarding and in turn he felt he had done his best (*Utah Since Statehood* 2:905). Benjamin had served on various committees: roads and bridges, territorial militia, petitions and memorials, counties, claims, herding and herd grounds, and education (Journals of the House of Representatives). Shortly before the end of his last term, Benjamin was appointed to a committee to determine the legal boundaries and area of the Territory. In commenting on this work, the leaders of the Church stated, "The promptitude of the committee in filling the duties assigned them is praise-worthy while the result of their labors is a work of permanent benefit" (*Journal History*, 14 January 1867). Turning from politics, Benjamin focused all his attention on his family. Regardless of their continual challenges, they were able to draw from a deep reservoir of faith.

> In 1868 the grasshoppers threatened to devastate the land in our part of the state. The people were alarmed and used every device they could think of to spare us from impending famine. One day when their wings had developed, the hoppers flew high in the air, in such numbers that the sun was obscured. A strong wind from the east blew them out over the lake and they settled on the water and all were drowned. Later we saw grasshoppers washed ashore in masses a foot deep for miles along the shore. Thus by the hand of providence, our people were again saved from starvation. We all considered this as great a deliverance as the crickets that were destroyed by the seagulls. (Harriet Naomi LeBaron, Biographical Sketch)

By 1869 Benjamin was no longer concerned with the pressures of poverty. He prided himself in having the largest fruit orchards owned by any one man in Utah (Benjamin Johnson, "A Life Sketch"). Along with making a profit from his orchards, he prospered through gardening, operating a nursery, and manufacturing brooms and syrup. Benjamin was not content, however, in this material success alone. He believed that "we are rich only as we are grateful to the Lord; and too often measure our own blessings as compared with what others possess" (*MLR* 236).

Although he had been successful in lifting the burden of poverty from his family, he did not feel at peace. As a barrier from the outside world, Benjamin surrounded his homes with flowers, shrubs, and a forest of trees—both fruit-bearing and ornamental. He wanted the homes to be attractive, pleasant, and to meet all their needs, but he also believed he must protect his family from what he believed were harmful outside influences. This concern, along with limited interaction and social life for young people, resulted in many youth marrying relatives or those from their own community.

Benjamin's desire for seclusion was complicated by the arrival of the transcontinental railroad in 1869 which brought an end to isolation for the Mormons. As industry grew and outside influences poured into the area, he noticed a change in conditions and also in the Latter-day Saint people (*MLR* 238).

President Brigham Young insisted that the Saints develop agriculture as the primary industry because food, clothing, and shelter were their more urgent needs. He knew there were rich mineral deposits in the territory, but he feared that mining would bring an influx of hostile people. However, the minerals were discovered, and the railroad brought in people who were seeking wealth. Many of the Saints were afraid that lust, gambling, and the evils in the mining camps would destroy the faith of their children (Carter). Benjamin's years of experience among the non-Mormons, combined with his views of raising his family, caused him much anxiety. He wrote,

> Our earnest prayer for so many years that the Lord would "hide from our enemies the treasures of the earth, that they come not to defile our inheritance," was being forgotten, when all so suddenly, mines were discovered in every direction, causing strangers to flock into our midst. To me this was a fearful evil, to bring baneful consequences to us, and I loathed the thought of coming again in contact with the outside element. Although I knew that such would be the case, I was yet unprepared to see introduced among us their vices, or to again suffer their persecutions. And now I felt ready for their sake, to sacrifice all and move my family away to some secluded place, if only safe from such evils. (*MLR* 238)

Despite Benjamin's fears for the spiritual welfare of his family, he was unable to move because of his health problems. For twelve years Benjamin's health had continued to deteriorate. To find the cause of his infirmity he sought the help of three prominent surgeons. Believing his problem to be a tumor they operated on him. Complications followed, however, and for three weeks he was seriously ill. Through the kind attention of his family he gradually regained his strength (*MLR* 238-39).

Once cured, Benjamin again concerned himself with seeking isolation for his family. President Young and several other brethren and their families left Salt Lake City to spend the winter in St. George. Because Benjamin was now enjoying a degree of prosperity, he decided to do the same (*MLR* 240). Thus, on 23 November 1870, he and some of his family left Spring Lake and after travelling for fifteen days, arrived in St. George. Here they met relatives and friends and were pleasantly greeted by President Young and members of the Council of the Twelve (*MLR* 240). Since there were now five Johnson brothers and a sister in St. George with their families, they held a family reunion. The following article appeared in the *Deseret News*:

> St. George, Dec. 30
> DESERET NEWS:-A Reunion Festival of the Johnson family, ancient Mormons, met of the 28th inst. Joel H., Joseph E., Benjamin F., George W. and William D. , with one sister, Esther W. LeBaron, with their families amounting to seventy-seven persons, partaking of the feast; representing four generations, three of which were born in the Church. President Young, together with many old friends participated.

> The descendants of Ezekiel and Julia Johnson number 228, in this Territory, none of whom ever raised hand or voice against Zion. (Deseret News, 30 December 1870).

As they sat in the Social Hall, a long-time friend of the family recounted some family history. Benjamin wrote,

> President George A. Smith alluded to historical family incidents; said he became acquainted with the Johnsons while journeying together from New York to Kirtland in 1833; since which he had known each member personally; that my brother, Seth, was with him in Zion's Camp; that my brother David, died from overexertion in work for the Kirtland Temple; that our mother was married to his father, and our family was now perhaps the largest family in all Israel, and of all the members not one had yet apostatized or been convicted of crime; and of them all there was not one unwelcome to the name of Smith; and if we were not of the Smith family then he belonged to the Johnson family. (*MLR* 241)

Establishing the Johnson Settlement

While in St. George, Benjamin had occasion to meet with the First Presidency. During one of these meetings, President Young suggested that the Johnson brothers colonize the Scootempah or Rock Spring Valley, about twelve miles east of Kanab. As Benjamin believed this was a good opportunity to get his family to a secluded place, he and his brothers accepted the offer.

In January 1871 Benjamin and his brothers Joel, William, Joseph, and George; their brother-in-law David T. LeBaron; and nephews, Sixtus, Nephi, and Elmer Johnson, along with some of their wives, left St. George to explore Rock Spring Valley. Describing the canyon, Joel said,

> We accordingly went out and found a beautiful canyon half to a mile wide and several miles long covered with grass with small springs coming out at the foot of bluffs on each side and a small beautiful stream running from the mouth of the Canyon, with plenty of building rock, fencing timber, and fire wood, and plenty of excellent grass for meadow and stock range extending for miles around. We were highly pleased with the place and concluded to accept the President's offer. Therefore we made arrangements for some of us to move there in the spring and start co-operative stock

> association for herding stock and dairy purposes. ("Mormon Ghost Towns," *Our Pioneer Heritage*)

A family council was held and the land and water were divided among the family members. After a few days they returned to St. George where they began making preparations to establish the new settlement which they had named "Johnson." (*MLR* 241-42)

Anxious to prepare for the move, Benjamin returned to Spring Lake in February 1871. Leaving the pleasant climate of Southern Utah, he and his wife travelled through winter storms over terrible roads. While they were travelling through a canyon in deep snow, a wagon wheel broke, leaving them stranded a long way from any settlement. Having no one to help them and no way to make repairs, their condition looked grave. They were relieved when Joshua Sylvester came along and offered to help. He had materials to fix the wagon wheel and then carried much of their load to Spring Lake (*MLR* 242).

Upon arriving home, Benjamin announced his new plans to the family and invited all of them to accompany him. Two daughters, a son, and their families agreed to go. They hastily gathered the supplies and equipment they would need for colonizing, and prepared to leave Spring Lake. Benjamin wrote,

> With a zeal and hope born more of fear than knowledge, I hurriedly arranged for speedy return to Johnson, the new place, filled only with a desire to get away from the present outside influences, with my eyes shut to all present advantages of home comforts, society and education for my children. (*MLR* 243)

After a tiresome journey of four weeks, Benjamin and his family arrived at Johnson on 7 April 1871. He was disappointed with the reaction of some of his family, who after looking around, were quite unimpressed with the area. They did not see it as he did, and they did not have the same motives for moving there. After a short stay, most of them returned to Spring Lake (*MLR* 243).

Determined to achieve his dream, Benjamin, with the remaining family members, began the task of building a settlement. As a seasoned colonizer, he realized that much hard work lay ahead, especially burdensome without help from his sons. He set up camp in what became known as "Uncle Ben's Grotto." Benjamin said,

> [It was] a circular opening like an amphitheater of two or more acres, surrounded by a precipitous wall with woodstudded cliffs far above. The overhanging rock around this enclo-

> sure gave us deep and ample shelter from storms, was a cool retreat from heat, and partial protection from Indian hostilities, to which all new settlements were more or less liable; while wood in abundance we could toss to our camp fire from cliffs above. A spring dug within our rock shelter afforded plenty of water. So, while our food supply would last we had nothing to do but work.
>
> We planted hundreds of orchard trees, thousands of grape vines and cuttings, with all desirable in a garden, purposing largely for a grain crop without a thought that water could become scarce for some 80 acres of field crops, besides our trees and garden. (*MLR* 244)

About the last of May, when the weather became hot, Benjamin was alarmed to find that their water supply had dried up. The running stream they had found in the winter was now gone and there was no water available for irrigation. Determined to succeed, Benjamin dug ditches to springs that were higher up. They planted seeds in damper places and dug wells, but to no avail. In desperation, Benjamin and his family carried hundreds of gallons of water each day with the hope of saving the costly trees, vines, and seeds. His two little girls, Ann and Jenny, carried over 10,000 gallons of water from the wells quite a distance away. But the effects of the hot sun and sandy soil were too much and most of the crops withered and died. The few remaining plants were destroyed by swarms of grasshoppers (*MLR* 244-45).

Benjamin now showed the characteristics which made him a great colonizer. His unbending determination combined with hard work and initiative, often kept him going after other men had quit. He would not accept defeat as long as he could see a glimmer of hope. Continuing his search for water, Benjamin and his nephew went about three miles into the mountains where they found a small pond. There they cleared the land, prepared the soil for planting, and dug ditches to irrigate their crops. But there was not sufficient water.

Although Benjamin was discouraged, he felt comfort in the knowledge that he had done everything possible to succeed and realized that the experience had been for a purpose. He wrote,

> I knew the Lord did not want me there, but had permitted me to come and learn a lesson for my own good. The Lord knew I had been willing to sacrifice for the good of my children, and he had accepted my offering. I could now look upon our labors and rejoice, even in our disappointment. I knew it was of the Lord, and our home was to be yet at

> Spring Lake. I could now see, as I had been told that the Lord had a purpose in bringing us again in contact with the outside world, as another test to see if our children could be enticed away, to become like them. If this be the case, why should I try to avoid it by taking my family away from an experience needful to all?
>
> This all came plain, as though spoken to me, and I was now as anxious to return as I had been to come. (*MLR* 245-46)

Benjamin and his family bid adieu to this place of toil, sacrifice, and disappointment, and returned to Spring Lake on July 27th. However other families later moved into the Johnson settlement and built up the area. It eventually became a town with a brick schoolhouse, which was also used as a church, but by the turn of the century only a few families remained.

Back in Spring Lake, Benjamin saw things differently than he had before. As he gazed upon his green fields and orchards laden with fruit, he felt as "one from banishment returning to Paradise" (*MLR* 247). To add to his happiness, on the day following his return, family and friends celebrated Benjamin's fifty-third birthday complete with a brass band (*MLR* 247).

Experience with Goats

In the fall of 1871 Benjamin and his brother, Joseph, became involved in an unusual business venture. Joseph knew where he could purchase a flock of Cashmere goats which, it was claimed, had been imported from Tibet. The goats were said to be very prolific and produced long, silky hair which was easily dyed and made into beautiful and luxurious wool. It was also believed that these expensive animals would do well in the climate of southern Utah. Benjamin was immediately interested in obtaining the goats because much was being published regarding the manufacture of expensive cashmere shawls (*MLR* 247). Also, Church leaders were encouraging new textile industries. A few years previously President Young had promoted the silk industry (Jensen 841-43).

Hoping to gain assistance for the goat venture, Benjamin discussed the idea with Elders Erastus Snow and John Taylor. Both were interested and a meeting was held in Salt Lake City to organize a joint stock company. The company consisted of John Taylor, President; Erastus Snow, Vice President; Joseph E. Johnson, Secretary; and Benjamin F. Johnson, Superintendent. About ten thousand dollars worth of shares were sold for fifty dollars each (*MLR* 247-48). Elder Taylor invested one thousand dollars, and Benjamin and Joseph also invested heavily (Journal History, 5 December 1871).

The goats arrived in Salt Lake City the latter part of November. It was decided that they should be driven to Johnson, in southern Utah, for the winter. A few days later the following article appeared in the Salt Lake Herald:

> CASHMERE GOATS: —We had a very pleasant call yesterday from Joseph E. Johnson, Esq., of St. George, and his brother Benjamin F. Johnson, Esq. These gentlemen are superintending the shipment south of a flock of Cashmere goats. One hundred and thirty-three goats were shipped, of which sixteen died on the way, six, we believe, will be taken to the Sandwich Islands, and the remainder of the flock will be driven south, as a cooperative herd.... We wish the gentlemen all success in their enterprise. (Journal History, 5 December 1871)

Benjamin's son-in-law, D. C. Babbitt was given the responsibility to move the herd from Salt Lake City to Spring Lake. Along the way, some of the animals became frightened and ran into the hills. It took quite a while to recover them. While herding the goats into a coral in Springville one of the females, valued at over $300, escaped without being noticed. Two men found the goat and, mistaking it for a sheep, killed it for mutton. They were arrested for grand larceny.

On 24 December 1871 the goats, a flock of Benjamin's sheep and one baggage wagon left from Spring Lake in the care of two of Benjamin's sons, B. Farland and B. Samuel, assisted by a man named Townsend. Benjamin followed with his wife and son a few days later, and they hurriedly pushed on while weather and feed were good.

The herd attracted a lot of curiosity and speculation as they were moved through the communities, and Benjamin received many offers to buy stock in the company or to purchase some of the goats. A businessman in Beaver inquired concerning the price of a pair of goats. Hoping to discourage him, Benjamin quoted him $350. The man agreed to the price and bought the two goats. Benjamin found the sale fortuitous, because the money was needed to cover their immediate expenses.

Their journey was filled with unexpected hardships. It was difficult getting the animals safely across the Virgin River (*MLR* 248-49). One night while the company was camped one hundred miles from their destination, a wind storm arose. In the middle of the storm, the female goats began giving birth but many of the kids died before Benjamin and his sons could care for them. They gathered the flocks close to the wagons and built a fire with grass to warm the sand. By burying the new kids in the dry sand, they were able to save a few of the many born that night. In the morning, they wrapped the surviving kids in blankets and continued to Johnson, arriving the evening of January 23rd (*MLR* 250). Many of the kids which had been saved were disowned by their mothers, so Benjamin found bottles and hand-fed them. They were confident that they would eventually recoup their investment (*MLR* 250).

The goats had been purchased with the assurance that they were "nearly full blood" and some had been imported from Asia, but there was no proof of these claims. While he cared for the goats, Benjamin studied their character and read all he could about them. As his knowledge increased, he became convinced that the whole business was nothing but a fraud. He wrote to Elder John Taylor conveying his concern. In answer, Elder Taylor expressed satisfaction with what they had done. But Benjamin realized the extent of their predicament when the wool began dropping off before shearing time, and he learned that there was not a machine in that part of the country which could work the wool. Seeing the unprofitable nature of this venture, Benjamin resigned his post, left the goats and sheep in the care of his nephew, Sixtus, and returned home the end of March (*MLR* 250-51).

After Benjamin left St. George, some of the goats were lost in the mountains, and the remainder drowned while crossing the Colorado River. Thus ended the hope of beginning a cashmere industry in the Territory. The only income Benjamin realized from his investment and labors was the money received for the pair he sold and compensation for the one which had been killed (*MLR* 251-52). For the second time within a year, Benjamin had found disappointment at Johnson.

Perseverance Against Disappointment

When Benjamin returned home he learned that a fire had destroyed most of his property at Spring Lake. Benjamin's daughter wrote,

> When I was about 7 years old, my father's house caught fire, starting in the broom factory and it went through the whole house. Father was away, everyone large and small ran to help put it out, some throwing water on it, others carrying things out in the city lot, clothing, bedding and most necessary things. The small children were sent into the big library to carry out the books but they threw them in the dirt and water and nearly every book was spoiled; the fire was extinguished before it reached the library. It burned thousands of dollars worth of machinery, furniture, etc. and most of the living rooms were burned up. Several new saddles and other

> things stored upstairs were burned, also a patch of broom corn which they tried hard to save, caught fire from the sparks and went too, making a great loss to my father. (Harriet Naomi Johnson LeBaron, Biographical Sketch)

In the summer of 1872, Benjamin built a steam sawmill at about 10,000 feet elevation up in the canyon. Leaving his farm in the care of his sons and sons-in-law, he devoted all his time and energy in trying to make the sawmill a profitable business. Although in ill health much of the time, he continued to work into the winter. During December a snow storm closed the canyon denying workers access to the mill and trees. Benjamin and his crew shovelled out and cleared the road so work could proceed (*MLR* 253-54).

Working along the steep walls of the canyon was hazardous for the men, and Benjamin prophesied that everyone who remembered his prayers and held sacred the name of the Lord would not be harmed. He worried that some of the "most profane outsiders" would be offended, but Benjamin observed that they said their prayers regularly and guarded their tongues.

> With the exception of one—and he born in the Church—I heard of no other profanity in the canyon and he felling a tree upon himself, was brought down the canyon upon a stretcher, and for a time supposed to be dead. We ministered to him and he lived; the only serious accident through the winter. (*MLR* 254)

The sawmill expanded until Benjamin was required to hire additional help to manage it. Soon, however, he realized the business was losing money because of faulty record keeping. In the summer of 1873, Benjamin closed the mill, feeling he had been "greatly robbed" by those he had trusted. Discouraged with the lumber business, he turned the management of the mill over to family members. In April 1874, it caught fire and burned to the ground, an estimated loss of ten thousand dollars (*MLR* 255). Benjamin said, "This was a hard blow upon all, especially upon me, as the mill was yet unpaid for, our houses unfinished, our farm unfenced, and many claims for lumber standing due." Then in Benjamin's pioneering spirit he added, "we must cast about for some other enterprise" (*MLR* 255-56).

Industry and Horticulture

Benjamin was always looking for additional ways to provide for his family which would also bring new industries to the community. In 1876 Johnson and Sons, who had the largest mulberry crop in Utah County, raised bushels of cocoons and offered free silkworm eggs to anyone who was interested (*Deseret News*, 5 March 1876). Benjamin had the finest fruit orchards in Utah. Because he believed that canning his own fruit would bring a greater profit he decided to open a cannery (*MLR* 256). Canning as an industry was undeveloped in Utah, and there was much to learn. Benjamin said, "We were ignorant as to the process, and we must learn by experiment. But what had my life been but an experiment? And how else had I attained to any knowledge?" (*MLR* 256).

One of the problems they encountered at the cannery was how to release the air from the cans of boiled fruit without allowing the juices to escape. After considerable experimentation, Benjamin said,

> We had started in faith, determined not to fail, and at last stumbled upon the secret, which was simply to reduce the heat of boiled cans by a few moments' immersion in cold water. We now proceeded with better success, yet many cans were imperfect, we still suffered loss, but not enough to discourage us. (*MLR* 256)

By continuing to improve his methods, Benjamin's fruit became esteemed as the best on the market. He took pride in knowing that his canned fruit was even shipped outside the territory. In reporting to the *Deseret News*, Benjamin proudly wrote,

> Although we are but a small settlement, our gardens and orchards are the largest and our class of fruits perhaps the best of any in the Territory. Johnson and Sons have engaged in the canning of fruit which they have so far made a success. They are now arranging to enlarge their gardens, and as early as possible to greatly extend their orchard, with a view to a commercial business in fruit. Their canned fruit sent east last fall, as well as their dried fruits, gave the highest satisfaction, and they think that if the citizens of Utah would devote themselves to the cultivation of stone fruits, the price and demand for Utah fruits would be greatly increased, and to this objective they are turning their more full attention.
> Fraternally yours,
> B.F. Johnson
> (Deseret News, 5 March 1876)

Benjamin also became known as a pioneer in horticulture (Deseret News, 7 June 1882; Journal History, 7 June 1882). He made vast contributions to Utah's horticulture through experimentation with plants. In addition to discussing his findings with others and showing people his methods and results, he wrote a number of letters to newspapers. The *Deseret News* printed the following,

> Spring Lake Villa
> October 26th, 1875.
> Editor Deseret News:
>
> I see in your issue of the 19th reports upon the Compton Surprise potato. The past Spring a friend brought me two potatoes of that kind that weighed scant half a pound each...[one of] which I planted and I have just dug, and weighed one hundred and eighty pounds from it; and a few were evidently lost. So to beat that you must call up the man who can report a greater yield.
>
> I believe that [this variety of potato] could, under the most favorable circumstances and culture, be made to yield one thousand bushels per acre.
>
> Yours,
> B. F. Johnson.
> (Deseret News, 26 October 1875; Journal History, 26 October 1875). [For more detail and humor, see pp. 208-211]

The Reformation—Proving His Integrity

During the winter of 1874–75, following a national depression, President Brigham Young inaugurated a reform movement called the United Order. Through this he hoped to improve the Saints' standard of living, provide better care for the poor, and motivate the Saints to keep the commandments. As part of the United Order, he advocated that all surplus property or profits be given to the bishop, who would distribute them according to needs (Roberts 5:484-90). This movement began in St. George and spread to other areas, including Spring Lake. Benjamin accepted the principle gladly and was rebaptized to show his resolve to devote himself and his possessions to the gospel (*MLR* 257-58).

When the United Order was instituted in the Santaquin area, Benjamin, a member of the Santaquin Ward, was selected to be the vice-president. Because of his position, some members of the ward became jealous. Benjamin believed that the past problems were stirred up by the new bishop of the ward. He wrote,

> I had spent twenty-five years of my life's best years in toil and sacrifice in colonizing Santaquin and Spring Lake and developing the country.

> I will not stop to explain as to how things occurred or even to call names, but will say that indignities were offered me, both in public and private, until in the fall of 1876, it was told to those going to St. George with President Young that Brother Johnson was becoming apostate. (*MLR* 257-58)

While attending the dedication of the St. George Temple, Benjamin learned that false rumors were being circulated about him. No accusation could be more upsetting to Benjamin. Throughout his life he had endeavored to live so that his loyalty to the gospel and the Church leaders would be above reproach. It was important to him that the Brethren respect and trust him. His first reaction to the rumors was that they were a joke, but in finding that this was not the case, he took the matter to Erastus Snow, his stake president. After explaining the situation, Benjamin requested that the Church leaders test his faithfulness in some way (*MLR* 259-60).

When ordinance work commenced in the St. George Temple, very few people participated. It seemed that the members generally did not understand the importance of this work. The First Presidency decided to send missionaries to all the settlements in the area to "wake up the people and teach them their privileges and duties." Benjamin and two other brethren were called to visit the northern settlements. He was concerned about the assignment because of the rumors, and he didn't know how the members would receive him. Benjamin also felt that even after all his missionary experiences, he was not an adequate preacher. He wanted to shrink from the calling, but realized this was exactly the sort of test he had asked the brethren to give him. He turned to the Lord, seeking strength from Him (*MLR* 260-61).

Although their mission lasted only about a month, Benjamin felt that through his service he had been able to prove himself. He wrote,

> The Lord had taken me at my word, and I was satisfied, in the kindness and confidence with which I was everywhere received and listened to. It seemed a pleasure to my companions that they could use me to do most of their preaching. (*MLR* 261)

Soon after this missionary effort, the temple was busy with members doing work for the dead.

The Dream, Then the Call

After spending some time working in the temple, Benjamin returned to Spring Lake. He was grieved to find the spirit of antagonism still existed in the neighboring settlement. With feelings of great concern, he prepared to attend a two day conference in Provo the last Saturday and Sunday of May 1877. The night before leaving for Provo, Benjamin had a dream.

> I thought I was with [the Santaquin bishop], who standing by a boat, ordered me to get on board, which, desiring to be obedient I did, with a reserved thought that he should not take me with him from the shore. As he sat down with his back toward me, to take the oars to push from shore, lying upon my back I quietly and unknown to him, put my left leg over the side, and rolled myself out upon the beach; and looking up saw a man, who, pointing to another boat said, "There is a nice safe one prepared for you," which I took with a feeling of deliverance from an unnatural and irksome association. My dream caused me to marvel, I felt it had a meaning but had never thought as to how it might be fulfilled. (*MLR* 262)

Benjamin traveled to Provo and attended the conference. At the Saturday meeting he saw his bishop sitting on the stand and couldn't help but have negative feelings toward the man. Because the principle of loyalty to Church leaders had been important to Benjamin, this inner conflict between his distrust of the bishop and his allegiance to the bishop's priesthood office greatly upset him. He wrote,

> I prayed most earnestly that I might die, rather than be left to dishonor the high calling of an Elder in Israel, which I greatly feared I should, if existing conditions continued. I did not enjoy the conference, and asked the Lord to take away my bitterness of feeling or let me die to be rid of it.
>
> I returned home Sunday, not wishing to remain longer, crestfallen and disappointed.
>
> I had not thought it possible that President Young had understood my feeling and condition in Santaquin Ward; and a possibility that Spring Lake could be organized as a ward had never dawned upon me until the next morning after our return from Provo. Brother Clark came and said that after I had left the Conference President Young had called for me to come to the stand to be ordained Bishop of Spring Lake Ward. This was indeed a surprise, and I could now see the full meaning of my dream, and I knew it was of the Lord—a relief from a bondage of feeling I cannot describe. I was ordained Bishop by Apostle John Taylor, and organized a ward, mostly of my own family. (*MLR* 262-63)

Because of this experience, Benjamin did some soul searching. He had always felt a need to be respected by his Church leaders and to protect his reputation. Few offenses were as disturbing to him as having someone darken his name. In examining himself, Benjamin said, "My great fault is in not loving those who injure or offend me, and Brother _____, with all his faults, may be in many respects my superior" (*MLR* 263).

The conference in Provo was one of the last contacts Benjamin had with President Brigham Young who died 29 August 1877. Of this modern Moses and latter-day Prophet, Benjamin wrote,

> Of Brigham Young as President of the Church, I will again bear this as a faithful testimony that I do know and bear record that upon the head of Brigham Young as chief, with the Apostleship in full, was by the voice of the Prophet Joseph in my hearing, laid the full responsibility of bearing off the Kingdom of God to all the world.... I do know that this my testimony is true.
>
> From his young manhood, all through his life, in close observation I saw him through every calling, rise to become Israel's great chief, holding every key of the Priesthood and power pertaining to the Kingdom of God on the earth and the salvation for the dead. (Benjamin Johnson, Gibbs Letter)

Although Benjamin prospered in his many business pursuits, his family was not as united as they seemed to be in times of poverty and famine (*MLR* 257). These concerns became a burden which he felt he could no longer carry. Being "borne down with the ingratitude" of his family and realizing his own weaknesses and faults, Benjamin sought divine help to work out his family problems. He told the Lord he could stand it no longer, and wished to turn himself, his family and all he possessed into His hands, to deal with as should be for their good and His glory. Benjamin returned to the house, went into the family room and sat down. He recorded,

> There was a terrible roaring in the air, it grew dark, the wind became terrific. The family, alarmed, came to me in their fright, wondering at my calmness; and as the hail came in torrents, driven by a whirling cyclone, I told them it would take but ten minutes and all our harvest would be done. In less than that time not one square rod of the hundreds of acres of field crops, orchard and gardens, was left—everything stripped to the ground, the orchards denuded of their leaves. The clouds rose from three points and meeting

> formed a cyclone funnel directly over our heads, and all occurred in less than half an hour. (MLR 266)

Although they lost everything, Benjamin felt that the Lord blessed them so that his family was never in real want. Benjamin learned valuable lessons from this experience, but he was disappointed when his family continued in the spirit of complaint, murmuring, and selfishness (*MLR* 267).

Benjamin gained a desire to become more Christlike. He said, "I am more determined now in patience to bear, to drop all authority or austere manners in government, and to harmonize my feelings to the wish and spirit of my wives" (*MLR* 267).

Benjamin hoped he could change his family by transforming himself. Instead of being authoritarian and dictatorial with his wives, he was determined to become more patient, charitable and kind.

Chapter IX

A Call to Mexico—Colonizing Arizona

Early in 1882, Benjamin's brother Joseph asked him to again try colonizing in the south. Although Benjamin felt his land was already too small for his large and rapidly growing family, being almost sixty-four years old he had little desire to face such a task. After forty years of sacrifice and service, Benjamin wanted to spend his "evening years" in the comfort and beauty of their home at Spring Lake (*MLR* 268).

Benjamin wrote to Elder Erastus Snow to ask his advice in the matter, and arrangements were made for them to meet in Salt Lake City at the upcoming Church conference. During the meeting Benjamin was told that he and his family would be called to move south and establish a colony in Arizona.[15] He talked the matter over with the First Presidency and other Apostles, who told him to immediately begin making the necessary arrangements (*MLR* 269). Although he did not want such an assignment, he began to prepare.

Soon after returning home, Benjamin received a letter from President John Taylor, the new President of the Church, asking Benjamin to come to his office at once. The following day, Benjamin took a train to Salt Lake City where President Taylor informed him of new federal legislation prohibiting the practice of plural marriage. The public had been incensed over the Church's practice of plural marriage since it was first publicly taught in 1852. When the Saints sought statehood ten years later, they were turned down, and an anti-polygamy act was passed by the federal government which made it illegal to marry more than one wife. With the completion of the transcontinental railroad in 1869, Utah was no longer isolated, and the practice of plural marriage became more publicized. The public was alarmed to see it continue in spite of the federal law.

[15] The first Latter-day Saints to visit Arizona were the members of the Mormon Battalion. From their reports Church leaders were interested in Arizona as a possible location for Mormon communities and many Saints were called to colonize there between 1870 and 1890.

In October 1880 Governor Murray of Utah stated, "Mormon polygamy is a practice which is punished as criminal in every part of the Republic, but flourishes unchecked in Utah" (Roberts 6:4).

In March 1882 Congress passed the Edmunds Bill which amended the previous anti-polygamy law and defined polygamy as a crime. Any person convicted of contracting a plural marriage could be punished by a fine not to exceed $500 or five years imprisonment or both. The law further defined plural marriage as "unlawful cohabitation" and made this offense punishable by a fine not to exceed $300 or six months imprisonment or both (Roberts 6:41-45). Anyone living the law of plural marriage was subject to arrest under the Edmunds law (*MLR* 269-70).

President Taylor asked Benjamin if, instead of colonizing in Arizona, he would go to Mexico to help locate a place of refuge for those who needed to flee to safety. Benjamin realized that, considering his age, this assignment would be very difficult, but he also recognized that the call came from the President of the Church. He wrote, "I told [the First Presidency] I was subject to God and His servants, and ready to try to do anything required of me" (*MLR* 269). Benjamin was especially pleased that all his family, including sons and sons-in-law and their families, and his brother Joseph were called to go with him (*MLR* 270). President Wilford Woodruff of the Council of Twelve Apostles set Benjamin apart for his mission and gave him a blessing. He also told Benjamin that Brother A. F. Macdonald would set up a base for supplies near Mesa, Arizona to assist in establishing the settlement. They were to meet in St. George in four weeks, on the first of June.

As Benjamin returned to Spring Lake, he was enthused with the spirit of his calling but concerned that he could not be ready within four weeks. He was also not sure he could persuade his wives to accompany him, for most of them had many children or were burdened with sickness. Upon arriving home, Benjamin called all his family together and read them the instructions he had received and explained the object of their mission. He wrote,

> As I was becoming aged and worn I needed the companionship of a wife for comfort, and of my sons to strengthen and sustain me, and asked for volunteers to go with me. A number of my sons were willing and would be ready, but of my five wives not one could afford the sacrifice. (*MLR* 270)

From Utah to Arizona

Undaunted, Benjamin made preparations to leave. Being in debt, he realized that he must sell his homestead to pay his debts and obtain the necessary materials for his new assignment. Since there appeared to be no prospect for a buyer, he became concerned and went to the Lord for help. He said,

> I asked the Lord for guidance, considered carefully the price for my possessions, and concluding upon a sum I could afford to take, I told the Lord that if it was his will that I should sell and go immediately with all my family to send a buyer, to give me the price I had fixed upon. If no buyer came I would take it as a sign that I was to move slowly in the matter. I had hardly told my family my feelings, and purpose, before an offer came, in amount more than the price I had thought to ask. And so it was the sign I had asked of the Lord. I closed the sale. (*MLR* 271)

Benjamin sold his farm for $5000, paid off his debts, and got his finances in order. In preparation for his departure, Benjamin was released as Bishop of the Spring Lake Ward, which was mostly comprised of his own family. In reflecting on his five years of service as Bishop, he said, "I knew the Lord had accepted our endeavors to sustain the good character of our ward; our tithes and offerings were well paid; there was no drunkenness or profanity, or Sabbath-breaking; our meetings were spirited" (*MLR* 271).

Benjamin was to be accompanied by six of his sons, a son-in-law, and his wife Sarah Jane, who decided to join him. With all arrangements completed, Benjamin was prepared to leave his comfortable surroundings. As he contemplated this new challenge Benjamin observed,

> It is now the 20th of May, 1882, and we are about ready for starting to find and make another home in a far off and different clime, among a strange people, perhaps of another tongue, say good-bye to the land of our birth; and I must leave most of my dear ones and the graves of my loved ones. And now at 64, with age and infirmities creeping upon me I am going to life's pioneering, perhaps to return not again to the place of so many years of love and labor, of hope and fear, of sorrows and joys; but with the promise of his servants that the hand of the Lord shall lead and open the way. As a son of Abraham, I am willing to go, to do my best, and trust my remaining days to the will of Him who is true and faithful to His obedient children...The clinging embrace and tearful kiss of those I so much loved, inspired courage and renewed within me the hope of happier days in another land. (*MLR* 272)

For thirty years Benjamin had been in colonizing and serving the Church and the public. When it became known that he had left for another assignment, the following article appeared in the *Deseret News*:

> 7 June, 1882. Southern Colonists.
>
> Elder B. F. Johnson, of Spring Lake Villa, disposed of his farm, orchards and canning establishment a short time since, and has gone southward as the advance guard of an extensive colony, to found and build up new homes. The colonists were undetermined as to their future location, but purposed examining the Gila and Salt River Valleys in Arizona, as well as those of the Yoko and Janas in Old Mexico.
>
> Speaking of the passage of the advance party, through Silver Reef, Iron County, the "Miner" of that place remarked as follows:
>
> Mr. Johnson, the promoter of this exodus, is 64 years of age, patriarchal in the fullest sense, being the father of forty living children, 22 of whom are married. Of the number there are 25 sons. This advance party consists of seven families, 25 persons in all, with eight vehicles, well equipped, which will make camp and remain in the vicinity of St. George until the 10th inst., when another contingent will join them in their journey over the southern deserts in search of "the promised land." Mr. J. E. Johnson, of this city, brother of B. F Johnson, and who, like him is a pioneer in horticulture in Utah, will accompany the party. (Deseret News, 7 June 1882; Journal History, 7 June 1882)

When Benjamin arrived in St. George, he found that his brother Joseph was not yet prepared to leave, and that Brother Macdonald would not be ready for quite some time. In order to help Joseph, Benjamin bought him supplies, a wagon, and a carriage. While they waited, his sons found jobs hauling copper ore using Benjamin's wagons. This proved costly to Benjamin, however, for some of the wagons broke and his best mules were stolen (*MLR* 274).

After this unexpected delay and expense, and without any forewarning, Brother Macdonald informed Benjamin that the Macdonald company was going to leave for Arizona the following day and that Benjamin's group should be ready to go with them. But they were unable to leave on such short notice, and the Macdonald company left without them. Benjamin merely said, "Our having to wait for him [Brother Macdonald] in St. George, and his cold notice of leaving us, did not inspire a feeling I wish to record" (*MLR* 274).

A week later, as the Johnson company prepared to leave St. George, Benjamin noted how sad the people were to see his brother go. Joseph had held places of honor and public trust and had gained the respect and love of all. The evening before they left, Joseph's friends gathered in a large hall to express their sorrow at his leaving and to wish him well in his new assignment (*MLR* 274).

On 22 June 1882 the Johnson company started on their long journey south with Benjamin F. Johnson as President or Captain, Joseph E. Johnson as Chaplain, and William S. Johnson as Captain of the Guard (*MLR* 275).

Because they were late in starting, the company had to go one hundred miles out of their way to find a safe place to cross the Virgin River which was swollen by spring run-off. The weather was extremely hot, and the deep sand and winding river slowed their travel and made the journey perilous. One evening, as they were looking for a suitable place to camp, they came upon a beautiful open space near the river, which appeared to have everything they needed. The group was eager to stop, but Benjamin felt prompted otherwise:

> I drove my light vehicle upon the green grass so inviting, and stopped to look around, but a voice within me said, "Go on." I looked ahead and saw a high ridge to go over, and my feelings said "No," but the voice said, "Go on over the ridge." My hand involuntarily drew the mules back to the road, still wondering why I did so and fearing all would be offended. But I went on, the company following up and down a long, rocky dry way, and going nearly two miles we came upon a high table of flat rock, which offered nothing inviting, but safety. Here we camped, and I greatly feared I had given offense but nothing was said, and we put our stock upon higher ground.
>
> We soon heard thunder with fearful lightning and wind—a tempest was upon us which continued till near daylight with a dreadful roaring. In the morning we saw that the valley was covered with rolling flood of thin mud, from mountain to mountain. We beheld the fearful picture with wondering astonishment, and with joy and gratitude to God that by his angel we were so marvelously led to the only safe spot for many miles upon the bank of this river.

> Had we camped at the place first chosen, all would have been overwhelmed; and we learned that a wagon with salt had camped there, and the teamster narrowly escaped with his life, losing his wagon and load; and the dry ways we had traversed the day before were now impassable. (*MLR* 275-76)

The company could not travel until the flood had subsided and the mud had dried. They now faced the problem of having enough drinking water, as there was none near their camp except thick, red, muddy water. When the supply in their wagons was gone, the members of the company and the live-stock began to suffer. Benjamin could not see a solution to this crisis, but had confidence that they would not suffer long. His twenty-year-old son, William S., fell asleep while considering the matter and saw in a vision a spring of water in a green spot. When he awoke he took his gun and, following his impressions, went up into the foothills. He saw in the distance the green spot pictured in his vision, and soon came to the spring of which he had dreamed (*MLR* 276). The spring was up a smooth wash about three miles from camp. With their wagons and teams, they were able to carry about a hundred gallons of water back to camp. Benjamin likened their experience to Moses providing water in the desert for the Israelites.

After waiting five days for the ground to dry, the company was able to commence their journey. It was now early July, and they were suffering from the blistering heat. Some local settlers warned them that there were fifteen miles of deep sand just ahead of them, which could only be crossed with light loads but plenty of water. When they reached the sand, Benjamin observed that the hot wind blowing off the sand felt like a furnace blowing into his face. That night as they camped near the sand, Benjamin pondered upon what course of action they should take and realized the need for divine intervention (*MLR* 277). He said,

> Late at night I laid down, but was too anxious and fearful to sleep, feeling we were again in peril. But I did not forget the promise while earnestly calling upon the Lord, it began to thunder and a heavy cloud came almost over us. I asked the Lord to let it rain and wet the sandy road; but none came to us, and I felt disappointed and sad that we must pull through the deep, dry sand that could so easily have been made wet for us.
>
> Fearful, yet in hope we started, and coming at once upon the sand found to our great surprise and joy that the road had been deluged with water, although the rain had not reached

> us, not half a mile away. I felt ashamed that I had been so fearful, and we all felt certain the angel had filled the road with water for our special blessing. (*MLR* 277)

On 7 July the company safely crossed the Colorado River at Lee's Ferry and that night had a pleasant journey over forty-five miles of desert (McClintock 219). It was a relief to know they were over the worst of the trip. The remainder of the journey was over good roads with grass and water readily accessible.

On the night of 22 July, Benjamin's group passed President Macdonald camped near the road. After starting two weeks later and going a hundred miles out of their way, Benjamin and his group would be in Mesa before President Macdonald (*MLR* 277).

Benjamin was pleased with their success and the spirit among the group: during more than a month of travel, there was not one complaint or unkind word. All were in good health, the teams were in good condition, and not one animal had been lost on the way. However, without mentioning a specific incident, Benjamin commented, "from a wife loved too much I may have expected too much. In my Eden there was the serpent of discontent. I was worn with infirmity, weary with fatigue, and petulant, and perhaps selfishly looked for sympathy more due to another" (*MLR* 277).

On the morning of 23 July 1882 the company arrived in Mesa, Arizona. There they rested at the home of Joel Johnson, the eldest son of Benjamin's brother Joseph. Joel had come to Arizona the previous year (*MLR* 278).

Establishing a Settlement

With temperatures souring to 110 degrees or more, the company moved to Tempe, a cooler location, where they established a base for future migration to Mexico (*MLR* 278). The Johnson family were the first members of the Church to settle in Tempe, which later became a Mormon settlement (McClintock 219). Benjamin is recognized as the founder of the Tempe Ward in the Maricopa Stake (Maricopa Stake Quarterly Historical Report, 22 July 1882).

Typical of his industrious nature, Benjamin set out to find a means of providing for his family and soon found employment hauling hay and grain. He was told that sixty miles from Tempe at a place called Gila Bend were thousands of acres of good land with water available for irrigation. Benjamin and some of his family set out to see the property.

Benjamin's age, frequent illness, and many years of hard labor, began to affect his ability to work. He wrote,

> We started soon, but I was tired, worn, and almost an invalid; my strength was not equal to my ambition. We stayed the first night at Phoenix where I became quite ill with fever, which increased until I was unable to sit up to ride. We had forgotten some points in description to the place, and passed it twenty or more miles; and finding we were lost, and being now so sick they feared I would die, they turned with a feeling to drive for home as fast as possible. Coming opposite the place we had come to visit and meeting a miner, he accompanied us to Mr. Webbs. (*MLR* 279)

Here Benjamin received excellent care, and his health improved. When Benjamin was able to examine the property, he estimated that there was sufficient water and land to provide for ten thousand people. He purchased the property for four thousand dollars, paying half the amount himself. Benjamin and three of his sons decided they would settle there (*MLR* 279-80).

A Trip to Mexico

Benjamin was still weak when he returned to Tempe, but he felt he had to travel to Mexico and find a location for the settlement there. Benjamin, President Macdonald, and several other men left for Mexico the first part of September 1882. Although Benjamin had been given the responsibility of building the settlement, President Macdonald, whose calling it was to assist Benjamin, took over all leadership responsibilities from the first (*MLR* 280).

Along the way, the company visited with members of the Church who had colonized southern Arizona. They travelled through dangerous Apache territory and camped at the old San Bernardino ranch near the Mexican border.

President Macdonald called everyone together and outlined his plan to purchase and colonize the ranch. He asked Benjamin if he now wished to take the lead in accomplishing their objective. Benjamin, who had many years of experience as a colonizer and had been given the responsibility to build the settlement, expressed his feelings that it was not the right place. President Macdonald called on someone else who accepted the assignment, but Benjamin did not have faith in this arrangement.

After returning to Tucson, they learned that the San Bernardino ranch had already been sold to someone else (*MLR* 280-81). Several months later three general authorities visited the ranch and confirmed Benjamin's evaluation that it lacked everything necessary for establishing a settlement.

Family Disappointments

After failing to complete his assignment in Mexico, Benjamin returned home too disappointed and sick to even drive his team. Although discouraged, upon returning home, he rejoiced with the news that three of his wives, Harriet, Sarah Melissa, and Susan, and their younger children, were travelling to Arizona by train. Benjamin went to Maricopa and eagerly awaited their arrival. He was unaware that they had accused him of neglect and complained about him to the leaders of the Church. In coming, they hoped to obtain money and property Benjamin had left in Utah (*MLR* 282).

Of their reunion, he said,

> Arranging everything for their comfort, I awaited them at Maricopa with arms hungry to embrace them; but our meeting was in every respect just what I hoped it would not be, apparently cold, and dead to love or care for me.
>
> Bringing a larger carriage for the others, I had given the one in which I came to Sarah Jane and her mother, an old lady, in full expectation of finding a place and comfort with them.
>
> And so, when late in the evening, coming to camp after riding as baggage through the day, I found myself the "man between two stools," and having no place offered me, and too proud to sleep with my driver, I sat out, alone, through a late November night, in a condition of physical and mental discomfort that I trust may never be endured by those who occasioned it. (*MLR* 282)

This was a low point in Benjamin's life. After spending a lifetime struggling for his family who meant more to him than his own life, Benjamin now felt he had been completely rejected by his wives.

Benjamin returned to his settlement at Gila Bend, discouraged, disappointed, and despondent "with the sorrow of living bereavement." With no apparent hope for the future, Benjamin set out to be alone with his thoughts while he explored some of the land he had purchased. Life seemed dark to him as he moved around his new property. As he walked through forests of mesquite and palo verdes, he paid little attention to landmarks and direction. When he turned to go home, he realized he was lost. The November night was turning cold, and he was without his coat or food. He tried to start a fire with the few matches he had, but without success.

> Reflecting, I asked myself what there really was for me to fear? I had knowingly done no wrong, had always sought to know and do my duty; I had not come to this land for any vain purposes; and if my work was done and the Lord would

> now accept me, what had I to lose? And in reality—what had I now to live for? My wives were willing to sell me for pottage, and those more dear than life were my accusers to bring reproach upon my old age. These were my thoughts as I stood alone pondering, when a voice asked, "Why do you not call upon the Lord?" which I at once did, and asked that if it was His purpose that I should still live to labor for His kingdom, that He would open my eyes to see the way of my return.
>
> Looking around I then saw a high point or bank I had not before noticed, and climbing its top I saw away in the distance, in another direction, green trees that I knew grew upon the Gila River, and I could now understand how I had become lost.
>
> With hurried walking I got home before dark, a little wiser, and the current of my thoughts a little changed, knowing that the angel had still been with me. (*MLR* 283)

More Bereavement

When Benjamin received word that his brother Joseph was seriously ill, he was grief stricken. As youths they had been particularly close, and although they had been separated most of their adult years, they were hoping to spend their declining years together in this new settlement. As soon as Benjamin learned of Joseph's condition, he rushed to Tempe to be with him. Seeing his brother in the throes of complicated pneumonia wrenched his heart. Although Benjamin administered to and prayed for him, he feared Joseph would not recover. Benjamin was afraid that he would be left without the one person who really understood him and was his closest friend and confidant.

> My children may be a source of great happiness, my hope of the future; may minister to my wants with loving hands—in caressing affection; but they are not my contemporaries, they were not the companions of my childhood or of my youth, to emulate my aspirations in manhood or middle age. (*MLR* 284)

While with Joseph, Benjamin received a letter from their eldest brother, Joel H.[16], stating that he and one of his sons planned to come to Arizona to join them. But in the same mail was a telegram saying Joel had suddenly died (*MLR* 284). A few days later, on 17 December 1882, Joseph also died.

With Joseph's death and Benjamin's failing health, it appeared unlikely the family would be able to establish the settlement at Gila Bend. Benjamin turned the land back to the original owner, who offered to return all payments and reimburse them for the improvements they had made to the property. With this Benjamin received back his original investment.

Benjamin's wives continued to show a spirit of unkindness toward him, and he seemed to feel that all they wanted from him was his property. The same selfishness that had been common among them years before continued to plague the family. Benjamin observed, "As Israel clamored for a King, so clamored the women for property" (*MLR* 268).

A committee was formed consisting of sons of each of the three wives and President Macdonald who acted as chairman. Benjamin's property in Mesa and Tempe was divided equally among the wives in proportion to the numbers in each family. A son of each of the three wives was assigned to help his mother care for the property. Benjamin looked upon this transaction as "greatly relieving the burden of my hands to make it heavier upon my heart" (*MLR* 286).

A Call as Patriarch

Since leaving Spring Lake, Benjamin had not held any official Church position. President John Taylor recognized Benjamin as a deeply spiritual man, and wrote to inform him that he would be ordained a patriarch by the first member of the Council of the Twelve who visited that area.

On 7 January 1883, Benjamin was ordained a patriarch by Elder Brigham Young Jr., son of the late President of the Church (*MLR* 286). Throughout the remainder of his life, Benjamin was active in giving patriarchal blessings.

Progress in Agriculture

By importing a wide variety of plants from California, Benjamin soon had his two acre plot in Tempe looking like paradise. Within two years he had built a large nursery and established an apiary with nearly one hundred bee hives (*MLR* 287). Through careful attention and hard work, Benjamin built both these projects into lucrative businesses. His vast accomplishments in such a short time attracted attention throughout the region, including Utah. The *Territorial Enquirer*, reported,

[16] Joel H. Johnson is also the author of the popular LDS hymn, "High on the Mountain Top" (*Hymns of The Church of Jesus Christ of Latter-day Saints*, number 5).

> Our old friend, B. F. Johnson, formerly Bishop of Spring Lake in this county, is following his old and favorite pursuit—horticulture—at Tempe, Maricopa County, Arizona. He and his sons have a very extensive nursery there embracing a quarter of a million trees of almost every description. (*Journal History*, 19 Dec 1884)

Public interest increased among many of the Utah Saints, and Benjamin was invited to send a detailed report of his successes to the *Deseret News*. In part he wrote,

> A WONDERFUL COUNTRY
> A LAND FLOWING WITH HONEY AND OTHER THINGS IN PROPORTION
> Tempe, Arizona, Oct. 23rd, 1884
>
> About the first of April last I imported from California 70 swarms of bees, 25 of which were paid for by the citizens of Mesa. On their arrival about two-thirds of the bees were dead. I kept them all in my care until the first of June, when all the hives, by careful manipulation, were again well filled with bees and so had full swarms to give to those who had paid for them. Our bees were laid down at Maricopa station at a little less than Seven dollars per hive.
>
> From our 45 stands of bees we extracted not less than
> TWO TONS OF HONEY
> and multiplied them into 200 swarms, which we found to be very bad policy, as we were not able to provide tight hives and it being the dearth season, and not being able to give them the care they needed, no less than 50 of the weakest colonies were destroyed by bee moth. Had they been kept at the number of about 100 swarms we could have easily attained four tons of honey in all.
>
> But the bee is not the only marvel of increase in this land of almost constant spring and summer. I have just come from
> MEASURING A FIG TREE
>
> One of nearly a hundred that I put out as cuttings not 20 months since. It is 1O feet high and near to 10 feet through the limbs, and five inches in diameter of wood at the surface of the ground, and now ripening its third crop of fruit. I also found many trees in my nursery from peach pits planted the past spring, over nine feet high, and grape vines from cut-

> tings planted the spring previous have produced as high as 35 or more pounds of fruit.
>
> Could you take a look at the flowers in front of my door, you would see nearly fifty oleanders that were cuttings the past spring, and now some of them are five feet high and bowed down with the weight of their loveliness. On some of them I counted 15 large festoons of flowers.
>
> And then the pomegranates put out at the same time have also been in bloom and will produce fruit another season, and the olive also, which is long in starting from cuttings, is already over three feet high. But all this is more than you have asked, and perhaps more than you will thank me for. (*Deseret News*, 5 November 1884)

Whenever he was able, Benjamin promoted industry and beautified the landscape. One of his grandsons, William Farland LeBaron, fondly recalls,

> He had a pleasant home and lovely landscaped grounds with fine garden and fruit orchard. I know because he often needed me to hoe weeds and do his irrigating. His garden always seemed too big but he said he liked to grow more than he needed as the Indians or someone else might need some. He was always happy to share with his friends—white, Indian, or Mexican.
>
> He loved horticulture, birds, and bees, and was always experimenting with new varieties of flowers, fruit, nuts, and vegetables.
>
> Whenever B. F. Johnson stayed for a few weeks in one place during his extensive travels, he either started a nursery or planted trees and grapes and flowers. Like Johnny Appleseed, I suppose he left a much longer trail of not only apples but so many other varieties of important food-producing fruits, shrubs, and vegetables, that only a very few of the most important can be mentioned here. Many large trees are still growing in Salt Lake City that he planted, also at Spring Lake, and Santaquin where apple, peach, apricot, and cherries are still bearing. The same was the case in Tempe, Mesa, Arizona; Deming, New Mexico; Diaz, Juarez and Dublan of Mexico (Interview with William Farland LeBaron).

A Mission to Mexico

Although Benjamin was sick and sometimes seemed tired of life, he held to the hope of establishing a settlement in Mexico (*MLR* 284). Perhaps his interest was fueled by a lengthy letter he received from President Wilford Woodruff, President of the Quorum of Twelve, dated 7 December 1882. President Woodruff outlined the assignments of the Twelve to various Indian areas. Then he said,

> I am in hopes that there will be an opening in some part of Mexico for a settlement of our people. I hope you will get a settlement [there] that will suit you and be a benefit to you...We as the Quorum of the Twelve have been commanded of the Lord to now turn our attention to the Lamanites and preach the gospel to them which we are now endeavoring to do...[Missionaries] have lately baptized 27, and some of them have had visitations from messengers who have informed them that they must be baptized and follow the Mormons as they are the head; that there will soon be a great war throughout the land—only among the Mormons there will be peace. One of the messengers talked with one of the Indians from 6 to 8 hours and instructed him in those things he could not tell but he is now doing a great deal of good among his tribe. The Lord is at work among them and it is our duty to work among them and preach the gospel to them and administer the ordinances of the gospel unto them. (Wilford Woodruff, Letter to Benjamin Johnson)

In the fall of 1884, Elders Brigham Young Jr. and Heber J. Grant stopped in Mesa on their way to a mission among the Yaqui Indians, one hundred miles south of Guaymas on the California Coast. They hoped to make a treaty with the Indians which would allow the Saints to settle in Southwestern Sonora (Romney 53). A meeting was held in Mesa to select men to accompany them, and Benjamin's name was mentioned as a possible candidate. Elder Young said he feared Brother Johnson, now sixty-six years of age, was too old to endure the hardships. But Benjamin said,

> I desired much to go, and felt the spirit of the mission almost thrilling me; and I told the Lord that if he was willing I would go and be valiant and stand in my place. Again my name was called, and Brother Young said he feared I could not do without my tea and coffee, as all who went must keep the "Word of Wisdom." I said he might try me if he would. (MLR 288)

Although it may seem strange that a man of faith like Benjamin would not be keeping the Word of Wisdom, it is important to note that it was not emphasized in the early history of the Church like it is today. It was President Heber J. Grant, who was President of the Church from 1918 to 1945, who emphasized it as a commandment. Benjamin did occasionally drink tea and coffee, although not with the approval of some of his family members. This is illustrated in the following experience related by Harriet Naomi Johnson LeBaron, one of Benjamin's daughters.

> When I was eleven years of age I went with my sisters Ann and Jenny and father [Benjamin] to Salt Lake City to conference. We stayed with our Aunt, and Ann and I decided to help by washing the dishes. We piled them up and as we were moving the table back it fell apart and most of the dishes were broken. I was so stunned I could not move. Auntie took me in her arms and told me she was glad because most of the broken dishes were cups and saucers and now she would not have to serve tea or coffee anymore. (Harriet Naomi Johnson LeBaron, "Biographical Sketch")

It was decided that Benjamin could go on the mission and Elder Young promised to take care of him if he became sick. (*MLR* 287-88). When the group was organized, Benjamin was chosen to be the chaplain. They left Mesa on 18 November 1884. Along the way the expedition was joined by other missionaries which expanded the company to about twelve wagons (*MLR* 288). When they arrived at the Mexican border, Benjamin was surprised to meet an old friend. Benjamin said,

> Here I visited my old schoolmate, the once great Samuel Brannan, the millionaire, now living in great poverty with a Mexican woman, in a poor Mexican hut, decrepit with palsy. As I looked upon him with pity, I thought, "Oh! how art thou so fallen!" In boyhood we were companions; in manhood he was brilliant as a speaker and writer. He came by the ship Brooklyn to San Francisco in 1847[17], and through the discovery of gold soon amassed wealth. He met President Young soon after his arrival in Salt Lake[18] and vehemently urged a removal to California. He was told that Salt Lake was the place for the Saints; and that if he sought only

[17]The *Brooklyn* arrived in San Francisco on July 31, 1846. See *California Saints*, by Richard O. Cowan and William E. Homer, BYU Religious Studies Center, 1996.

> for riches he would die poor and friendless which had now been fulfilled, as no wife or child was left him. In 1852 on my way to the Sandwich Islands without purse or scrip, I met him in San Francisco, and although then one of the richest men on the coast, he gave me nothing to sustain a cause he had once loved and ably advocated. Learning we were going to the Yaqui country he told me that in the Maximilian War, he advanced the Juarez government one million dollars which was still his due; that the government ceded to him the Yaqui country, and that his going there to claim it had stirred up that people to rebellion and he was now waiting for another grant elsewhere from the Mexican government. (*MLR* 289.

Comparing Sam Brannan's illustrious past with the pitiful condition in which he now lived, Benjamin commented, "To die in poverty while waiting for the Mexican government! Poor Sam! To have worked for the Lord would have paid him better!" (*MLR* 289)

In Mexico, Benjamin and a few others met with the governor of the territory to learn what they could about the Yaqui Indians. They were told that the Indians were fighting against the Mexican government because the Mexicans had tried to sell and use land which the Indians claimed was given to them by the King of Spain. The missionaries were warned that they would be in great danger if they travelled into Yaqui territory, and that many had done so and had not returned (*MLR* 290, 294-95).

In spite of these warnings, the company continued their journey to the coastal city of Guaymas where they made arrangements to travel down the coast aboard a large single-masted fishing vessel. When the people in Guaymas heard that the missionaries planned to travel into Yaqui country, they became quite excited. They gathered on the wharf to warn them that they would be killed. A Catholic priest told them to go to confession to be absolved of their sins before leaving. One of their group, Valenzuela, was swayed by these people and returned to the camp at Hermosillo (*MLR* 291-92).

The boat set sail amid a clamor of warnings but returned to shore and anchored for the night when a strong wind came up. Being the stormy season, the rain fell in torrents. Because the ship was not equipped for passen-

[18]Brannan met President Young in Wyoming before the Saints entered the valley. See *California Saints*.

gers, Benjamin slept on three sacks of corn which were partly sheltered by the hatch.

The following day the company sailed down the coast, a trip which lasted four tedious days. Back on shore they met some natives who agreed to lead them to a Yaqui village. The natives told them that they would have to cross a flat of mud and water about two and one-half miles wide. With Natives carrying the baggage, they started across the mud, which was closer to five miles across. Benjamin related,

> In this tiring and tedious tramp, Brother Young was signally unfortunate in his avoirdupois [stoutness or hefty of body] and No. 6 boots, both tending to his greater depth in the mud. And here was my advantage and triumph, both in being web-footed with No. 10 boots, and in being like Pharaoh's lean kine, for I was the only one of the party that passed through that terrible ordeal with dry feet, which took nearly three hours to wallow through. (*MLR* 293)

The elders were kindly received at the Yaqui village, but were told that the tribal leaders were not there. The missionaries arranged a meeting for that evening.

> At night around the small fire of sticks and bamboo the natives gathered to listen while Brother Ray as our interpreter gave them a brief history of the coming forth of the Book of Mormon, the record of their forefathers; and that we had come to tell them of these things to prepare them for greater knowledge and blessing that would come to them as a people. They listened eagerly and by earnest inquiry sought to obtain all the knowledge they could upon the subject. Although late and we were tired, they could hardly permit the subject to drop, and long sat talking among themselves after we had retired for rest (*MLR* 293).

The weather was damp and cold, and Elder Young took a chill and became sick. The next day he was to meet with one of the chiefs, but because he was so sick, President Macdonald and Benjamin were sent in his place. As the chief and fifty other Indians sat on the ground listening to the gospel message, Benjamin was reminded of his experiences in the Sandwich Islands. He said, "The Yaquis were in physiognomy, dress and mode of living very much like the Hawaiians were on the seacoast" (*MLR* 294).

That night the missionaries held their final meeting with the Indians. All the principal natives gathered around the campfire and listened eagerly, late into the night. They said they would wait anxiously for the day when the Book of Mormon would be brought to them in Spanish and asked how long they would have to wait. They were told they could expect it in six months (*MLR* 295). (Ten years later, Benjamin said that the Spanish Book of Mormon had not yet been taken to these people [*MLR* 295].)

Concerned for the welfare of Elder Young, whose condition grew worse, the company made a hasty departure the following morning. As Elders Grant and Young were preparing to leave for Utah, Benjamin had one more visit with Elder Young. Benjamin wrote,

> Brother Young, seeing me from his window, sent for me, and on coming to him he said, "I am glad you are come, Brother Johnson, for I wished to see you again and bless you. You have disappointed my expectations, and have cared for me when I had fears of your not being able to endure the trip. I have been glad you came and I say, "God Bless you, Brother Johnson." Your face is one of the first in my remembrance, and you have from my earliest childhood been in the front rank of the kingdom, faithful in every calling. And now if there is nothing for you in reward what can there be for me? Who have not so long labored in faithfulness. And now we as Apostles say to you as the Lord said to my father[19]—Go your way and provide comfort for yourself and family, and let no public calling hereafter bind you. Your labors have been enough and we release you from every public labor but such as you volunteer to accept. And as to your Mexican Mission you shall move in that just as you shall desire. You may stay where you are or go elsewhere as you may desire, and gather your family around you just as it shall please you and them; and the Lord shall be with you all your days ...And as for your family trouble do not take that to heart, but remember that all good men have lacked appreciation at home. My father had his troubles, Heber [C. Kimball] the same; and who ever suffered greater peril in his own home than did the Prophet Joseph? You just take things natural, and go right along and all the good will follow you. (*MLR* 296–97)

Elder Young's generous blessing and consoling words were "like oil upon troubled waters of an overburdened heart," and brought tears of joy

[19]See Doctrine and Covenants 126, a revelation through the Prophet Joseph Smith to President Brigham Young.

and sadness at parting (*MLR* 297). Benjamin felt a great bond of love for Elder Young. He said,

> Brother Young was still sick with fever, and contrary to his fears for me, and his willingness to care for me, it has been my privilege while still in health to assist in caring for and ministering to him in sickness, and afterwards providing for his comfort. I had now so learned to know and to love him that I felt it almost a robbery that I had not [known] him in the past. (*MLR* 296)

When Benjamin arrived back in Tempe on 26 December 1884, he learned that Presidents John Taylor and Joseph F. Smith of the First Presidency were in Arizona. They had gone to Mexico to locate a suitable place for a colony. On their way home they held a meeting in Mesa and although Benjamin had a severe case of pleurisy at the time, he attended the meeting and visited with the brethren. President Taylor and his party of twenty-four were dinner guests at Benjamin's home the following day.

Opposition to the practice of plural marriage was becoming more and more intense. Church leaders were concerned that the members were not receiving justice in the courts. In 1884 President Taylor had written to the president of one of the Arizona stakes, in which he said,

> A general attack is being made upon our liberties throughout all the territories where our people reside. It is said that prosecuting officers in making this raid are acting under instructions from the department at Washington. Whether this be true or not, there can be no question that there is apparently a concert of *action on their part to push our people to the wall and to destroy our religious liberty and with it our religion itself.* (italics the writer's)...In Utah Territory God-fearing men, whose only offense is that they have obeyed a command of the Almighty, are thrust into prison while appeals are pending in a higher court, being refused bail, a boon which should be granted to every person not guilty of a capital offense. In Arizona we learn that the same course is being pursued, that to be accused before any of these courts is equivalent to being convicted. Our counsel has been and is to obtain a place of refuge under a foreign government to which our people can flee when menaced in this land. Better for parts of families to removed and go where they can live in peace than to be hauled into jail and either incarcerated in the territory with thieves and murderers and other vile char-

> acters, or sent to the American Siberia in Detroit to serve out a long term of imprisonment. (Romney 51-52)

Along with other polygamists, Benjamin was in constant danger of arrest. Shortly before President Taylor's visit, Benjamin wrote a letter to the *Deseret News* in which he said,

> Of course polygamists are being hunted for, and men who are so morally and physically rotten that they require a bandage to hold themselves together, are the ones here and elsewhere who are howling themselves hoarse about "Mormon" corruptions. Quite a number of the citizens of Mesa have been indicted by the grand jury and have given bonds....and I think the end is not yet (Deseret News, 5 November 1884; Journal History, 23 October 1884).

Prior to leaving Benjamin's home, President Taylor gave him a blessing. He counseled Benjamin to go "underground" to avoid arrest. He also advised him to go to St. George and help care for his brother Joseph's family.

Although Benjamin realized it would be a considerable personal sacrifice, he immediately made preparations to leave. He left one hundred thousand trees and vines, his bees and his property and gardens in town. His sons were able to care for them but they were also very busy with businesses of their own. Benjamin knew that all his property would suffer without his personal attention (*MLR* 299).

Benjamin left his comfortable home on the night of 3 February 1885. Along with others, he travelled by lumber wagon to Maricopa and then to Salt Lake City by train. Their journey took them through Los Angeles and San Francisco and he was amazed at the growth of those cities since he had last visited there in 1852 (*MLR* 299-300).

The Underground

In Salt Lake City, Benjamin was impressed with the changes both in property and people. Many places which he had once owned were now of great value. While he was pioneering new settlements and homes, and struggling with the wants of a large family, his old associates who remained in the city had become wealthy. He wondered if they would even want to recognize him.

Benjamin went to President Taylor's office and met with a number of the Apostles and other friends. He was asked to give Brothers F. Little and H. Clawson letters of introduction to Judge Hayden and other public officials in Tempe and Phoenix. He was also released from his assignment to purchase land in Mexico (*MLR* 300). Benjamin spent time visiting friends and relatives and giving patriarchal blessings. He was honored to speak at meetings in the Tabernacle and a ward chapel.

Although his health greatly improved while he was in Salt Lake City, Benjamin found the trip south to St. George exhausting. The last sixty-five miles were over the roughest public roads in all of Utah, and the buckboard was so crowded that he had to hold his bedding and satchel. Benjamin arrived in St. George almost paralyzed by fatigue (*MLR* 301).

Upon his arrival Benjamin was warmly received by many friends and relatives. For the next two years, Benjamin gave patriarchal blessings, did genealogical research, attended the temple, visited relatives and friends, and was frequently called upon to speak in church. At this time he began writing an account of his life entitled *A Life Review*. He also wrote a twelve-page letter to President Grover Cleveland regarding the persecution of the Mormons for plural marriage (*MLR* 302-12; Appendix). After his brother Joseph's death, Benjamin felt there was not much left in life for him, but these new activities gave him renewed enthusiasm and vitality (*MLR* 311).

In July 1885, Benjamin was visited by Jacob Hamblin. He said:

> My old friend, Jacob Hamblin, a "nobleman in disguise," being like myself on the underground, spent with me a few mutually pleasant days, comparing notes of our experiences; and on leaving I blessed him with a full heart, as though I would see him no more on this side of the veil, which proved true, as he died on return to his home. (*MLR* 304)

On his sixty-eighth birthday, Benjamin wrote, "But my spirit is still young, and only in a pace more slow, with greater inclination for rest, do I realize that I am becoming aged" (*MLR* 311).

Sarah Jane, Harriet Naomi, and two sons, came to visit Benjamin in St. George, which brought him great joy. While in St. George they attended the temple and received their second annointings and other ordinances for themselves and their dead. When Harriet Naomi and her sons returned to Spring Lake, Sarah Jane chose to remain in St. George to help Benjamin with temple work.

During President Woodruff's visit to St. George, Benjamin had a long interview in which they discussed the mission to Mexico. President Woodruff seemed satisfied with Benjamin's efforts and advised him to remain in St. George with his family.

In September Benjamin moved into the former home of President Brigham Young. While there, he devoted much effort to genealogical correspondence and research. Regarding this work, Benjamin wrote,

> I had now been in St. George over one year, and although much of the time in poor health, earnestly sought, by writing many letters to obtain a knowledge of my mother's kindred, to get the names and dates of their dead in order to do the necessary temple work for them. I now felt that my labors for them had been accepted. But I had obtained no knowledge of my father's family and kindred, and my heart yearned anxiously for the privilege of becoming a savior to my father's house, as had been promised me; and I had not forgotten my vow to the Lord in the endowment house in 1875, which I felt ready and anxious to fulfill. Oppressed by these feelings I went to the Temple to finish my present work and bring away my clothing, but in conversing with Brother Farnsworth, Temple Secretary, upon the subject of my being through, he asked me why I did not take up the Johnson list of nearly 1000 names, all of Massachusetts, and their genealogy from early 1600 down to near my father's time. His question aroused new thoughts, and the spirit of them filled me, and as a vision, it was opened before me and I saw they were my forefathers and that they were waiting for me to move for their redemption. And as it were a voice said to me, "The Lord heard your prayer and has opened your way. These are your kindred; you now have the key of parentage [as the oldest member of the family], and it is yours in birthright to lead in your redemption. It is of the Lord, in answer to your prayer."
>
> My aversion to that list was now turned to joy in possessing it my soul was filled with gladness. I knew it was a revelation from the Lord; and I felt now with all my heart to fulfill as I had vowed, "Even though in poverty to do the work for my father's kindred if the way ever opened for me to do so. The way was now open, and the privilege mine. (*MLR* 308-9)

Sarah Jane received word that her aged mother had died in Tempe. She was grief stricken, and returned to Arizona.

Being in exile, Benjamin was continually on guard and was almost arrested many times. He felt great loneliness as he could not live with his family. These conditions reminded him of a time of terror as a youth in Missouri. To his daughter Cassie he wrote,

> Perhaps it will not now be wise for me to be out much, as telegrams from Phoenix may be sent to officers in [St. George] to be looking for me. But I am in no way scared. I was, when only a boy [in Missouri] in far greater jeopardy of life and liberty than the prospects of a prison now...Of course, I wish to see ...all of my children who *do love me*, and I constantly feel that only for their confidence and love and sympathy, would I even feel that I could continue my labors on this side of the "*Better Home.*" (Benjamin Johnson, Letter to Cassie)

In spite of this, he felt that he could not complain for he was not in prison like so many others. His philosophy was that what God permits or ordains must be for the best.

Benjamin received a letter from his son, James F., informing him that he was coming to take him home to Arizona. Benjamin replied that with three indictments against him, he was afraid to go back to Arizona. But the family insisted, so at the risk of his liberty, Benjamin prepared to leave St. George. Leaving was not easy, for he had made many "kind and dear friends," but Benjamin was glad to be with his son, James F., again. Benjamin wrote,

> How gladly I welcome the son, who through love and self-sacrifice, has been to me a source of comfort; and in him I have not only a son but a counselor, companion and friend. He has come a long journey at much expense to bring me home. (MLR 313–14)

En route to Arizona, Benjamin enjoyed a pleasant reunion with his family and friends at various stops along the way. Of their visit in Spring Lake he wrote,

> I visited that old home where so many of my children were born: where so many of life's vicissitudes had overtaken me: where joys and sorrows had so often mingled in my cup. Happiness in this life is not without alloy, for He who was greatest of all was "a man of sorrow and acquainted with grief." So let the anguish and disappointment be forgotten, and like Him cherish with gratitude the good received; and with a feeling to forgive and forget every unhappiness of the past, I turn away, in sadness but not with regret, feeling assured the Lord had led us to a land and home of great usefulness and blessing. (*MLR* 314-15)

Other family members joined Benjamin for the trip to Arizona. They travelled by train, arriving in Maricopa on 13 March. Benjamin rode the last thirty miles to Mesa hiding under a wagon cover on a hot day because he was still subject to arrest.

Not knowing what course to pursue, Benjamin frequently discussed his problem with church leaders and Judge Hayden, a friend to the Mormon people. Benjamin was told of plans to establish a colony in Mexico and in May received a letter from Elder Erastus Snow inviting him to come to Mexico to see the proposed area. With the pressures of imminent arrest upon him, and not having the money to fight his case in court, Benjamin accepted the invitation (*MLR* 315-16).

In Mexico, Benjamin met John Squires, an old acquaintance from Salt Lake City. Brother Squires, himself in exile for plural marriage, was living alone in a tent and teaching in a small school. Benjamin commented that Brother Squires' home in Salt Lake City was a palace compared to his tent and observed, "I would not like to be so buried while still alive" (*MLR* 317).

Arriving in Colonia Juarez, Benjamin and Elder Snow examined several sites for the proposed settlements, and Benjamin purchased property in the city. Elder Snow told Benjamin about seven thousand acres of choice land which could be bought for $6,000 and offered to purchase it for him. Upon investigation, Benjamin found it to be all that Elder Snow had claimed. Although he could see great possibilities in the property, Benjamin hesitated because of his family circumstances. He asked himself, "are we united enough to acquire so rich and desirable an inheritance?" The following day, while Benjamin was trying to make his decision, the property was sold to someone else and the matter was dropped (*MLR* 318-20).

As Benjamin prepared to return to Arizona, he was disturbed by the paradox in which he found himself. His fear of arrest kept him from finding peace with his family in Arizona, yet he was physically unable to begin again without them. The trip home took them through dangerous Apache territory, so they travelled quickly. Anticipating his return to Arizona, Benjamin wrote,

> June 12, 1887, Sunday. Quite worn, I would have gladly rested, but the rest of our party are anxious to get home. But where for me is home? Perhaps the "Pen" for a term of years, or to continue as a wanderer. (*MLR* 321)

Arriving in Tempe they found everyone well and glad for their return.

In July, Benjamin learned that his wife, Sarah Melissa was very ill. Upon visiting her, he found she was having "spells of sinking and at times very low." He went to Tempe and brought his wife, Harriet, to care for her sister. Before leaving, he and his sons prayed for and administered to Sarah. He wrote,

> Power was given to rebuke and cast out from the house every spirit or power opposed to health, fellowship and union. All felt the power, and a feeling of old-time confidence and love gushed from her heart. She asked me to come tomorrow, and with a feeling that I ought to remain with her, yet not being invited to stay, I returned to Tempe. (*MLR* 322)

This feeling of mutual love was only brief, however, and in the following days their relationship grew worse again.

Unable to relax and enjoy the fruits of his labors, Benjamin resented the attitude and actions of those wives who shunned him. He wrote,

> I spent a portion of the day at my son-in-law, Wm. J. LeBaron's where were assembled a number of my children and my wife, Susan A., who has not spoken to me since my return from over two years' exile, hiding from the penalty of the law that she might have the privilege of being the mother of her own dear children, and of attaining the highest and almost sacred blessings ever on the earth bestowed upon woman. But therein is manifest the cunning of the evil one in destroying family union, and the faith of the youth of Zion. (*MLR* 322)

Benjamin, now in his sixty-ninth year, had to stay in hiding to avoid arrest. He frequently moved when he was warned by family or friends that the marshals suspected where he was. Of one occasion he wrote,

> Aunt Hannah came and told me her girl, Winnie, while on her way from Phoenix this morning, heard men say they were coming for Johnson tomorrow morning. I concluded to leave the coming night, but in the afternoon, as I sat writing, a knock at the door drew my daughter to it, and she saw the men described by the girl. She gave me a hint, and I dodged out the back into the garden thicket and through the orchard, to my son Frank Carlton's to await darkness, when, with S. Openshaw, D. T. and Wm. J. LeBaron and some of my own boys I left, and about midnight arrived at the Johnson ranch, where we remained through the night. But I was sleepless, pondering the subject as to what I should now do, or where to go to avoid the "pen." (*MLR* 322)

It was learned later that the two men were not trying to arrest Benjamin but had come to see him for business reasons.

The constant fear of arrest and being unable to appear in public or visit friends and relatives as he desired, greatly distressed Benjamin. As he considered having to again flee from his home, he commented,

> I have now a comfortable residence, surrounded with the choicest fruits and flowers with every convenience and comfort for my age and infirmities. If I have to leave it, where or when shall I be able to procure another. Never before did I so feel the need of a home, or so highly value its comforts. But as the Lord wills, so may it be; and if in this life there is no place for future home and peace, through faith and patience I may still hope to find it where the heartbeats of disappointment, anxiety and yearnings are all stilled within the mother's bosom. (*MLR* 326)

Through the summer months, Benjamin continued to move quietly among the homes of his family members. He kept occupied by giving patriarchal blessings, writing, and carrying on his business as best he could.

On Sunday, 23 October 1887, Benjamin had dinner with Governor Zulick and other public officials from Phoenix. They discussed the indictments against Benjamin and his many years in the underground. All the party seemed friendly and sympathetic and promised their influence in his behalf should he submit himself to the court (*MLR* 326).

The following month, Benjamin learned that writs had been issued for his arrest. At the suggestion of Judge Hayden and others, he submitted a "plea for justice and personal liberty," to the District Judge and Prosecuting Attorney. In the plea, Benjamin explained his background and outlined his reasons for practicing plural marriage. He explained that he had married all his wives prior to the Edmunds Law and that since coming to Arizona in 1882, had not lived in unlawful cohabitation at any time (*MLR* 326-28). The following day Benjamin was informed by his stake presidency that they had promised the federal officers that he would give himself up and appear in court in two days. Being tired of life in the underground and having confidence in his stake presidency, Benjamin travelled to Phoenix.

The Trial

At the appointed time Benjamin submitted to arrest. He was treated with kindness and respect by the marshal and members of the federal court. Initially he entered a plea of "Not guilty," but after consulting with his attorney and church leaders, he changed his plea to "guilty ...of unlawful cohabitation," hoping to expedite the suit. Of the events which followed, Benjamin wrote,

> In reply he [the judge] said that as I had now plead guilty, he would be obliged by law to pass sentence, which he regretted to do if I was not guilty; and looking up the law's penalty for unlawful cohabitation, he asked me if a fine of $75 would hurt me much? On which one of the sons came forward and deposited that sum upon the desk. Attorney Briggs Goodrich, one of the most eminent lawyers in the territory, who would accept no fee for his services, but taking me by the hand said, "Not one dollar, Uncle Ben, not a dollar. I did not work your case for money, but for my friendship for you. Still there is a favor I would ask—I wish a copy of your statement made to the Judge and prosecuting attorney in plea for justice. I want it to file away as a memorial specimen of Mormon spirit and pleading." I promised him a copy, and in a short time a messenger from his Honor was sent saying he had ordered a rebate of $25 from my fine, which amount was lying on the desk for me. (*MLR* 329-30)

In reporting these events, the following article appeared in the *Deseret News*:

> In Arizona.
>
> A few days ago Elders B. F. Johnson, A. F. MacDonald, Jesse Steel, Don M. LeBaron and Orson Richings, who have been under indictment in Arizona for some time, for unlawful cohabitation, gave themselves up, and on being arraigned in court pleaded guilty. The first named was fined $75 and the others $100 each. There are now no cases under the Edmund's law in our sister Territory. (Deseret News, 21 January 1888)

Freedom at Last

Benjamin found great joy in his new freedom. He was free from the fear of arrest and able to appear publicly again. For the first time in three years he walked openly through town to visit friends and family (*MLR* 330).

His joy was brief, however, for in December less than a month later, he suffered a severe attack of pleurisy which continued all winter. In March he wrote, "I have now a painful cough with hemorrhage to show me that without immediate relief my lungs may become affected beyond recovery. And a grave doubt arises as to my long remaining above the sod" (*MLR* 332).

Fearing that the end was near, Benjamin tried to make amends with his family, but without success. In despair he recorded,

> As I have just made another fruitless effort to effect a family reunion, I can now more fully realize the combined power that is against me, while age and infirmity are lessening my ability to resist or patiently endure it. And in view of this cruel condition sustained by those to whom I have given my life's best offering—to whom I was never disloyal or untrue as a husband, I feel a sadness that leaves no desire to remain longer in this life than to properly prepare my manuscript, "Life's Review," and to put in order papers that may interest my children after I am gone. (*MLR* 332-33)

As Benjamin's condition worsened he began coughing up blood and was convinced that he would soon die in the same way his father had died. He told his wife, Sarah Jane, that he felt he had only two weeks to live, and from what she saw of his condition, she too believed his time was brief. That night Benjamin had a dream which told him he would get well. The following morning his decaying lungs were sound and well, and he was again in good health. He felt like "one coming through a resurrection back to life and hope" (*MLR* 333-34).

On 5 June 1888, Benjamin learned of the death of Elder Erastus Snow of the Council of the Twelve. They had shared many experiences during the early years of the Church. When the Council of Fifty was organized, Benjamin and Elder Snow were the youngest members. They were given a special charge by the Prophet Joseph Smith who urged them to remember when they were old to bear testimony of his teachings pertaining to the Kingdom of God as it should be established upon the earth (*MLR* 334). Benjamin was sure that there was now no one living, who was more personally acquainted with the Prophet Joseph Smith than he was.

Feeling lonely and forsaken by his wives, Benjamin wrote to President Woodruff seeking permission to marry again:

> Tempe, A. T. July 24th, 1888
> Pres. W. Woodruff
> Dear Brother
>
> This young woman through the suggestion of the wife with whom I live and by her own choice has consented to remain with us and fully expresses a wish to go with us to Utah and become my wife, and the object of this writing is to obtain for this your sanction and blessing.
>
> Each of my present wives have comfortable homes of their own and I am fully able to supply the same for another.

> Will you please write me at the earliest that I may know your mind to govern myself thereby in regard to my going [to Utah].
> Awaiting reply, I remain,
> Truly your brother and fellow servant,
> B. F. Johnson
> (Benjamin Johnson, Letter to President Wilford Woodruff)

There is no record that Benjamin married again. Although he greatly desired the love and attention of a companion in marriage, he recognized the presiding authority of President Wilford Woodruff.

On 28 July 1888, Benjamin celebrated his seventieth birthday. As he reflected upon the many experiences of his life, he wrote,

> I am left to wonder that so much of joy and gladness, so much of grief and sadness, so much of hopes and fears, so much of love and yearning, so much of deathless affection, so much of poverty, and toil, so much of sickness and anguish, so much sorrow and tears with death and mourning, could be crowded into the brief space of one short normal life. (*MLR* 336)

Benjamin continued his experiments in horticulture, developing new varieties of plants. During the fall of 1888, he imported large quantities of fruit trees from Alabama. He also exported many trees and bees to the Mormon colonies in Colonia Juarez and Colonia Diaz, Mexico (*MLR* 338-39).

Benjamin was recognized as an authority in the field of horticulture. Articles which he wrote on the subject were published in newspapers, and many people came to him to order plants and obtain information on caring for them. Benjamin was pleased with the effect he was able to have on non-Mormons, or "outside people" as he called them. They seemed to marvel that a Latter-day Saint, especially a polygamist, could have advanced ideas.

Benjamin was also a member in the Beekeepers' Association, which was "an important corporation of business men." Because of his reputation in horticulture and his contributions to the bee industry, he was elected President of that organization at a meeting held in Phoenix. He felt that this broadened his association and influence with non-Mormons and hoped it would decrease opposition to the Church.

Benjamin was zealous in sharing his testimony with everyone he met. He believed that his business associations were the reason the Lord was keeping him at Tempe. On 14 June 1890, Benjamin baptized J. M. Crosby and George W. Ingram, who had been prominent preachers in their own churches. They became active members of the Church in Arizona (*MLR* 340-47).

Opposition to the practice of plural marriage began again after Territorial Governor Lewis Wolfley made a public attack on Mormon polygamists in the fall of 1889, soon after being appointed Governor.

Benjamin was so incensed by the Governor's attack on the Church that he wrote a letter which was printed in the *Arizona Gazette.* He said,

> Tempe, Arizona, October 26, 1889.
> Open letter to his excellency, Governor Lewis Wolfley:
> My dear Governor:
>
> As we should be good Republicans as well as fellow citizens, suppose we have a little whisper together on this troublesome Mormon question. Now as to Mormon morality, Governor. Is it really so much more immoral in a true sense to bring home a second wife, where all concerned are agreeable, than to keep mistresses, Governor, did you ever hear of a pauper among the Mormons? Or of a house of ill fame? A gambling hall? Or a whisky saloon? Until they were forced upon them by carpet bag, federal officers of their territory? And as to our "Christian and Moral Law," now Governor, I have read the Bible through again and again and I find that plural marriage was common in the days of Christ and His Apostles. Yet they failed by any word to admonish or reprove it and while nearly all the men of whom and by whom the Holy Bible was written were polygamists; and as Christ so honored plural marriage, how can we call laws Christian, enacted against it?
>
> And how, my dear Governor, do the Mormons differ from other political parties, voting for their friends instead of their enemies? To me, Governor, a man would appear an idiot who would vote for his pronounced enemy. And I am quite of the opinion, Governor, that if they would conclude to vote with us it would greatly diminish that deformity, so apparent while they vote with the Democrats.
>
> And regarding their numbers in our territory, Governor, is there any constitutional law to forbid even eighty [thousand] instead of eight thousand to find homes in Arizona? and suppose, Governor, that no one was allowed to become a citizen but those who were above criticism, whom everybody loved,

what place of use would there then be for you and me, Governor.
Respectfully,
B.F. Johnson
(*MLR* 341-43)

Benjamin's letter created considerable sensation which later developed into animosity. Although Governor Wolfley, a bachelor, had the reputation of being "a man of sterling qualities and high ideals," he was released from office before his term expired because of his lack of executive ability and public support (Arizona Historical Review 3:3:11-12). Benjamin believed that the reason the governor was removed from office was because of his attack on the Church.

As opposition to plural marriage increased, Benjamin was the object of an editorial attack in the *Arizona Republican*. He said that the editor portrayed him as "a Mormon horror, with a dozen wives, and a hundred children living within the broad light of Christian civilization" (*MLR* 347).

In June 1889, Benjamin again wrote in defense of plural marriage. His article was entitled "My reply to the Republican's: 'Mormonism as an Issue'" and printed in pamphlet form by the *Arizona Gazette*. According to Benjamin, the reaction to his article was frightening. He said that they "raked up all the hear-say crimes and horrors of Mormon history through sixty years and poured them all upon my devoted head, and then [they called] for the strong arm of the law to take into its iron clutch the criminal wretch that I am made out to be" (*MLR* 349).

With his loss of prestige, the intense opposition to his beliefs, and the fact that he was growing old, Benjamin found himself getting physically weaker, and he could no longer endure hard labor. However, Benjamin still enjoyed the occasional visits from general authorities and loved the association of his children and grandchildren. On his seventy-second birthday, 28 July 1890, he was honored with a birthday party attended by over two hundred family members and friends.

In 1890 Benjamin noted that The Church of Jesus Christ of Latter-day Saints was now completing its sixtieth year of existence, and he felt that the Church was half-way to the Second Coming of Christ. He supposed that there would be another sixty years in which to preach the gospel, gather the Saints, redeem the center Stake of Zion, build the holy Temple, convert the Lamanites, rebuild Jerusalem, and receive the Ten Tribes from the North. At the beginning of the year, Benjamin had expected to see conditions improve and move quickly toward the fulfillment of these prophecies, but by November it was obvious that this was not so.

Benjamin's writings about plural marriage, and particularly his denunciation of the laws of the land allowing "persecution under the guise of prosecution," had fanned a flame which built an inferno of opposition. Public resentment toward him continued to increase until it was once again not safe for him to remain in Arizona.

Chapter X

Exile in Mexico

As resentment toward the Saints increased, Church leaders became concerned for the safety of those living the law of plural marriage. On 7 December 1890, Benjamin was warned by his stake president that in order to avoid arrest for unlawful cohabitation he must leave for Mexico immediately. President Hakes also informed him that others would be fleeing with him. Benjamin knew he had lived within the law, and it seemed unreasonable to charge him with unlawful cohabitation. However, since his first wife had died and his others were all considered to be illegal, he either had to remarry one of them under the law or be imprisoned. Benjamin refused to be forced to choose between his wives, therefore his only alternative was to go into exile (*MLR* 351).

Quickly and secretly, Benjamin and his family worked through the night, gathering supplies for the journey. He was ready by four o'clock the next morning. Benjamin wrote,

> With feelings known only to those of similar age, circumstances and conditions of health, I again, in the winter season, bade adieu to a home of comfort and dear ones, to take my chance and find as best I could a place for shelter and safety. (MLR 352)

Although the train was scheduled to leave at five in the morning, it was detained for five hours. After waiting in an open room with no heat, Benjamin caught a cold which became so severe that he feared he might not recover. But once again he felt the Lord's blessings, and he was able to continue his journey.

Although as early as 1882, Church leaders had gone into Mexico to locate a proper site for a settlement, Colonia Diaz was not established until 1885. Some of Benjamin's family were helping to build the area, and Benjamin had assisted by shipping trees and bees to them.

Benjamin arrived at Colonia Diaz on 14 December 1890 and was warmly greeted by his family (Romney 53). He was invited to stay with the bishop's family who was also the son of his youngest brother, William.

The members frequently sought counsel and patriarchal blessings from Benjamin. He enjoyed a particularly close association with Elder George Teasdale, a member of the Quorum of the Twelve Apostles who was presiding over the Church in Mexico. Elder Teasdale often called upon Benjamin to speak in various church meetings. One Sunday, he put his arm around Benjamin and said that "hereafter in public meetings I was to occupy the seat next to him." (*MLR* 353-56)

The winter of 1890–91 was a time of much sickness for the Saints in Mexico. With epidemics of smallpox, diphtheria, and other diseases, Benjamin spent much of his time caring for and administering to the sick. After continuously laboring for several weeks and being unable to stop the spread of smallpox, the leaders knew they needed divine help. Benjamin wrote,

> A number of persons exposed to smallpox now have incipient disease and send for Apostle Teasdale to administer to them. He came to council with me and for [the] sake of others who would be exposed, we feel it not wise to visit them until our duty is made more plain. So we retired to a private room and together called upon the Lord to show more plainly our path of duty. We asked Him that the terrible disease might be stayed, and its power be broken among the people, which it at once was, and from that hour no case of smallpox was developed among the Saints at Diaz. (*MLR* 358)

When conditions improved, Benjamin tried to persuade his wives to join him, but he received no response from any of them. However, he continued to move ahead with his plans to settle in Mexico by selling his property in Tempe and Mesa at a great sacrifice. He also had most of his nursery stock shipped to him so that he could relocate his business.

The prospect of facing his remaining years without the kind attention of a wife troubled Benjamin. He sadly wrote, "At no period of my life did I feel the want of a home with its comforts, as at present" (*MLR* 357). Under these discouraging conditions, he considered taking a wife from among the Saints in Mexico, but he knew there were no new plural marriages being sanctioned by the Church. In his journal Benjamin wrote, "My wives do not wish to come to Mexico, and to enjoy the comfort and sympathies of a home I would be compelled to look elsewhere, which the 'manifesto' does not permit" (*MLR* 362).

The previous September, President Wilford Woodruff had issued the Manifesto (see Official Declaration-1 in the Doctrine and Covenants), which discontinued the practice of plural marriage. Benjamin recognized and sustained the man he knew to be the Prophet of God. Regarding this, his son, Ellis said,

> To him, as he taught his family, and exemplified in his life, the Revelation on Polygamy was a divine and sacred commandment of God, and in the same measure was the Manifesto both sacred and binding.
>
> The main theme of his teaching to members of his family was "OBEY THE COUNSEL OF THE HEADS OF THE CHURCH, FOR THEY ARE PROPHETS OF THE LORD. UPON OBEDIENCE TO THIS WILL DEPEND YOUR HAPPINESS HERE AND HEREAFTER." (Ellis H. Johnson)

Many years after Benjamin's death, some of his descendants made false claims that he had secretly passed on to them "keys" to practice plural marriage. Those who make this claim and blacken the name of Benjamin Franklin Johnson, may one day have to answer to Benjamin as well as to God. His life and teachings bear witness of the divine origin of the law of plural marriage as received by the Prophet Joseph Smith, as well as the revelation received by President Wilford Woodruff halting the practice. One of Benjamin's close associates testified, "I have never heard B. F. Johnson say anything that was contrary to the teachings of the authorities of the Church. He told me many times that if I always followed the leaders of the Church I would never go wrong" (Horne).

Through the summer of 1891 the people in Mexico suffered a severe drought. Benjamin's nursery and gardens failed, and his losses were great. For the Saints, the prospects appeared bleak. Benjamin's daughter, Harriet Naomi Johnson LeBaron, and her husband David Tully LeBaron, were also in Mexico at that time. Regarding their suffering, Harriet wrote,

> We moved to Colonia Juarez, Chihuahua, Mexico where we all lived together in one small house. We were advised by our leaders to go there, but it was a very hard year and we nearly starved after dividing the fruit, flour and other things we had brought, with others who were out of provisions. During this time of famine, David walked fifteen miles to find some greens that he heard were growing along a water ditch, but he could not find any and had to walk the fifteen miles home again, tired out and hungry. I had nothing to give him to eat, but took a pan and went to several who had borrowed from us and told them how hungry we were, but they had none to give. I went home discouraged. Geneva

> shook out the bran sack and got a little bran, and I made some dough and baked it on the skillet to divide among us.
>
> In the spring we planted a garden, but the mice ate it up. President Erastus Snow came and upon seeing our sorrowful conditions, told us we could go if we chose. By this time I was so weak I had to go to bed, and they took me in the bed so I could hear him speak. David asked if I wanted to go back to our old home. I was so ill and discouraged that I told him I did not care what happened to me. He put my bed in the wagon and we went back to Tempe. (Harriet Naomi Johnson LeBaron, "Biographical Sketch")

Benjamin's troubles were complicated by ill health, and he considered returning to Arizona. However, since his wives had refused to follow him into exile, his pride would not allow it, and so he remained in Mexico.

In August, Benjamin received a letter stating that since prosecution of polygamists had decreased, his family and the stake presidency wanted him to return to Mesa. For reasons of comfort and health, Benjamin considered the possibility.

The drought continued, and conditions became critical. Almost no crops had been raised, and the cattle were starving. On 25 August 1891, the Saints gathered together in a church service to seek divine intervention. Benjamin was called upon to offer the benediction to the meeting. He wrote,

> Being called to make the closing prayer, with a feeling of assurance, that he would, I asked the Lord to send rain, to make the earth and its perishing cattle glad, that His saints might have cause to rejoice in His mercy and blessing. Clouds soon overspread the sky, and rain is still [two days later] coming in abundance. (*MLR* 363-64)

The rain continued for several days.

A week later Benjamin and Elder Teasdale travelled to Colonia Juarez to dedicate a church building. They were surprised to find that only four miles from Colonia Diaz the ground was still dry. The rain had fallen only at Diaz (*MLR* 364).

When Benjamin's health permitted, he gave patriarchal blessings, accepted speaking assignments, and visited relatives and friends. On 25 November he received more letters from his family urging him to return home. Benjamin decided it was time to go.

Before his departure, the Saints in Diaz expressed their love and respect by honoring Benjamin with a surprise social. Friends and family gathered for an evening of spontaneous music, recitation, dancing, speaking, songs, and feasting. Regarding the occasion, Benjamin wrote,

> With full hearts and a "God bless you" from each, all returned to their homes, leaving me to ponder the kind words of Apostle Teasdale, of the Bishop, of Sister Teasdale and others, loving words spoken for my comfort, which I would not repeat, but my eyes were not dry while listening to them. (*MLR* 367)

Benjamin had planned to travel to Arizona with a company, but just as they were preparing to leave, a little girl Benjamin was particularly fond of became very ill. He remained behind to help care for her and give her a blessing. Assuring her that she would get well, she soon began to improve.

After a year in Mexico Benjamin found it difficult to leave, but he knew that he must return to Arizona. He bid farewell to his friends and family, and travelling by train, arrived in Mesa in December 1891.

Chapter XI

The Evening of Life

Soon after his return to Arizona in December 1891, Benjamin caught a severe cold and was so sick he often felt he was going to die. He longed for the care and attention of one of his wives but none of them came to see him. His children cared for him, yet somehow it was not the same as the care he hoped for from a loving wife. In his journal he wrote,

> Such can never be my feelings toward the dear mothers of my children, for no matter the distance or the sacrifice, were they in sickness, tribulation, or real want, my feet would hasten to minister to them, comfort and bless them. I do not write this in feeling of reproach, for I am not without fault, but that our children, in a coming time may comprehend in a degree the great love I ever cherished for their mothers (*MLR* 370-71).

After eight weeks Benjamin's condition improved slightly but he was still too weak to get out of bed for another month. Being unable to attend church meetings for three months, ward leaders brought the sacrament to him. While still sick in bed, yet renewed in spirit, Benjamin continued to write *A Life Review*, which he felt was a duty he owed his posterity (MLR 371).

In the spring of 1892, Benjamin's wife, Sarah Jane, decided to leave Tempe and purchase a home in Mesa. She invited him to live with her. He wrote, "I am wondering if the time is come for women to rule over us and if so, I should gracefully submit" (MLR 373).

When the purchase of her house fell through, Benjamin proposed that they build and own a home jointly. Sarah Jane agreed and Benjamin was pleased that their relationship was improving. In time, their home and surrounding gardens were considered the finest in Mesa (MLR 381).

The dedication of the Salt Lake Temple was scheduled for the spring of 1893, and some of the Arizona Saints planned to attend. Benjamin wanted to participate in this historic event but was afraid his poor health would not permit him to travel. As the time for their departure grew nearer, his health improved, and he was able to make the trip.

Benjamin was warmly received by his family living in Salt Lake City and was thrilled when the First Presidency assured him a seat at the temple dedicatory services. Following the dedication of the temple on 6 April 1893, he attended General Conference. Benjamin spent time visiting relatives and friends and giving patriarchal blessings.

When Benjamin returned home, he continued his church activities and writing. Many of his articles on agriculture were printed in Arizona publications. Benjamin built up his orchards and resumed his canning business. In the World's Fair edition of the *Arizona Gazette* on 28 September 1893 B. F. Johnson, Sons and Company were recognized for producing up to four thousand cans of "superior quality peaches, apricots, and grapes" (Melvin 15). He tried to rekindle interest in a milling company he and his sons had owned in Mesa, but because of his losses in Mexico, he found it difficult to re-establish himself (MLR 374). Although he had suffered much financially, Benjamin retained his faith in an overruling providence (*MLR* 383). Through hard work and frugal management, he once again became well established in business. In a letter to the *Deseret News*, 17 August 1895, he described the prosperous conditions in the Mesa area.

> The present season here is one of general health and good abundance in field crops and fruits; the peach, pear, plum, quince, pomegranate, with the coming orange, olives and other fruits are in plenty. We yet have little market to encourage the producer and so in money matters times are still hard. I am told of 500 tons of stacked hay that sold within the last few days for less than that many dollars. This is a country of great abundance just now in everything but money, and in that it is improving a little. Our steam roller flouring mill is a success and is now furnishing a fine commercial brand.
>
> Our summer has been dry and rainless. The river was low for a time but showers are now coming, canals are overflowing, and all appears green and verdant again.
>
> "Uncle Ben." (Maricopa Stake History, 17 August 1895)

Struggles with Loneliness and Rejection

Although so many people had high regard for Benjamin, he felt that those who mattered most had forsaken him. For many years he was disappointed with the lack of closeness, love, and support he received from his wives.

Benjamin's feelings of sorrow and rejection increased as he got older. Of his five remaining wives and forty-five children, few of them lived in close proximity. Because of the limited attention he felt he received from them, he poured out his feelings in letters to his children. In one letter he wrote,

> Your mother is still confined mostly in bed & I fear her affliction may be dangerous.... I call there occasionally to learn of her welfare but she has never asked me to come to see her. But I would do anything possible for her comfort.... When I think of what as a family in unison we should have been. . . it brings a feeling of lonely disappointment that words do not express.... The *disjointed, unloving* & *scattering* condition of the family fills me with a sorrow that is hard to put away (Benjamin Johnson, Letter to Heber and Lizzie).

A year later Benjamin wrote,

> What I feel most and would most impress others is the disgrace reflected upon me through dissertion [sic] by the mothers of my children .... I love all the mothers of my children & would turn my back on no one that would in a wilfuly [sic] spirit return to me & I pitty [sic] more than I blame any one.... Now with these conditions, altho [sic] yearning for companionship, what hope can I have of finding among strangers the sympathy & care refused me by those I have loved from their childhood *more* than my life & to whom I have given *all* but the small remnant of life still left to me. (Benjamin Johnson, Letter to Heber and Lizzie)

Benjamin struggled with deep feelings of rejection and loneliness, but his writings give little insight as to how the problems developed. Although it was a great challenge for multiple families to function as one, he did not seem to feel that living the law of plural marriage was the root of the problems. In 1903 he observed in retrospect,

> And while I can believe that to some plural marriage was a great cross, yet I cannot say so from my own experience, for although in times that tried men's hearts, I married seven wives, I was blessed with the gift to love them all; and although providing for so many was attended with great labor, care and anxiety, yet there was sympathy and love as my reward. And there is not one of my children or their

> mothers that are not dearer to me still than life. (Benjamin Johnson, Gibbs Letter).

Benjamin's fifth wife, Sarah Melissa Holman Johnson, expressed her feelings about plural marriage when she said,

> I want to express my sentiments in relation to plural marriage. In it I find happiness, joy, peace, love and beauty.... Six wives.... have raised our families under the same roof, having separate rooms. Children of six mothers raised in the same dooryard, most of them grown to young manhood and womanhood, are devotedly fond of each other as brothers and sisters, all of them intelligent and full of the spirit of the Gospel. We can have a dance, singing choir, theater or any social entertainment independent of any outside our own family ("Our Pioneer Heritage," *True To The Faith*).

In two letters written in 1896 and 1901 we gain more insight into the deep hurt Benjamin was feeling [See Appendix for copies of these two letters]. Although addressed to his fifth wife, Sarah Melissa, the last of the two has the heading "Open Letter to My Family" in which Benjamin wrote,

> This letter...is adapted to each of the mothers of my children, I wish it preserved to be read by all, even as an open letter to all my children.... To the last day and hour of my life and by the last breath I draw, I shall continue my protest to the cruel injustice of being left as I now am, wifeless and alone.

In a letter to his son Heber in 1901, Benjamin sadly wrote that it was becoming rare that any one could find time to call on him (Benjamin Johnson, Letter to Heber and Lizzie). His family seemed to be more aware of his needs and feelings after he was gone. His granddaughter Nettie Johnson wrote,

> We lived so close to him when we were in Mesa and would stop in on our way to town, and grandfather would be there sitting in his chair in his room or in the garden. I remember him so well. I realize now how lonely grandfather was in his last days and how thoughtless we must all have been. We could have done a lot of things we didn't do (Nettie Johnson).

A Support to His Family

In January 1894, Benjamin noted the anniversary of the birth, marriage, and death of his father. He was impressed with the growth and contributions of the Johnson family. He wrote,

> We have found nearly two thousand that by birth or marriage are kindred in the Johnson family tree. No doubt by far the largest number of descendants from any one pair of parents who received the gospel and died within the Church and of all who were born in or have married into the Johnson family up to the present, no one has yet apostatized from the Church, and of my own family of children, grandchildren and great grandchildren, as one branch of the Johnsons we are now over three hundred in number (*MLR* 382).

Although Benjamin's descendants were many, he made continuous efforts to build his relationships with each one and to help them and strengthen their faith in the gospel. In a letter to his son Ellis Hills who was serving a Church mission in the southern states, Benjamin wrote,

> I am pleased indeed with the tone and spirit of your letters. They show that you are trying to build your manhood upon a love of the Gospel with a knowledge of its truth, which is the only foundation which will stand when the "Storms with floods shall come."
>
> . . .God bless and keep you all the time under his care.
>
> Affectionately your father.

Benjamin's daughter, Harriet Naomi Johnson LeBaron, reflected upon the important times in her life when her father was there to teach her and give her support and encouragement. She said:

> Father bought large tracts of land surrounding our homes and we therefore had meadows covered with trees, flowers and springs of water. There was a meadow and grove near our home where my happiest childhood days were spent herding sheep and picking flowers. It was customary for us all to meet in one room when the bell rang at prayer time, both morning and evening, where the older members of the family took turns praying. This was the cause of much love and unity in our family.
>
> In July 1865, father had just finished blessing and naming Emma Geneva, [my sister], when I went outside and fainted, falling against the house. I soon broke out with scarlet fever, which left my legs so weak I could not walk for months, and

> was unable to go to the prayer room until fall. On the first day that I went to the prayer room, father offered me a big red apple if I would walk to him. I slid off mother's lap and tried to walk, but fell to the floor. Father picked me up and gave me the apple.
>
> When Geneva was six months old she contracted pneumonia and was very sick for about six weeks. She got so bad that mother sent me out to get father to come and dedicate her to the Lord. He took her in his arms, and while he was blessing her I was crouched down at his feet, and I distinctly heard a voice say, "She shall live and not die," and then father repeated those words, which he had heard also. Geneva was instantly healed (Harriet Naomi Johnson LeBaron, Biographical Sketch).

It was Benjamin who took Harriet to Salt Lake City when she was only fifteen years old, and introduced her to her first cousin—who soon became her husband—David Tully LeBaron. She recalled,

> While there, David Tully LeBaron and I became interested in each other and we became engaged.... He claimed me as "his girl." I would not go back to school, as my mind was more on housekeeping and preparing for marriage (Harriet Naomi Johnson LeBaron, Biographical Sketch).

Harriet developed serious complications with her first pregnancy. She recalled,

> I was very ill during the pregnancy and at the end suffered so much for five days that mother ran out of the house so she would not see me die. They decided to hold a prayer circle, and my husband, father [Benjamin], brothers and doctor, all knelt around my bed, never taking their hands off me until the next morning when my baby was born (Harriet Naomi Johnson LeBaron, Biographical Sketch).

Although Harriet's life was preserved, the baby died. Harriet and her husband, David, lost six of their ten children in death. Then Harriet wrote,

> I awoke one night and found David awake. I asked him what was the matter. He said that he had dreamed he was in a Council Meeting where more missionaries were called and he was one of them. All those in the meeting, that he recognized, were men who had died. I was very sorrowful and cried because I felt sure it meant that he would die. He begged me to stop and not think it meant death because he

> did not want to leave me, but I felt that he also thought it did mean his death. At that time there was an epidemic of pneumonia and David, being Mayor [of Mesa], felt it his duty to care for the sick. For several weeks he hardly stopped to rest, until he took the disease and passed away June 1st [1899] after being ill for one week (Harriet Naomi Johnson LeBaron, Biographical Sketch).

Their son, Homer Neal, was three years old when his father died, but he recalled,

> Grandfather's home was situated just across the street from us and after my father's death he would come to our home almost every day to try and help and comfort us. Well do I remember many times sitting on his knee and hearing him tell of early Church experiences, of the Prophet Joseph—his friendship and fine relationship with the Indians, etc. (Interview with Homer Neal LeBaron).

In 1901, a company of forty-two persons—most of whom were Benjamin's family members—left Arizona to homestead in southern Alberta, Canada. One year later, he bid a sad farewell to his wife, Harriet Naomi Holman Johnson, his widowed daughter, Harriet, and her children, Ella Eve, William Farland, Homer Neal and Theiss Ralph. Harriet went to Canada in hopes that the colder climate would be better for the health of her children. She recalled,

> [My father] stood on the platform at the depot as I left for Canada. He put his arms about me and with tears in his dear eyes he said, "My dear girlie, I'll never see you again, but don't forget, I will always be near you to keep watch over you. You're going a new country; do all you can to build it up—plant trees and make homes; pray always with your children and they will never leave you but will care for you to the end. Teach them to love the gospel above all else in life and they will remain true to its principles" .... I never saw my father again but many times during the long years since, I've felt his presence and his words of counsel have come back to me when I needed them. May the day be hastened when I can join him and mother (MLR 386).

It is somewhat ironic that these painful separations were, in part, a result of the spirit of colonizing and pioneering which Benjamin had passed on to his posterity.

Benjamin enjoyed every opportunity to visit with his family, especially on his birthdays. His grandson, William F. LeBaron recalls,

> Grandpa was always happy when the 28th of July came and the entire population would assemble to celebrate his birthday. He loved his friends, but was especially fond of his own wives and children, and seemed extra kind to the grandchildren; took care to learn all their names, treated them not as babies but as people and he enjoyed giving each one a Patriarchal blessing as soon as they were old enough (William Farland LeBaron).

Benjamin's birthdays were always newsworthy events. On his seventy-sixth birthday the *Deseret News* reported,

> Yesterday a part of the family of Patriarch Benjamin F. Johnson, to the number of 144, and thirteen friends of the family, met in the grove of Don M. LeBaron, in Nephi Ward, to celebrate the seventy-sixth birthday of the Patriarch. A pleasing sight it was, to see our Patriarch, looking hale and full of life, despite his 76 years, surrounded by so many of his children, grandchildren and great-grandchildren, although many were unavoidably absent, and by a few of his many friends. Had it not been a family reunion the grove would have been too small to shelter his many friends, and therefore a general invitation could not be extended.
>
> The table being cleared, the family choir gave a greeting song, followed by a short address from the Patriarch, touching upon his childhood and youth, passed amid the sorrows, cares and fires of persecution in Ohio, Missouri and Illinois. Responding to a call, short addresses were made by James H. Martineau, Bishop Samuel Openshaw and J. M. Crosby, all bearing testimony founded upon many years personal knowledge of the integrity of Brother Johnson and his unswerving devotion to the cause of God during his sixty-three years' membership in the Church.... not a feeling except that prompted by love or friendship was manifest. At the conclusion the patriarch bestowed a fatherly blessing upon all, and we separated with a feeling that such reunions should be more frequent (*Deseret News*, 4 August 1894).

His Final Years

Benjamin bore his testimony whenever he had the opportunity. One of the last great public honors to come to him was at General Conference on 6 October 1900. He was called upon to be the concluding speaker in the afternoon session. Although his remarks were brief, they represent how he felt about the Church and the gospel. He said,

> My dear brethren and sisters, it is a pleasure that I did not expect, to have the privilege of standing here to bear my humble testimony to the truth of the words this day spoken in your hearing—the truth of the great fact that God has set His hand to the accomplishment of the great purpose of gathering together all things in one Christ. I feel to express my gratitude that God has given me the privilege of living in this day of the harvest time of the earth—a period toward which all energies, all desires and hopes have been directed from the earliest times. I know that Joseph Smith was a Prophet of the Most High God. It is a pleasure to me to look around upon this vast assembly and say to you that this is my testimony, and that I know that the work in which we are engaged as Latter-day Saints, is the work of God Amen .(Conference Report 41).

As Benjamin became one of the few living members of the Church who had experienced early Church history and been a close personal friend of the Prophet Joseph Smith, he received much recognition and was a popular speaker. In 1903 the First Presidency asked him to record some of his memories (Benjamin Johnson, Letter to President Anthon H. Lund). He did so in a lengthy letter to Elder George S. Gibbs, secretary to the First Presidency (See appendix for a copy of this letter).

The largest gathering ever held in Benjamin's honor was in celebration of his eighty-seventh birthday on 29 July 1905. About 300 family and friends dropped by throughout the day to wish him well. Many tributes and testimonies were given of his worthy life of service. In response, Benjamin said,

> I know the Gospel is true. I know the Book of Mormon is true, as I know that my soul lives; and before the bar of eternal justice before which I must stand shortly, I testify to you that these things are true. I know Joseph Smith was called of God. Though but a boy when I first saw him, I felt the presence of pure intelligence in him. I knew then and I know now that Joseph Smith was and is the great prophet, who talked with God the Father, and the Son, and has revealed to

> him the truths of eternity, that will save mankind. And I desire to bear this testimony particularly to my children, for this may be the last time (*Deseret News*, 26 August 1905. For a complete account of this article, see the Appendix)

Near the end of Benjamin's life, his daughter, Melissa Almera, and her husband, Don Carlos Babbitt, moved into his home to care for him ("Almon Whiting Babbitt", *Our Pioneer Heritage*). Benjamin grew weaker as he got older and one day he fell through the french doors. With his pride hurting more than his body, he wept and said, "If I am going to be weak like this, I want the Lord to take me!" Benjamin was gone in two weeks (Rose A. Openshaw, Grandfather Johnson had a Birthday).

Before he died, he bore his final testimony regarding the experiences and principles which had guided his life. He made a plea to his descendants that they would follow the living prophets of God, as he had done. Benjamin's grandson, Samuel J. Johnson, recorded,

> I was at the bedside of my Grandfather, Benjamin F. Johnson, when he died and heard him give his last testimony. When he called his children around his bedside, with a twinkle in his eyes, he mentioned the Prophet's name.
>
> He said, "Children, listen to my last testimony. Joseph Smith was a Prophet of God, faithful and true to the end of his days: I know, I traveled with him, slept with him, lived with him. I was his Bodyguard, Private Secretary, and Business Manager for years. I have always loved and revered him and all his successors, as I know them all to be Prophets, Seers and Revelators. I was one of the first persons he mentioned plural marriages to and he asked for my sister, Almera. The Manifesto has been given by a Prophet, Seer and Revelator. It is just as binding on us as the first, for all the keys of the Priesthood are held by the President of this Church. May God bless you and help you to follow the leaders of the Church" (Affidavit on file with the author).

Benjamin Franklin Johnson died on 18 November 1905. The following article appeared in the *Deseret News*:

> FUNERAL OF B. F. JOHNSON
>
> Honored Patriarch closes Eventful Career in 88th Year
>
> Mesa, Maricopa Co., Ariz., Nov. 20.
>
> The funeral of Patriarch Benjamin F. Johnson who died Nov. 18, was held in the Latter-day Saints' tabernacle yesterday, Bishop James M. Horn presiding. The speakers were

> Elders F. T. Pomeroy, Noah Brimhall and President Isaac Dana, all eulogizing the noble, upright life of the departed. There was a large concourse of people in attendance to do honor to his name and his remains were followed to the Mesa cemetery by a cortege a mile long.
>
> He has ever been a faithful, consistent member of The Church of Jesus Christ of Latter-day Saints, and was Patriarch in the Maricopa Stake, where like Abraham, and Isaac and Jacob of old, he not only blessed his own children "concerning things to come" but hundreds of others. And many of them bear testimony of his prophetic words being fulfilled on their heads.
>
> He was beloved by all who knew him. He had the pure love of God in his heart, which was abundantly manifest in his remarkable love for his fellow men.
>
> "Uncle Benji" was over 87 years of age, and for years his birthday had been annually celebrated by his friends and descendants of whom he has a great number in Utah, Arizona, Mexico and Canada. For years he has been a patriarch in the Church, and has converted many people to his faith. He was fond of telling stories of early Church history, and of the Prophet with who[m] he was so intimately acquainted. He was a man much loved by both the old and young people in his neighborhood, and his memory will long be held in loving esteem by those who knew him (*Deseret Evening News*, 6 December 1905).

Although Benjamin's mortal ministry had come to an end, his posterity and influence continue to increase. Seventy-five years after his death there were 15,778 known descendants (*Descendants of Benjamin Franklin Johnson*, B. F. Johnson family, Arizona Branch).

Memories of Benjamin

Benjamin impressed and inspired others. His dignity, his intense faith, and his love for others made an indelible mark upon those who came in contact with him. His appearance and demeanor particularly impressed the youth.

A fifteen year old boy considered Benjamin to be one of the leaders of the Church and was greatly impressed as he watched him go to and from church in his long swallow-tailed coat and hat, all in black, and using a cane (Brundage).

A granddaughter observed,

> He was proud and fastidious, dressing carefully and rather than be caught with a patch on his garments however inconspicuous, he would tangle with the cold, at one time travelling in freezing weather without an overcoat, due to a darn [mending] concealing a small burned spot.
>
> Attired usually in a dark suit, his dignified and impressive appearance, augmented by the cane he carried and the massive gold ring adorning his finger, created an illusion of grandeur, and we children stood a little in awe of him, according him much of the reverence due kings (Oppenshaw, "Grandfather Johnson had a Birthday").

At stake conferences, or when a general authority visited Mesa, Benjamin usually met with them and enjoyed the privilege of entertaining them in his home. It was well known that "Uncle Ben" would be one of the main speakers at every conference (Interview with William LeBaron).

Whenever he was asked to speak, he drew a large crowd, and everyone liked to hear him (Riggs). A young deacon's quorum president said,

> I was always pleased when Patriarch Johnson was called on for a sermon, for when he spoke about the Prophet Joseph Smith, which he always did, before he was through, his face would light up and a light would shine all around it like a halo. It was thrilling to watch that light (Henry C. Watson to Rose A. Openshaw, "Grandfather Johnson Had A Birthday").

Joseph E. Robinson, former president of the California Mission, related a most unusual experience he had with Benjamin. He said,

> I saw Patriarch Johnson for the first time at the conference June 14, 1902. I was sitting on the rostrum with Apostle Hyrum M. Smith, J. Golden Kimball, Pres. Hakes and other brethren, when the door, at our back opened and Bro. Johnson came in.
>
> I recognized him at once as the one I had seen in a dream when I was a lad 8 years of age. I arose and offered him my chair and trembling with suppressed emotion, called him by name. He was much surprised and replied, "That's my name, but I do not remember of ever having met you before" and asked me how I knew him. I told him he never had met me but after [the] meeting I would tell him how I knew him. When the services were over...I said, "First I

> should like to ask you two or three questions...Did you ever know the Prophet Joseph?"
>
> He drew himself up proudly and said, "I should think I did. I was his confidential secretary and advisor for a time in the early days of Commerce, or Nauvoo, and he married my oldest sister for one of his plural wives."
>
> I said, "Were you ever a military man?"
>
> He said, "Yes, in a way. Joseph chose me to succeed Hyrum as his aide-de-camp in the Nauvoo Legion, but owing to conditions immediately following I did not fill that position, however, later I became an officer in the first [militia] of the state of Deseret.
>
> Then I asked him if he ever used tobacco. He was somewhat ashamed and said, "What made you ask me that?"
>
> I said, "Because I wanted to know but I did not want to be offensive in asking."
>
> "Well," said he, "at the time when you are speaking, I am ashamed to admit it [but] I used to sometimes smoke a cigar." Then I told him of a dream wherein I saw the Prophet Joseph Smith talking with the other men. One of the men seemed on more intimate footing with the Prophet, than either of the others—tall, straight, lithe in figure, with black hair cut rather long, piercing dark eyes, an aquiline nose, and a hearty infectious laugh. He carried a cane and smoked a long black cigar. Next to the Prophet his likeness was fixed upon my childish mind.
>
> Years after in telling my dream to Judge James Lewis, who was well acquainted with the Prophet, he said, "You have given a most accurate description of [the Prophet], and that dark military looking man you speak of was a man by the name of Johnson, who was closely associated with the Prophet."
>
> That was the reason I knew the name of Bro. Johnson when I first saw him in [the] meeting at Mesa so long afterwards.
>
> I treasure very highly my acquaintance with Bro. Johnson and a wondrous Patriarchal blessing he gave me (Joseph E. Robinson, Letter to C. S. Sellers).

In appreciation for his influence in her life, Ruth M. Fox, who later served as the General President of the Young Women's Organization, wrote the following poem:

To Benjamin F. Johnson

In feebleness, dear Uncle Ben
My gratefulness I try to pen;
I fain would have thee know that I
Thy name will cherish till I die.

I would that these few lines may be
A bond of love twixt thee and me,
For kindly words from thy lips fell
Which healed my heart and all is well.

A noble patriarch art thou
That thou canst graft so green a bough
Upon thy fruitful Family tree
But worthy I will try to be.

In blessing me thou shalt be blessed
To what extent can't be expressed,
But know the influence of thy love
May op'n for me the gates above.

And let the love of God divine
Into my heart and bosom shine
That I like thee may send it forth
To bless the sad and sore of earth.

And like the Patriarchs of old
Thy words and deeds though not all told
Shall follow down the stream of time
And shed their rays on thee and thine.

Say wilt thou not be blessed indeed
In yonder realm where thou shalt lead
If too the Father I shall tell
This is the man whose heart did swell

With sympathy and love for me,
And helped my heart from sin to free
That I might choose the broader way

That leads to life and endless day.

I honor him, our Uncle Ben,
As one of thy most noble men
And when his crown shall given be
Place one bright gem in it for me.

(*MLR* 379-80)

The feelings expressed by Sister Fox are representative of the respect and love which many people had for Benjamin.

Chapter XII

Legacy of Faith

> I have so many wonderful memories of my dear father, his love for his children, his deep concern for their welfare has always drawn him near to me in times of distress and trial. When I heard his "Life Review" read I lived again the days we all lived together as one big happy family. I could see all us children with our mother come trooping in for supper at the call of the supper bell. I can see our happy home evenings when we had our home dramatics. I could see the barrels and barrels of pickles stored down in the cellar, the women at work on their looms, the boys in the tannery and best of all there was father in our midst, telling us about the Prophet Joseph and his early missionary experiences. Never did father turn me away without answering my countless questions; patient, kind, faithful, understanding and true, my father was all of these virtues to me. His deep love for the gospel and his firm knowledge that God lives will always remain fresh in my memory. "Pray to God just as you would talk to me, and He will hear and answer you," he would say (Harriet Naomi Johnson LeBaron, MLR 385–86).

Four principles a granddaughter learned from Benjamin are:

1. Anything obtained with compunction of conscience will never do its owner any good.
2. We are rich only as we are grateful to the Lord.
3. Disunity, contention and ingratitude are the forerunners of poverty.
4. We never really own anything until we have paid for it with a price—the price of self-sacrifice (Openshaw, Grandfather Johnson had a Birthday).

A granddaughter wrote the following:

There are so many things to admire about B. F. Johnson. His great faith and courage. His pride in learning and self-education; his humility; his forgiveness of those who wronged him; his trust in his Heavenly Father to help him through every trial; his trust in his guardian angel—to prompt, to guide, or save him from harm.

He would not have us believe he was a perfect man. There were many instances when pride overcame him, or faults, weaknesses or failures to give obedience to some in authority, caused him sorrow, and he speaks often [of] bitter lessons learned, of blessings denied. But he always repented, and leaves us with the feeling that, if only others, especially his children or *their* children might profit, the mistakes were not without meaning.

He was sympathetic to women and children and all those whom he felt [were] downtrodden. He was generous, almost to a fault, giving away food, shoes, guns and such supplies as were often needed to sustain his own life, and loved ones. He was always a great friend to the Indians.

His love of beauty is seen in the trees, shrubs, gardens and flowers he planted where ever he went. But woe to the child who pulled his turnips for a turnip fight, or picked the flowers without his consent.

His love of animals is shown in his attachment to his horse, Ranger, and his dog, Ring, who were faithfully buried in the family garden beside his departed children.

It was said by a prominent government official from Washington, D. C. to Cassandra J. Pomeroy, [daughter of B. F. Johnson], as she was introduced to him, "Your father is a walking encyclopedia. A self-made man, but never in my life have I met one better informed. He can talk intelligently on any subject from soil to the stars. Young lady, you should be proud of your heritage."

Indeed, he was more than an intelligent "talker," he was an industrious *doer* in many fields of endeavor, and [he] achieved remarkable success. He was [a] doctor, druggist, lawyer, gunsmith, missionary, brick-maker, home-builder, colonizer, explorer, pioneer, legislator, lumberman, bee keeper, horticulturalist, industrialist. He engaged in commercial canning, in sheep raising, in silk-worm culture. For

> his large family he made shoes, had a broom factory, molasses mill. He was an author, bishop and a patriarch. He was beloved by all who knew him. He had the pure love of God in his heart, which was abundantly manifest in his love for his fellowmen (Nix).

> Yes, that big old house still lives in my memory, with all its pleasure of being together, the morning and evening prayers, the talks to us and truths explained, the recounting by our parents of hardships endured for the gospel's sake, the teachings of a wise and venerable father who had been so closely associated with the Prophet Joseph Smith and tried always to impress on us the need of praying always, morning and night, that we might be guided by the Holy Spirit to choose the right path, and follow the gospel plan. Such teachings were never to be forgotten. They were a great safeguard for us all through our lives, as well as a help in keeping us close to the Lord in our childhood and youth.
>
> After training in this way for a while, the mothers were instructed to teach their children in their separate rooms how to act, to train sons and daughters how to take the lead. In this way they learned to carry on in their own homes when they married. (Pomeroy 3)

> The greatest of all the good things our wonderful pioneer parents left to us was their firm and unwavering testimony of the divine origin of The Church of Jesus Christ of Latter-day Saints, and the example of their untiring devotion to the restored gospel which we were taught to obey as we were taught to love the Lord our God with all our hearts and pray to Him always for guidance and protection. May we inherit their unwavering faith, their tireless devotion, their unfailing loyalty and their dauntless trust in the promises made to the faithful. Such a heritage is beyond all price, means more to us—much more—than all the riches of the world.(Pomeroy).

In 1951, Elder John A. Widtsoe of the Quorum of the Twelve Apostles spoke to a group of young people in Mesa, Arizona. He encouraged them to live good, clean lives, to live the Gospel and to follow God by following the example of the Prophet Joseph Smith. He then said,

> If you would be like him, study the life of Joseph Smith—and if you really want to know him—go to the life of his most intimate friend. Oh, I don't mean Oliver Cowdery, or Martin Harris, or any of those associates. I mean his most intimate friend and companion, with whom he spent many hours; a man who pioneered here in Arizona. Maybe some of his descendants are here in this audience, children or grandchildren of Benjamin Johnson (Nix).

After the meeting one of Benjamin's granddaughters, Norma G. Nix, introduced herself to Elder Widtsoe. He then said,

> He was a great man, your grandfather...But you should be doing something about his book [*My Life's Review*]. You should be circulating his book. It is a fine literary production and the history—there is something you can find no place else, especially concerning the early days of the Church (Nix).

A Noble Heritage

Thirty-five years before Benjamin's death, at a time when life was full of sorrow and uncertainty, he had received the following patriarchal promise:

> I say unto thee be of good faith and of good cheer for better days await thee. The Lord hath heard thy petitions and knoweth the integrity of thy heart and is satisfied, therefore be at rest in thy mind and put thy trust in the Arm of the Almighty and thy pathway shall be made strait and thou shalt fulfill thy mission here upon the Earth and fill up the measure of thy days and accomplish a work for which thy name shall be held in honorable remembrance and handed down from generation to generation, and written in the Lambs Book of Life. Thy posterity shall also be numerous and bear thy name in honorable remembrance and I say unto thee let thy faith fail not and thy days and years shall be lengthened according to the desires of thy heart (John Smith).

These divine promises have been, and are being, fulfilled. To countless thousands of Benjamin Franklin Johnson's posterity his name is "held in honorable remembrance and handed down from generation to generation." Indeed, we are grateful beyond measure for the life of this noble ancestor.

Appendix A

Report of Benjamin's Last Birthday

Deseret Evening News

Mesa, Arizona, Aug. 15—The eighty-seventh anniversary of the birth of patriarch Benjamin Franklin Johnson occurred on July 29, 1905, and his children and friends prevailed upon him to be "at home" during the day. An announcement to that effect was made in the Mesa Free Press, and as a result probably as many as 300 people gathered at some time during the day to shake hands with the venerable patriarch and receive his hearty blessing. Preparations in the way of light refreshments had been made and the guests were treated to grapes, cantaloupes, lemonade, ice cream and cake.

Elder F. T. Pomeroy received the guests and took charge of the gathering, and about 4:30 PM he called the people to order, and after a hymn and prayer, he gave a brief sketch of the life of "Uncle Benji," from his boyhood days in New York, where he received the Gospel when 13 years of age, until his arrival in Arizona many years ago. He stated that probably there was no one now living that was so intimate with the Prophet Joseph Smith, during his life time. He had been the close friend and confidential business agent of the Prophet, from Kirtland until the hour of the Prophet's martyrdom, and for a number of years before his death he acted as his private secretary. Thus the lives of the two had been very close, and his mind, which today is bright and keen, is a veritable storehouse of incidents of the Prophet's life.

He first met the Prophet Joseph Smith at Kirtland in 1833, and was present when Brigham Young and the Twelve were chosen to lead the Saints, and witnessed the transfiguration of Brigham Young.

Elder Pomeroy referred to the numerous posterity of the venerable Patriarch, numbering in all about 800 souls, and said his second wife, who now was with him, and present, was given him by the hand of Joseph Smith himself.

He further said that for one to see his family of children, grandchildren and note the intelligence, morality and the elements of good citizenship they possessed was ample refutation of the common estimate placed by the world upon the tendencies of polygamous marriages formerly practiced among the "Mormon" people.

Uncle Benjamin is proud of his posterity, and well might he be, for in no community do you find a finer looking, brighter lot of men and women than his sons and daughters and their children to the third generation, who are a credit to any community. His posterity possibly numbers larger than any man of his generation.

President C. R. Hakes; also addressed the assemblage. He recounted vividly many of the events in the life of this good man that were a great lesson the people enjoyed. He bore a faithful testimony to the worthy life of the patriarch, and admonished his children to always remember the testimony of their father.

Uncle Benjamin then addressed the assembly and for an hour he stood up and recounted the stirring scenes of the early rise of the Church. There was something majestic about him as he bore a strong testimony to the life and divine mission of Joseph Smith and the cause that he gave his life to establish.

The Patriarch said in part,

"I know the Gospel is true. I know the Book of Mormon is true, as I know that my soul lives; and before the bar of eternal justice before which I must stand shortly, I testify to you that these things are true. I know Joseph Smith was called of God. Though but a boy when I first saw him, I felt the presence of pure intelligence in him. I knew then and I know now that Joseph Smith was and is the great prophet, who talked with God the Father, and the Son, and has revealed to him the truths of eternity, that will save mankind. And I desire to bear this testimony particularly to my children, for this may be the last time."

Benjamin then related some of his experiences with the Prophet Joseph Smith and Brigham Young. He concluded by testifying, "I knew then where the cloak of the Prophet fell. I remembered then what he had said, and I knew and still know that Brigham Young was a Prophet of God and the true successor to Joseph Smith, and I know that the successors to Brigham Young were the chosen of heaven."

In answer to the question to what Joseph Smith's feelings were towards the United States government, "He was loyalty itself," was the reply of Patriarch Johnson. "How could he be other than loyal when the Lord revealed to him that this government was raised up by Him, and that He had inspired the men who brought forth the Constitution, and that it should endure,, and finally through it and the broad principles of liberty, religious and otherwise, it should leaven the whole earth."

At the conclusion of his address, all of the children present, about 50; filed by and dropped a birthday present, for "Father Johnson" and received his blessing.

The "at home" continued until 11 p.m. Among those present who were interested listeners, were a number of friends from Tempe and four Japanese, who with their gramophone, played some of the national airs of their far away homeland. The occasion was one long to be remembered by those who participated and all joined in wishing "Uncle Benji" many happy returns of the day. F. T. Pomeroy (26 August 1905).

Appendix B

Julia Hills Johnson Letter

(Original in possession of Rosy Williams, Henderson, NV. Used by permission)

Nauvoo [1846?]

May the 19 Dear Children I write a few lines to you as we have been disapointed about going to the west this spring, teams are vary hard to be got and Almon dont make many sales he Could but just get teams for Br Heywood and Fulmer

I hope you will make out to go with Joel and the rest on acount of your health, we have sent a few articles. Julia has sent you a coat cloth and bundle you may divide as you see fit I thought to send you a barrel of flour but got disapointed about geting it I send 16 pounds of sugar I send the rest a little aple and a few articles I meant to had you all some stockings but my health has ben poor and David has ben sick and I have not done much Wm send the pant cloth and hat &c Jane send the yarn I send Mary Ann Coverlet, the pink calico is for Julia D and the rest to them that need there each one a towel you cant think how I want to see you all I think David and Esther will send some thing and write as Joel can tell all the rest my pen is so poor I conclud your mother

Julia Johnson
tell the children there

Appendix C

Reflections by Benjamin's Children About Life at Spring Lake, Utah

The journals and histories of Benjamin's children indicate that when their family was growing up in Spring Lake it was a wonderful and happy time. The following are some of their reflections about these times.

The entire family was involved in their many endeavors to sustain themselves. Yet they also enjoyed many other activities such as fishing, hunting, and trapping. Utah Lake provided social as well as temporal benefits to the family. Benjamin's daughter, Cassandra, recorded:

> Our Spring Lake home was a few miles from Utah Lake, a beautiful body of fresh water that lies like a sparkling blue jewel at the mouth of Provo River with green slopes and towering peaks all around. It was a red-letter day when the big brothers could get away from the heavy work of field and shop for a fishing trip. With their seines they rowed out over the blue water and hauled in load after load of carp, suckers and sometimes a bass or mountain trout. The fish were brought home, cleaned and salted, ready to be dried, smoked or used right away. . . So the outing to Utah Lake was eagerly planned and awaited every year in June between spring planting and fruit-picking time (Cassandra 30).

Benjamin and his wives became expert in meeting the family's temporal needs and in making a profit through marketing their produce. A daughter recalls:

> Our "Pa" knew a lot about softening leather and had his own "lasts" to shape shoes and make the soles to size. Then he would ply his needle with the heavy waxed thread and peg them together with shoe tacks. Oh, that father, as well as our mothers, did know how to do everything for us that we really needed. . . Oh, so many things they could do for our home and our everyday needs that no one ever tries to do at home in these days. Most everything now is made in factories instead of by hand in our homes. Everything in that big house reflected their skill and handiwork.
>
> The clean whitewashed walls, the homemade rag carpet stretched from wall to wall over fresh clean straw from the wheat field and tacked securely in place. How grand the room looked with the new carpet! We had all helped to sew the carpet rags into balls during wintertime when we had to stay indoors. With the white lawn curtains at the windows and a bowl of beautiful fresh flowers on the center table the lamps trimmed and shining and chairs grouped around the fireplace. These simple things made a house a home to those wonderful brothers and sisters of mine. As long as we could all be together a big happy family — faces shining with health, love and intelligence, no palace could be more grand (Cassandra 21-2).

Benjamin was not only a hard worker but he also excelled in organizing, delegating and managing a large organization known as "B. F. Johnson and Sons" — which certainly included his wives and daughters. One daughter wrote:

> Summer work goes on! Benjamin F. Johnson, Sr., instructor and general manager, general — Yes! He looked like one — tall, straight, black hair and eyes, and long black beard.
>
> He calls his sons, several of them in looks very much like him, and sends them forth to take charge of the various lines of work to be done. One may go to the sawmill, another to the broom factory, another to the molasses mill, others out to mow the hay with their sharp scythe. Or it might be time to cut the wheat, barley, oats or other grain; all done with the scythe by hand labor, everything in its season and in those days by the hard way without help of modern machinery.
>
> Of the many projects and industries in which our family engaged not the least in importance was the canning. My, the loads and loads of fruit we had to prepare for the cannery! Here is where all the Johnson daughters came in for their full share of work. None were too small, except babies, to gather fruit from the trees or pick it up from the ground for feeding the pigs. The ground had to be kept clean and free from spoiling fruit, the good fruit sorted out for use. We smaller children could even pick the tomatoes for canning or run them through the sieve for our catsup — nothing wasted! We could cut and spread the fruit to dry apricots, peaches, and apples, and measure out the sugar into water for syrup that went into the cans of fruit as they were filled ready to go into the container that was lifted into the vat over the furnace where a log fire soon had them boiling hot. At the right time when the fruit was properly cooked big brother, Benjie, took the cans out, punched a hole in each to let the air escape; then resealed them with his red hot iron, rosin and bar of solder.
>
> Then came the job of labeling them before they could be placed on the cellar shelves. First came the paste-making — making the flour and cold water till free from lumps; then pouring in boiling water till it was clear, smooth and the right thickness for paste. Next, take a label from the stack and be sure its the right one! "B. F. Johnson and Sons," with the name and picture of the fruit the can contained.
>
> How wonderful those shelves all around the cellar wall looked, gay with bright pictures of peaches, pears, apricots, plums, apples, green gages and tomatoes. Many loads of these canned fruits as well as the dried ones went to Salt Lake City markets (Cassandra 23-4).

It was in the cellar that an amusing family incident occurred — amusing that is to all except Benjamin. Stored in the cellar were forty-gallon barrels of pickles, vinegar, catsup, molasses, applejuice and other commodities. They needed to be checked periodically to make sure that they were not fermenting or spoiling, which could cause an explosion. Benjamin had sent four of his sons to make this inspection and they found a barrel of applejuice which was beginning to turn to cider. After sampling this deliciously cold drink for some time, they then noticed a catsup barrel which was bulged. It looked ominous and they were trying to get each other to check it, when Benjamin marched in and demanded: "Why in tarnation are you fooling around wasting time down here? Get this job done and hurry up about it!" Ignoring their warning to stay away from the dangerous barrel, Benjamin grabbed the plug and pulled it out. There was an immediate explosion of catsup which sprayed out at him. His daughter, Cassandra, wrote:

> His hair and beard, so sleek and black were all red, dripping catsup. His eyes smarting, blinded as he yelled, "Where's the plug? Where's the plug, I say?" Yes, he was <u>seeing red</u>, too, as they all roared with laughter. My, but I was frightened and ran fast for Mother to help poor "Pa," I felt so

> sorry.
>
> Aunt Mary Ann, Aunt Harriet and my mother came in a hurry but they, too, saw first the funny side and joined in the side-splitting laughter. Then above the din roared our indignant father's voice. "Do something!" Mother, with her apron tried to mop the catsup from his eyes and ears. Others went for towels, water buckets and tubs for the cleanup job, and what a job! Catsup was dripping from ceiling and shelves into pools on the cellar floor.
>
> And our fine dignified daddy for once was abashed, humiliated, chagrined, <u>outraged</u> to be laughed at by his family. Weary but fresh and clean he came forth quietly only to retire to his bed a <u>sick man</u> and no one ventured to disturb him. He did not like the way his ladies had joined in the laughter at his expense while they with understanding hearts let it pass and the incident was closed. At least <u>I</u> was too young to dare say anything about it and don't remember ever hearing the catsup story mentioned again (Cassandra 25-6).

Among the many great qualities that Benjamin was known for was his empathy and love for others, especially the sick and the downtrodden. This was also a family characteristic. His wives and children generously provided service and compassion. Sarah Melissa, Benjamin's fifth wife, served the area as "a wonderful nurse." The sick would be brought from many communities as far away as Salt Lake City because of her "inspired ability to understand the symptoms of illness and to relieve pain." The Johnson home became a refuge for many who were suffering, some staying for months. One particular incident was recorded by Sarah Melissa's daughter:

> One hot summer day, [Sarah Melissa] noticed an Indian family across the road in the shade of a tree. They were bending over as if someone was sick. She went over to investigate and found a little boy suffering with fever and pain. She took the family to her home, made the child comfortable by her inspired nursing and usual simple remedies, instructing the mother how to care for him until the little fellow was recovered, and the family was able to go on their way. In appreciation for this kindness, the grateful parents gave to the baby boy the name of Aunt Lissy Johnson — by which he was always known. His Indian friends as he grew up, would laugh with side-shaking amusement telling Aunt Lissy of the Indian boy named for her (Cassandra 33).

Education was a high priority for Benjamin and his family. However, the responsibility for providing it was essentially theirs in these pioneering days. Benjamin's daughter, Cassandra, recalled:

> Then there was no free public school system. All had to pay for what learning they could get. . . The school teacher would live and board around, taking turns among the families to lighten the expense. . . Heating and lighting a schoolhouse, and obtaining and paying a teacher was a very big problem. . . It was so difficult to warm a large room. You could only warm yourself on one side if you were near enough to the huge stove or fireplace while you were freezing on the other side . . Spelling was most important. Spelling matches were great fun, as well as stimulating to our progress. But the younger children learned from an older brother or sister acting as teacher. (Cassandra 3).

Included in the family's education was a strong focus on the arts. Music was of particular importance to their cultural and spiritual life, as it was for many Latter-day Saint families. It was enjoyed in their home and through a choir they shared their talents with people in the area. A daughter wrote:

> That Johnson Choir — mothers, sons, daughters all joining in to make the mountains ring with echoes, as my eldest brother, B. J., lifted his baton to lead and direct while someone played the little old organ. It must have been inspiring for the Johnson Choir was well known throughout the valley and it was often remarked that you never found a Johnson who couldn't sing (Cassandra 45).

Benjamin and his wives were raised with a love for music. His mother, Julia Hills Johnson, had written a hymn that was published in the first Latter-day Saint hymn book which was prepared by Emma Smith and published in 1840. The words of this hymn, "The Joy and the Song" are:

We praise thee, O God, for the joy and the song
Which unto us this beautiful season belong;
We love and adore Thee, for light and for love,
And for all the rich blessings that come from above
The gates are wide open, they beckon us all,
Each to follow and serve at the sound of Thy call;
Through portals of praise and through Zion's fair gates,
We will pass on with songs to the work that awaits.

At last in that city, with its glories untold,
With its gates all of pearl and its streets of pure gold,
We'll give to the Savior, who dwelleth in light,
All the power and dominion and wisdom and light.

CHORUS:
Hallelujah! Hallelujah! O, the joy and the song!
With happy hearts and merry voices we the glad
Strains prolong (Terry).

Appendix D

Family of Ezekiel and Julia Hills Johnson

Benjamin Franklin Johnson's father, Ezekiel Johnson, was a son of Ezekiel and Bethiah Gurnsey Johnson and was born January 12, 1776, at Uxbridge, Massachusetts, and died January 13, 1848, at Nauvoo, Illinois. He married Julia Hills, daughter of Joseph and Esther Ellis Hills, January 12, 1801, at Grafton, Massachusetts. She was born September 26, 1783, at Upton, Massachusetts, and died May 30, 1856, at Council Bluffs, Iowa. To them were born the following children:

1. Joel Hills, born March 23, 1802, Grafton, Massachusetts; died September 23, 1882, Johnson, Kane County, Utah.
2. Nancy Mariah, born August 1, 1803, Northborough, Massachusetts; died October 30, 1836, Kirtland, Ohio.
3. Seth Gurnsey, born February 14, 1805, Royalton, Massachusetts; died February 19, 1835, Kirtland, Ohio.
4. Delcina Didamia, born November 19, 1806, Westford, Vermont; died October 21, 1854, Salt Lake City, Utah.
5. Julia Ann, born November 9, 1808, Westford, Vermont; died October 23, 1857, Crescent, Iowa.
6. David, born September 10, 1810, Westford, Vermont; died October 30, 1833, Kirtland, Ohio.
7. Almira Woodard, born October, 1812, Westford, Vermont; died March 4, 1896. Parowan, Utah.
8. Susan Ellen, born December 1, 1814, Pomfret, New York; died March 16, 1836, Kirtland, Ohio.
9. Joseph Ellis, born April 28, 1817, Pomfret, New York; died December 17, 1882, Tempe, Arizona.
10. Benjamin Franklin, born July 28, 1818, Pomfret, New York; died November 18, 1905, Mesa, Arizona.
11. Mary Ellen, born February 7, 1820, Pomfret, New York; died June 11, 1845, Nauvoo, Illinois.
12. Elmer Wood, born May 26, 1822, Pomfret, New York; died September 14, 1822, Pomfret, New York.
13. George Washington, born February 19, 1823, Pomfret, New York; died January 22, 1900, Moab, Utah.
14. William Derby, born October 27, 1824. Pomfret, New York; died April 13, 1896, Diaz, Mexico.
15. Esther Melita, born January 12, 1827, Pomfret, New York; died March 15, 1876, Salt Lake City, Utah.
16. Amos Partridge, born January 15, 1829, Pomfret, New York; died May 9, 1842, Macedonia, Illinois.

Appendix E

Family of Benjamin Franklin Johnson

Benjamin Franklin Johnson was born July 28, 1818, in Pomfret, Chatauqua County, New York, and died November 18, 1905, at Mesa, Arizona.

He married (first) Melissa Bloomfield Le Baron, December 25, 1841. Their nine children were Benjamin Franklin, Melissa Almera, Julia Didamia, Esther Melita, Delcina Elvira, Frances Belle, David Albion, Erastus Elmer, Leah Bloomfield.

He married (second) Mary Ann Hale, May, 1843. Their five children were Emma Jane, Joseph Ezekiel, Benjamin Samuel, Mary Ann, Vilate Elizabeth.

He married (third) Flora Clarinda Gleason and had one child, Clarinda Huetta.

He married (fourth) Harriet Naomi Holman and had eight children - Benjamin Farland, James Francis, Seth Jedediah, Harriet Naomi, William Sawyer, Emma Geneva, Marquis LeBaron, and Junius.

He married (fifth) Sarah Melissa Holman and had eleven children—Benjamin Julius, Brigham Moroni, Heber Franklin, Agnes Saria, John Angus, Sarah Melissa, Cassandria, Lionel Brand, Ellis Hills, Delightra Victoria, and George Albert. There were four adopted Indian children, Samuel, Elva, Kemo, and Daniel.

He married (sixth) Susan Adeline Holman and had eight children—Susan Celestia, Zina Susetta, Fanklin Carlton, Winnie Fredricka, Leofwin, Adeline Estelaa, Jestus Wanderus, and Nancy Lillian.

He married (seventh) Sarah Jane Spooner and had three children—Julia Ann, Sarah Jane and a son who died in infancy.

Appendix F

Benjamin Franklin Johnson to Sarah Melissa Holman Johnson Mesa, Arizona, May 10, 1896

My Dear Wife Melissa,

Last night you were with me in my dream. It seemed I was traveling a wearysome long and lonely road, and feeling tired and sad, sat down on a way-side seat to write. And looking around saw you seated on my left, partly behind me. I was glad you were there, and commenced to talk to you; when you said softly, "You should not talk to me, but should be with Someone Else." Your words seemed to arouse me, and forgetting all but my undieing love for you, I turned around on my seat and grasped you in my arms, and drawing you close to me said, "There is no one living I would love more, or more desire to be with than you, if you would but let me, and you could not treat me as you do, did you realize it."

I thought your arms came tight around my neck and tears were on your cheeks, while my heart and eyes were both full of the tears of Joy and Hope, and my dream so impressed me on awakening that I felt it a duty to tell it to you. For I know that the present condition of our feeling and fellowship is not right, and should not go with us to the great Beyond. For this life is the only place in which to contract sacred ties— To cultivate Love and Union in family Relations, other than by proxy, in which there is great loss, as all such will be left at side stations, instead of going directly through.

And while it is plain to me that the Springs of your life are weakening and liable suddenly to break, I am equally conscious that the long and weary journey of my life is fast nearing its close, That the margin now left me is narrow, a full sense of which inspires but the one regret— To leave the mothers of my children—the Wives I have so much loved, with no assurance that they would sleep by my side even under the sod, or be glad to meet me when free from this life's tribulations and cares. To once again see you together, each attended by the feelings that inspired you when the Veil was taken from your eyes, and those from the other side came to tell us of things that have been and are still transpiring. To again know that I had your love and confidence, that you were as then, all my own, I could willingly close my eyes in waiting a greater happiness in the joyes of that Sweeter "Bye and Bye."

I am aware that in the unhappy past you have pondered the subject of a Separation, and have felt toward me great aversion. While I can say in truth that my heart has always been loyal to you and my arms has been ever hungry to embrace you. And should not the great fact that the Lord has crowned our lives with so many pure-minded and noble children, preserving them to us until the present, stand as clear evidence of His goodness and Blessing upon our Union? And of his favor and mercy toward us even when so wicked and unkind to each other? To which at least I plead guilty towards all— And to restore myself fully would willingly make any atonement the mothers of my children could require for unkindness and or neglect—

You may say we are now getting old, and why care for the little happiness left to such relations in this life? But we should not grow old in Love for Each other. My body may feel aged but yet, to the last day and hour of my life, and by the last breath I draw, I shall continue my protest to the cruel injustice of being left as I now am by the mothers of my children, wifeless and alone.

And may the mercy of God never so fail those who through love for gain and for their own wills have so forgotten Love and Duty as to forsake their own still loyal and loving husband.

(Forsaken)
B. F. J.

Appendix G

Benjamin Franklin Johnson
Open Letter to My Family
Mesa City, Arizona T.
March 1st 1901.

My Still Dear Wife,
Sarah Melissa:

Your reply to my note, asking you to come to me as you had promised, or appoint a time and place for a meeting did inspire me with great hope, for its tone seemed earnest and sincere.

But after waiting so long I am left to the fear that I must wait on until the end. For in view of your deportment toward me through the long past you could not expect me to come to you without an invitation or appointment.

And now, by failing of both eyesight and health, I am admonished to remain at home when duty does not call me away, and I feel that the time now left to me should be used to a higher purpose than in recalling the many past lone and joyless years, through which, to me there was not one day of real happiness, nor one ray of real sunshine to cheer my earthly pathway. For never have I lain down at night but with the mothers of my children in my thoughts, to dream of them as once to me so loving and dear To awaken to the drear realities of their unforgiving hate—to paralyze every ambition and to inspire almost a contempt for life.

That I loved you all but too much, and more than you could reciprocate or comprehend is but too true. But I now realize that I have an austere and sometimes an unkind way of proving it to you. And while I know that even my anger or resentment grew out of anxiety for all you prompted me to leave you or others, when my heart yearned to remain— So easy to be offended— so impatient in contradiction, and so sharp and unkind in words has been my great weakness—the "Stone of my Stumbling, and Rock of my offence." I had loved you all, and cared for you in your childhood, and when you were married to me, although you were dearer to me than life, my government was more in parental authority than that of the Lover, which from a husband it should have been.— And so, under the burden of poverty, and a weight of anguish from nameless infirmities, such as few ever lived to endure, I still labored on for those I loved, weak in body, broken in spirit, and blind to consequences—to find myself deserted by those I had so loved, and for whom I had so labored. And then again forsaken by those for whom I had suffered and sacrificed all but life itself.

And now, aged, blind and infirm, still yearning for loving companionship of those "given to be with me," must I wifeless and homeless die alone? And must I bear to the grave all the sorrow and shame of the present conditions? Will only this satisfy the cruel pride of those who once did love me? If so, then let it Come. But if I have already suffered a four fold for sins more due to conditions of poverty, infirmity and hardship than real unkindness to you then you may beware, for God is just, and when I am gone that same cold wet blanket of your scorn,contempt and hate that has brought to me and to my children more of shame, sorrow, and regrets than words can express, will still remain a cover for you—To the name you bear a disgrace & to your children—A reproach upon that sacred law. Through which alone they could have had birth and being upon the earth.

Before leaving Spring Lake I saw my error in family government and the wrong it had done both to you and to myself. Ever since which I have been both willing and anxious to make any just atonement that would bring love and harmony back to me. But all my efforts have been repelled or ignored by you. And to me, you once loving and tender heart has become as of stone, untouched by even my tears or (pleadings) or repentance.

And now, my dear wife, let me once more, in humility before the Lord, say to you as by prophecy, or as the word of the Lord to you, that in as much as you will even now forgive me of all my trespasses as you have been forgiven of yours, and will in truth turn your heart and your face back to me—Then shall the Blessing of God with the light of His Spirit and of the favor of Heaven turn back to you in a fullness of joy, to make your last days your best days upon earth.

But God will not always be mocked, and the measure your meet must return to you. So, if you still refuse to forgive me, and neglect to do your part to remove the nasty blanket of unjust contempt thrown upon me by the mothers of my children, that has smothered all my happiness, and destroyed my usefulness for so many years—Then, as I have before said—Here or elsewhere it will cleave to you, with a weight of chilling coldness to make the mothers of my children a hundred fold more anxious for its removal than they were to provide it as a punishment for me.

God sent to us our children and we became their parents under covenant of eternal obedience, mine was made to the Father and yours was made to me, that in the law of obedience you would follow me back to his presence—Requirement of me to love you, labor for you, and by example and precept, in obedience, lead you through Holy Temples to Highest Blessings, back to the Father. All this I have done but so far as you would permit. But a "house divided against itself cannot stand," and as division in the head must affect the members, so it is already fearfully manifest in enmity and hatred between brothers who have been enlightened by the spirit of the Gospel Testimony while others are becoming infidel or reprobate in their lives—

Now let me once again say to you, as one of the dear mothers of my children, that just so far as you withdraw from me while I hold fellowship with God and his servants, just so far you are outside of the "true Vine", and of the Light and favor of God—And just so far as my sons separate themselves from me in their faith and Fellowship—just so far they are liable to darkness and doubt—to criticize authorities, and find fault and quarrel with each other, to become unworthy of the Holy Sacrament, which is the beginning of their end, if they repent not. And let me further tell you that just so long as you bear my name in the New and Everlasting Covenant, just so long I will be held responsible for you, and we both will be held responsible for our children. And in the day of Reckoning, if they do not fill their seats in the circle with us, then our seats will be vacant until they are brought back to their place in the fold—

And while our daughters may be given to sons of other parents, our sons with their wives will never attain to a majority to become the head of a vine unto themselves, for we are but a branch of the one great vine of eternal perpetuity and increase, and must grow together, equally dependent one upon another, and no authority or control can ever be sustained but in the light and right of parental love. While conjugal love alone can give the right to a "husband's rule over his wife—" And herein I now see was my great mistake in permitting austerity and apparent harshness to close up and shut out from common use that deep Fountain of love and affection which in my heart was always ready to gush into tenderness and overflow in tears of sympathy toward my loved ones all of whom were dearer to me than the apple of my eye or my own heart's blood.

Now dear wife would you say that these things are not true? Do you forget what was said of me by Prof. Brenan and the great O. S. Fowler? Both of whom placed me above all men in Payson for everything manly and noble and especially for my love, honor and justice to woman. While Prof. McDonald used almost the same words in placing me above all compeers at Tempe, and their words for me by inspiration, although they knew it not.

In my organization and my life's experience I am much like President Kimball though not so great and wise as he—and yet you heard one of his wives tell of his acts four-fold more cruel and unkind than anyone of you ever dared to accuse me—and yet he was the greatest of Prophets in Israel, honored of God and beloved by the saints; and the sorrows from ingratitude and disobedience in those he loved sent him too soon to the grave—Yet still he was not forsaken by all his wives, and left to die alone.

And now, let me before conclusion say that feeling again moved upon to write to you, I took up my pencil with earnest prayer that it might be guided by the spirit of humility and truth, and if it has not been so guided, then I am sorry indeed. I feel no unkindness to anyone, and I not only forgive all, but I try to pray for and pity those by whom I am wronged, or so misunderstood— You will perhaps refuse to read this letter—but I shall hope you will receive it kindly and read it in the spirit in which it was written. And if so, you will not always keep yourself from my presence or from my home. [five lines badly worn and indecipherable].

As this letter [indecipherable] much application where its contents, sentiment and spirit is adapted to each of the mothers of my children, I wish it preserved to be read by all, even as an open letter to all my children. For the day will come when the Light of inspiration will be seen shining through all family letters that duty has or may call me to write.

And let me still further say to all, both mothers and children that I forgive all for what I have been and am still made to suffer. [Indecipherable]. Yet to the last day and hour of my life and by the last breath I draw I shall continue my protest to the cruel injustice of being left as I now am, wifeless and alone.

And may the Mercy of God and his love never forsake those who have so forgotten love and duty as to forsake their own still loyal and loving

Husband (B.F.J.)

Appendix H

Benjamin F. Johnson to George S. Gibbs
April - October 1903

Dear Brother:

In resuming my answer to your scholarly and effusive epistle, I feel in every degree incompetent to the task. Especially do I feel the want of learning, and my writings, of course, must betray to you my poverty in classical education. Through childhood and early youth, my advantages, even for primary education, were the most meager. At seventeen, I attended the winter term of the grammar school taught by Wm. E. McLelland, in Kirtland, and presided over by the Prophet; at the same time attending night lectures in geography. These were my greatest opportunities for schooling, and in them was finished my school education; and if I have acquired in life anything further of worth, it has been as snatched from the wayside while on the run as a missionary, pioneer or while in Nature's great laboratory with the axe, plow, spade or garden implements. I have been hard at work to provide sustenance for that flock which the Father has sent to my special care. And while it may be a degree common, even with the youth of Zion, whose advantages so far surpass their parents', to look upon the aged as "black numbers," "old fossils," or "mossbacks," yet not one whit of that spirit do I feel in your letter, and my heart goes out toward you in love and blessing, as though you were indeed one of my own sons. And I most earnestly pray that the Lord will so inspire my thoughts and so awaken a remembrance of the past, that I may be able to write to you as by the voice of the spirit of my calling in the Priesthood of the fathers, of anything pertaining to the gospel principle or of our historic past, that may better equip you for that sphere of greater callings and responsibilities that await you as a son in Zion, in the lineage of Ephraim, and of the seed of the blessed.

Your thoughts in regard to the need of positive keys for interpreting our true position, condition and relation to the gospel, both in the past and for the future, strictly accord with my own, and to me it simply means that the spark of life or of light, brought with us at birth, thru a cumulative experience, has attained its present status in intellectual and physical power.

In infancy we were fed upon milk, and in childhood by a loving hand, while our mistakes were tenderly admonished. As we became older we began to grasp the principles and issues of physical life and the modes for its sustenance thru labors of our hands; while the gospel, as an alphabet, with its possibilities of reaching every principle of truth and light within the great science of eternal lives, is given to us as spiritual or intellectual food, thru which, by faith, we can forever grow in the knowledge and power of the Gods, to become in reality and fullness even the "Sons of God," with glory, exaltation, dominion and eternal progression, thru the procreation of endless lives.

And to how much of this greatness in knowledge and power have we yet attained? As well may little children in making their mud pottery claim perfection as sculptors, as for us to claim a fullness in the knowledge of Gospel principles, precepts, or powers.

When were we, as a people, ever able fully to live by the law given to us of the Lord? In 1831 and '32, we were tried in Missouri with the Law of consecration, in which we failed; in '33 we were given, in Kirtland, the Order of Enoch and the Word of Wisdom. The Order of Enoch was not fully honored, and after seventy years experience in accumulating wisdom many are not yet wise. While thru His mercy, the Lord in '36, gave us, when under His rod, the Law of Tithing in place of the former law, but how have we, as a people, fulfilled it? And again, when in '43 he gave us, by command the high and holy law of Plural Marriage, with the sealing power of the Holy Priesthood, did we, as a people, receive it in the spirit and purpose for which it was given? Or have we been slow in comprehending even the primary lessons and precepts of this life's mission?

And as for even our leaders being always filled with the light of their calling, to see the "end from the beginning," or always to discern correctly the thoughts and purposes of others, has not been, according to my experience or knowledge. Does not the Lord tells us in D. & C. Sec. 130, that the Holy Ghost may descend upon a man and not always remain with him? And do we not all, at times, feel that to be a reality, as did the Master, when thru mental anguish He "sweat blood at every pore," as also when upon the cross He cried out in agony of soul to His Father to know why He was forsaken? And to show a change of mood, even in our great Head, witness Him entwining a rope and in anger scourging out merchants and money changers from the temple and kicking over their tables, and in a gush of resentment toward those who hated Him he cries out: "Oh you Scribes and Pharasees, hypocrites, ye are of your father the devil, and his works ye do!" calling them "garnish sepulchres, full of dead men's bones," "robbers of widows and orphans, and oppressors of the poor"; and as though He would have them fight for the kingdom He had sent them to preach, He told those who had not swords "to sell their coats and buy one." But oh! how changed in feeling, when He, on the cross, could realize the enormity of their guilt and the greater sufferings consequent to them, and then with heart melted in pity for His murderers and those that hated Him, He cried to His father with entreaty that they be forgiven.

And just such phases, to a degree, have I witnessed in the life and character of our great Prophet, who stood in the presence of both the Father and the Son and personally conversed with them both; being often visited by Holy Angels, while continually receiving by revelation the word of the Lord to His people. And yet he was altogether of "like passions with his brethren and associates."

"As a son, he was nobility itself, in love and honor of his parents; as a brother he was loving and true, even unto death; as a husband and father, his devotion to wives and children stopped only at idolatry. And his life's greatest motto after 'God and His Kingdom' was that of 'wives, children and friends.'" And on one Sunday morning while sitting with him in the Mansion dining room in private converse, two of Emma's children came to him, as just from their mother, all so nice, bright and sweet, and calling to them my attention, he said, "Benjamin, look at these children, how could I help loving their mother; if necessary, I would go to hell for such a woman." And although at the time he had in the Mansion other wives, younger and apparently more brilliant, yet Emma, the wife of his youth, to me, appeared the queen of his heart and of his home.

But to return: Joseph the Prophet, as a friend he was faithful, long suffering, noble and true to that degree that the erring who did love him were at times reminded that the rod of a friend was better then the kiss of an enemy, "while others who sopped in his dish" but bore not reproof, became his enemies, and like Laws, Marks, Foster, Higby and others who hated him and conspired to his death.

As a companion, socially, he was highly endowed; was kind, generous, mirth loving, and at times, even convivial. He was partial to a well supplied table and he did not always refuse the wine that "maketh glad the heart." For amusement, he would sometimes wrestle with a friend, or oftener would test strength with others by sitting on the floor with feet together and stick grasped between them, but he never found his match. Jokes, rebuses, matching couplets in rhymes, etc., were not uncommon. But to call for the singing of one or more of his favorite songs was more frequent. Of those, "Wife, Children and Friends", "Battle of River Russen," "Soldier's Tear," "Soldier's Dream" and "Last Rose of Summer," were most common. And yet, although so social and even convivial at times, he would allow no arrogance or undue liberties, and criticism, even by his associates, was rarely acceptable, and contradiction would rouse in him the lion at once, for by no one of his fellows would he be superseded or disputed and in the early days at Kirtland, and elsewhere one or more of his associates were more than once, for their impudence, helped from the congregation by his foot, and at one time at a meeting at Kirtland, for insolence to him, he soundly thrashed his brother William who boasted himself as invincible. And while with him in such fraternal, social and sometimes convivial moods, we could not then so fully realize the greatness and majesty of his calling, which, since his martyrdom, has continued to magnify in our lives, as the glories of this last dispensation more fully unfold to our comprehension.

One small incident, among the many, I will relate to show his playful, familiar, kind and loving nature toward one who to him was as a protege or a younger brother. Soon after the Prophet's escape from Missouri and arrival at Old "Commerce," the future Nauvoo, in 1839, I was with him. The people had flocked in from the terrible exposures of the past and nearly every one was sick with intermittent or other fevers, of which many died. In this time of great sickness, poverty and death, the Prophet called his brother, Don Carlos, and cousin, G. A. Smith, as missionaries to administer to and comfort the people. And their being there two young Botanic medical students Doctors Wiley and Pendleton, he called them to prescribe medicine, and called me to follow and take general oversight and care of all the sick, which for weeks, I did, without even one night of respite for sleep. The forepart of September, Dr. Wiley became sick unto death, which soon occurred, after which the Prophet too had a violent attack of the prevailing sickness. And as Emma was in no degree able to care for him, it wholly devolved upon me, and both day and night, through a period of little less than two weeks I was hardly absent from his room: as almost his only food was gruel, and about the only treatment he would accept was a flush of the colon with warm water perhaps tinctured slightly with capsicum and myrrh, or a little soda and salt, both of which were prepared and administered by me in the room he occupied: and if any sleep came to me it was while lying upon his bed or sitting in my chair. At the termination of this sickness and fasting, he arose from his bed like a lion, or as a giant refreshed with wine. He went to President Rigdon with great reproof, commanding him and his house to repent; and called for a skiff, crossed the river, and finding Elijah Fordham in death's struggle, he commanded him to arise, which he did at once, and was made whole as also were others by his administrations.

But I am writing at too great length. Soon after the Prophet's recovery I too came apparently nigh unto death through a violent attack of the fever, through which my comfort was kindly looked after the Prophet.

About the middle of October a letter came to say that my dear mother and young sister were apparently near to death, in Springfield, Illinois, and were anxious for my return. And in my anxiety again to see my mother, I procured quinine, which was just becoming known as an antidote for fevers and taking it in large doses, my fever soon abated, and under it's tonic influence I fancied I had become well, and in great joy and hopehastened preparations to start for the home of my mother and kindred at Springfield. My horse was in the yard ready to mount, but I wished to take leave of the Prophet, with the hope of again to receive his blessing. Of the whole sum I had obtained with which to pay for an outfit and passage to England, with the twelve, when they should start, to which I had been called by the June Conference at Quincy, I had but one ten dollar bill, I said, "As this is all I have left, I want to pay a tithe of it." He saw I was weak in body and that my heart was sad in leaving him, so thinking to cheer and arouse me, when putting the nine silver dollars in my hand he playfully knocked my hand upward, and scattering the money all over the room. My heart was so full of tears, and my emotions must have vent, so forgetting all but the feeling that we were boy companions playing together, I sprang at and grappled him, as though to teach him a lesson, but the lesson was all to me, for on making one grand effort to throw him, I found myself in strength no more than a bullrush as compared with him, and as my strength was fictitious and my real recovery was but illusion, I collapsed and fainted in his arms. He placed me in repose, and did all necessary for my restoration and comfort. Then gathering up the scattered money, and after a period of delay, weak, trembling and desolate, yet determined to start, I led my horse to the other gate and as I was passing through, with the bridle on my arm, his hand detained me, and placing his hands upon my head, he seemed to pour out his soul in blessing me. He told the Lord I had been faithful to care for others, that I was now worn and sick, and that on my journey I would need his care, and he asked that a special guardian might go with me from that day and stay with me through all my life. And oh! my dear brother, how often have I seen through life the footprints of that angel, and knew that his hand had drawn me back from death.

The day after leaving Nauvoo my fever returned with all of its virulence. The next day, near night, I was found by the Prophet's brother William, lying helpless by the roadside, and the next evening I was found by strangers, being unconscious in the road, who kindly cared for me until I could again get upon my horse to finish the journey to my mother in Springfield, where I soon arrived, and remained very sick until Apostles Young and Kimball came in January to find me apparently nigh unto death with hemorrhage of the bowels. At leaving, they told me to take a mission East so soon as able to start, which I did through kindness of Brother James Standing, who, upon my bed in a sleigh took me a hundred and ten miles to Paris, Illinois. Turning home on bare ground, he left me in deep mud, alone, and near penniless, sick and among strangers, while borne to the earth by a burden of bashful ignorance—the long green of young manhood; but my "Angel" was always with me to open the way.

Now you see how I have wandered from the subject of your "Three Keys," but you said you wanted to learn more of my history and personalities, so what I have written may serve as a glimpse of my earlier life.

Now, returning to the subject, shall I tell you that just the other day at Quarterly Conference one of our best missionary speakers was led to say that "our Gospel was revealed as a whole, and not fragmentary," and I felt to tell him that the Gospel had not only been given to us by fragments, but that of the great science of Eternal Lives, we have not yet received or learned more than it's alphabet; and perfection here can only exist in parts or degrees. And while the Holy Ghost may not always remain upon a man, may not even a prophet to whom it was not yet all revealed, make mistakes, as in the baptism for the dead, and also in the prophet sermon at the funerals of a child of Winzor Lyon and King Follett, when he preached that children, "even infants, would sit upon thrones with dominion," which was published in the "Times and Seasons" at the time, but which, like President Woodruff, I am positive he afterwards reconsidered. And those who were with him in Kirtland, Missouri and Nauvoo, will remember many things in which his sanguine and prophetic hopes seemed disappointed.

The Prophet Joseph laid the foundation of our Church in a military spirit, and as the Master taught His disciples, so he taught us to "sell our coat and buy swords," but never did the sword fully prevail with us, not even with the Indians, and never before were we apparently so safe from them, or our outside enemies, as since the Lord, through the government, permitted us to be robbed of armed self protection; and even our mission martyers have generally been murdered after a show of resistance. And are we not beginning to see that charity is the life and core of our religion, and that love is the great life spring and centrifugal power of the universe, and in our gospel there appears no place for hate or resentment,—not even towards those that would nail us to the cross?

Yet neither in Kirtland, Missouri or Nauvoo, did we fully comply with this rule, and even in Utah many were left to cherish toward our poor Lamanite brethren, vindictiveness and hate; and in Missouri by Apostle Lyman Wight we were taught to "pray for our enemies," that God would damn them, and "give us power to kill them.." And while "three witnesses" with his counsellors and many of the apostles with their president, as also many others of our leading men, had turned their "heel" against the Prophet, how could he, in such disunion and enmity, always be strong in the might of his calling? And as the "eyes" of the Church, betrayed by those he loved who had so often "sopped with him" when there was little in the dish, under such disappointment and sorrow, may he not have been blinded even by his tears?

Jesus spent His life in teaching His disciples, and yet they did not understand Him or His doctrine. And altho He spent a long period after His resurrection in teaching them of the "common salvation," and although His last word to them was a command to "baptize all nations" yet Peter, the chief Apostle, had not yet swallowed it; and the Lord had at last to choke it down him, through his vision upon the housetop. And even after that, Paul "withstood" his partiality for the old law.

And now of your third Key, I do not feel to say much, as I fear I am writing in too great profusion, and that what I have written you will deem as of little worth. But from my standpoint of view, I can see that we have been in evolution since from before the world was, and that we were never without our agency, and never will be, unless we become the sons of Perdition, and that through our voluntary doings, or our failing to do. We foreordained, or elected ourselves to just the condition in which we were placed on earth; and we are now, through our works of good or evil, ordaining ourselves to the good or evil that awaits us in the great future. And I see that only through darkness do we comprehend the light, and that by their opposite do we comprehend the attributes and exaltation of the Gods. And just as we now love and care for our little children and foresee effects to them from causes, and have a purpose beyond their comprehension for their good, just so our Father has a purpose in everything relating to our condition here, for we are not here by accident or mistake, and that "all things must work to the good of those who fear God" and evolute in the "upward and onward;" and so I will thus leave your third key.

And then you would have "further truths from the teachings of the Prophet." And where shall I commence, and how shall I write to your understanding even the little I may have retained in memory? You will not forget that the march in science thru the last seventy years has in many things reversed the world's thought, changed its modes and almost its face, and is fast exploding the dogmas of outside theology. Well, the keys to all this knowledge was first committed to the Prophet Joseph, as a part of the gospel, for the world's benefit, for all of which he was derided. He was the first in this age to teach "substantialism," the eternity of matter, that no part or particle of the great universe could become annihilated or destroyed; that light and life and spirit were one; that all light and heat are the "Glory of God," which is his power, that fills the "immensity of space," and is the life of all things, and permeates with latent life, and heat, every particle of which all worlds are composed; that light or spirit, and matter, are the two first great primary principles of the universe, or of Being; that they are self-existent, co-existent, indestructible, and eternal, and from these two elements both our spirits and our bodies were formulated, and he gave us to understand that there were twelve kingdoms, or planets, revolving around our solar system, to which the Lord gave an equal division of His time or ministry and that now was His time to again visit the earth. He taught that all systems of worlds were in revolution, the lesser around the greater. He taught that all the animal kingdoms would be resurrected, and made us understand that they would remain in the dominion of those who, with creative power, reach out for dominion, through the power of eternal lives. He taught us that the saints would fill the great West, and through Mexico, Central and South America we would do a great work for the redemption of the remnant of Jacob. Of what he taught us relating to the Kingdom of God, as it would become organized upon the earth through "all nations learning war no more," and all adopting the God-given constitution of the United States as a Paladium of Liberty and Equal Rights.

But this, of itself, would require a long chapter, which must wait until the fulfillment of a prediction by the Prophet, relating to a testimony that I should bear, after I had become hoary with age, of thing which he that day taught to the circle of friends then around him of whom I am the only one living. So here I will leave this subject for your further interrogations, and proceed to give you, so far as I can remember the Prophet Joseph's last charge to the Quorum of the Twelve Apostles.

It was at Nauvoo early in 1844 in an assembly room, common to the meeting of the Council, or a select circle of the Prophet's most trusted friends, including all the Twelve, but not all the constituted authorities of the Church, for Presidents Rigdon, Law or Marks, the High Council nor Presidents of Quorums were not members of that council, which at times would exceed fifty in number. Its sittings were always strictly private, and all its rules were carefully and promptly observed and altho its meetings were at times oftener than monthly and my home at Ramus over twenty miles distant, I was present at every session, and being about the youngest member of the council, I was deeply impressed with all that transpired, or was taught by the Prophet.

Criticism had already commenced by those near him in authority with regard to his teachings and his doings. And we began now, in a degree, to understand the meaning of what he had so often publicly said, that "should he teach and practice the principles that the Lord had revealed to him, and now requested of him, that those then nearest him in the stand would become his enemies and the first to seek his life;" which they soon did, just as he had foretold. And to show you that under conditions then existing that the Prophet did not really desire longer to live, and that you may see how my mind was in a degree prepared for after results, I will briefly relate an incident that occurred at his last visit to us at Ramus.

After he had at evening preached with great animation to a large congregation and had blessed nineteen children, he turned to me and said, "Benjamin, I am tired, let us go home", which only a block distant, we soon reached, and entering we found a warm fire with a large chair in front, and my wife sitting near with her babe, our eldest, upon her lap, and approaching her, I said, "Now, Melissa, see what we have lost by your not going to meeting, Brother Joseph has blessed all the children in the place but ours, and it is left out in the cold." But the Prophet at once said, "You shall lose nothing," and he proceeded to bless our first born, and then, with a deep drawn breath as a sigh of weariness, he sank down heavily in his chair, and said, "Oh! I do get so tired and weary, that at times I almost yearn for my rest," and then proceeded briefly to recount to us some of the most stirring events of his life's labors, suffering and sacrifices, and then he said, "I am getting tired and would like to go to my rest." His words and tone thrilled and shocked me, and like an arrow pierced my hopes that he would long remain with us, and I said, as with a heart full of tears, "Oh! Joseph, what could we, as a people do without you and what would become of the great Latter-day work if you should leave us?" He saw and was touched by my emotions, and in reply he said, "Benjamin, I should not be far away from you and if on the other side of the veil I should still be working with you, and with a power greatly increased, to roll on this kingdom." And such was the tone, earnestness and pathos of his words to me then, that they can never be fully recalled but with emotion.

And now before fully returning to the council and subject in connection with the above, I will relate a dream told to us in council by the Prophet but a short time before his death, which was as follows: "I dreamed that by the Laws, Marks, Higby's and Fosters, I was bound, both hand and foot and cast into a deep well, soon after which I heard screams of terror and cries of 'Oh! Brother Joseph, save us, save us!" This cry continued until with my elbows and toes I had worked my way to the top, and looking out, I saw all of those who had bound me within the folds of a terrible serpent, that was preparing to swallow them, and I told them that as they had bound me, I could render them no assistance." This dream made upon my mind an impression never forgotten, and just as he related it, so it was fulfilled in his death; for those were the men that opened the way for his assassination.

And now returning to the council and the "Last Charge." Let us remember that by revelation he had reorganized the Holy Priesthood, and by command of the Lord (D. & C. 124 and

123) had taken from the First Presidency his brother Hyrum to hold as Patriarch, the sealing power, the first and highest honor due to priesthood; that he had turned the keys of endowments, to the last annointing, and sealing together with keys of Salvation for the dead, with the eternity of the marriage covenant and the power of endless lives. All these keys he held, and under these then existing conditions he stood before that association of his select friends, including all the Twelve, and with great feeling and animation he graphically reviewed his life of persecution, labor and sacrifice for the church and kingdom of God, both of which he declared were now organized upon the earth. The burden of which had become too great for him longer to carry, that he was weary and tired with the weight he so long had borne, and he then said, with great vehemence: "And in the name of the Lord, I now shake from my shoulders the responsibilities of bearing off the Kingdom of God to all the world, and here and now I place that responsibility, with all the keys, powers and privileges pertaining thereto, upon the shoulders of you the Twelve Apostles, in connection with this council; and if you will accept this, to do it, God shall bless you mightily and shall open your way; and if you do it I now shake my garments clear and free from the blood of this generation and of all men;" and shaking his skirt with the great vehemence he raised himself from the floor, while the spirit that accompanied his words thrilled every heart as with a feeling that boded bereavement and sorrow.

And now, my dear brother, after 60 years have passed, at 85 in age, I bear to you and to all the world a solemn testimony of the truth and veracity of what I have written above, for although so many years have intervened, they are still in my mind, as fresh as when they occurred; no doubt as a part fulfillment of a prediction by the Prophet relating to "testimonies I should bear of his teachings, after I had become hoary with age."

There were, dear brother, other teachings to that council, of which I am not at full liberty to write, but if I had your ear, I would remember that the Prophet once said to me: "Benjamin, in regard to those things I have taught you privately, that are not yet for the public, I give you the right when you are so led, to commit them to others, for you will not be led wrong in discerning those worthy of your confidence."

And now to your question, "How early did the Prophet Joseph practice polygamy?" I hardly know how wisely to reply, for the truth at times may be better withheld; but as what I am writing is to be published only under strict scrutiny of the wisest, I will say, that the revelation to the Church at Nauvoo, July 21, 1843, on the Eternity of the Marriage Covenant and the Law of Plural Marriage, was not the first revelation of the law received and practiced by the Prophet. In 1835, at Kirtland, I learned from my sister's husband, Lyman R. Sherman, who was close to the Prophet, and received it from him, "That the ancient order of Plural Marriage was again to be practiced by the Church." This at the time, did not impress my mind deeply, although there then lived with his family a neighbor's daughter, Fannie Alger, a very nice and comely young woman about my own age, toward whom not only myself, but every one, seemed partial for the amiability of her character; and it was whispered even then that Joseph loved her. After this, there was some trouble with Jared Carter, and through Brother Sherman I learned that "as he had built himself a new house, he now wanted another wife," which Joseph would not permit.

And then there was some trouble with Oliver Cowdery, and whisper said it was relating to a girl then living in his family; and I was afterwards told by Warren Parish, that he himself and Oliver Cowdery did know that Joseph had Fannie Alger as a wife, for they were spied upon and found together. And I can now see that as at Nauvoo, so at Kirtland, that the suspicion or knowledge of the Prophet's plural relation was one of the causes of apostacy and disruption at Kirtland although at the time there was little said publicly on the subject.

Soon after the Prophet's flight in winter of 1837 and 1838, the Alger family left for the West and stopping in Indiana for a time, Fannie soon married to one of the citizens there, and although she never left the state, she did not turn from the Church nor from her friendship with the Prophet while she lived.

And now, looking back through the stirring adventures and incidents of thrilling experience of the four years that followed, from 1838 to 1843, such as accompanying the "Kirtland Poor Camp," and arriving in Missouri just in time to take in all the experience of that period, such as imprisonment in Wilson's camp with for many—the Hauns Mill and McBride murderers as my guards, my wonderful escape and preservation, and my return the following summer to meet the Prophet at Nauvoo, with the terrible sickness that followed, both with others and myself; after which a two and a half year's mission to Canada and Middle States, all so full of change and thrilling incidents that all past experience of my life seemed as partly swallowed up or forgotten, but on meeting the Prophet at my return to Nauvoo, in June, 1842, he greeted me with great warmth, and almost at once installed me as his legal agent, with the right to use his name as I might be led in business transactions, especially as related to the Church lands and town property of Ramus, all of which were placed by my charge.

And now, in visiting my sister, the widow of Lyman R. Sherman, who died a martyr to the conditions at Far West, I found with her a former acquaintance, Sister Louisa Beeman,
and I saw from appearances that they were both in his care, and that he provided for their comfort; and as I was held closely to business, and my home at Ramus was twenty miles distant. I saw but little of them until after the Prophet, in early spring of 1843, had come to Ramus to teach me plural marriage, and to ask my other sisters to be his wives, an account of which I have heretofore given by sworn statement but will here repeat as it occurred.

It was Sunday morning, April 3rd or 4th, 1843, that the Prophet was at my home in Ramus, and after breakfast he proposed a stroll together, and taking his arm, our walk led toward toward a swail, surrounded by trees and tall brush and near the forest line not far from my house. Through the swail ran a small spring brook, across which a tree was fallen and was clean of its bark. On this we sat down and the Prophet proceeded at once to open to me the subject of plural and eternal marriage and he said that years ago in Kirtland the Lord had revealed to him the ancient order of plural marriage, and the necessity for its practice, and did command him then to take another wife, and that among his first thoughts was to come to my mother for some of her daughters. And as he was again required of the Lord to take more wives, he had come to ask me for my sister Almira.

His words astonished me and almost took my breath. I sat for a time amazed and finally, almost ready to burst with emotion, I looked him straight in the face and said: "Brother Joseph, this is something I did not expect, and I do not understand it. You know whether it is right, I do not. I want to do just as you tell me, and I will try, but if I ever should know that you do this to dishonor and debauch my sister, I will kill you as sure as the Lord lives." And while his eyes did not move from mine, he said with a smile, in a soft tone: "But Benjamin you will never know that, but you will know the principle in time, and will greatly rejoice in what it will bring to you." "But how," I asked, "can I teach my sister what I myself do not understand, or show her what I do not myself see?" "But you will see and understand it," he said, "and when you open your mouth to talk to your sister, light will come to you and your mouth will be full and your tongue loose, and I will today preach a sermon to you that none but you will understand." Both of these promises were more than fulfilled. The text of his sermon was our use of the "one, five and ten talents," and as God had now commanded plural marriage, and was exaltation and dominion of the saints dependended upon the number of their righteous posterity, from him who was then but with one talent, it would be taken and given him that had ten, which item of doctrine seems now to be somewhat differently constructed.

But my thought and wish is to write of things just as they occurred, and I now bear an earnest testimony that his other prediction was more than fulfilled, for when with great hesitation and stammering I called my sister to a private audience, and stood before her shaking with fear, just so soon as I found power to open my mouth, it was filled, for the light of the

Lord shone upon my understanding, and the subject that had seemed so dark now appeared of all subjects pertaining to our gospel the most lucid and plain; and so both my sister and myself were converted together, and never again did I need evidence or argument to sustain that high and holy principle. And within a few days of this period my sister accompanied me to Nauvoo, where at our sister Delcena's, we soon met the Prophet with his brother Hyrum and Wm. Clayton, as his private secretary, who always accompanied him. Brother Hyrum at once took me in hand, apparently in fear I was not fully converted, and this was the manner of his talk to me: "Now Benjamin, you must not be afraid of this new doctrine, for it is all right. You know Brother Hyrum don't get carried away by worldly things, and he fought this principle until the Lord showed him it was true. I know that Joseph was commanded to take more wives, and he waited until an angel with a drawn sword stood before him and declared that if he longer delayed fulfilling that command he would slay him." This was the manner of Brother Hyrum's teaching to me, which I then did not need, as I was fully converted.

Meanwhile, the Prophet, with Louisa Beeman and my sister Delcena, had it agreeably arranged with Sister Almera, and after a little instruction she stood by the Prophet's side and was sealed to him as a wife, by Brother Clayton; after which the Prophet asked me to take my sister to occupy room number "10" in his Mansion home during her stay in the city. But as I could not long be absent from my home and business, we soon returned to Ramus, where on the 15th of May, some three weeks later, the Prophet again came and at my house occupied the same room and bed with my sister, that the month previous he had occupied with the daughter of the late Bishop Partridge, as his wife.

And at this time he sealed to me my first wife for eternity, and gave to me my first plural wife, Mary Ann Hale, an orphan girl raised by my mother then living with us, who is still with me, and is probably the only wife still living with the man to whom she was given by the Prophet.

At the marriage of Sister Almera to the Prophet, there was still our youngest sister, for whom he manifest partiality, and would gladly have married, also, but she being young and partially promised to my first wife's brother, although reluctantly, the matter by him was dropped.

On learning from the Prophet that even in Kirtland "the Lord had required him to take plural wives, and that he had then thought to ask for some of my sisters" the past with its conditions and influences began more fully to unfold to my mind, the causes that must, at least in part, have led to the great apostasy and disruption in Kirtland. Without a doubt in my mind, Fanny Alger was, at Kirtland, the Prophet's first plural wife, in which, by right of his calling, he was justified of of the Lord (see D. & C. Sec. 132:59-60); while Oliver Cowdery, J. Carter, W. Parish, or others were not justified of the Lord either in their criticisms upon the doings of the Prophet, or in their becoming a "law unto themselves," thru which they lost the light of their calling and were left in darkness.

Fanny A., when asked by her brother and others, even after the Prophet's death, regarding her relations to him, replied: "That is all a matter of our own, and I have nothing to communicate." Her parents died in Utah, true to the church. And to my knowledge, was by President Kimball in the temple at St. George introduced as "Brother of the Prophet Joseph's first plural wife."

The marriage of my eldest sister to the Prophet was before my return to Nauvoo, and it being tacitly admitted, I asked no questions.

And as to the number that came into the plural order, before the Prophet's death, I can think of but five, whose names I will now attempt to recall, but the number soon after his death began to increase. But on the finishing of the Temple, with endowments that followed, the number was greatly augmented. And so there was at least a "few who had accepted" and practiced plural marriage from about 1842 to 1852, when the revelation was published to the world.

"How generally was polygamy practiced in Utah?" is a question that I am not qualified to answer, but from my narrow observation, I would "guess" that one-tenth of our church men married plurally, and that two-thirds of that number made a fair success in raising good families, and that the other third was more or less a failure. But my judgment is not to be fully relied upon.

Of the number of plural marriages in Joseph's day, I have already said of men there was but few comprising the Prophet and part of the Twelve, with a few others who were his confidential or bosom friends.

You ask if plural marriage was ever Manditory? If you mean by the Lord then I say yes; for it was by command to the Prophet from the first. But from the Prophet to the people, it came as counsel, which when personally given, was not always heeded. But no one who lived worthy of his priesthood and calling was deprived of a right to plural marriage. And just as it was a "happy privilege" for us in poverty and self-sacrifice to have our homes to preach the gospel, or to fill any calling in labors of love and charity for the salvation of the Father's children, thereby to learn their gratitude and love as our reward just so it was a privilege. For do we attain to real happiness but in administering happiness to others?

The first command was to "multiply" and the Prophet taught us that dominion and power in the Great Future would be commensurate with the number of "wives, children and friends" that we inherit here, and that our mission to the earth was to organize a nuclei of Heaven, to take with us, to the increase of which there would be no end.

And while I can believe that to some plural marriage was a great cross, yet I cannot say so from my own experience, for although in times that tried men's hearts, I married seven wives, I was blessed with the gift to love them all; and although providing for so many was attended with great labor, care and anxiety, yet there was sympathy and love as my reward. And there is not one of my children of their mothers that are not dearer to me still than life.

On my return in 1855 from a mission to the Sandwich Isles, I found that Santaquin, with the homes of my family and all that I possessed to the amount of thousands was destroyed or stolen by Indians in the Walker War, and my family homeless. And yet in 1856, although conditions appeared forbidding, council suggested that I take other wives; and feeling sure it was the voice of the Lord to me, with promise of His blessing, so I married three more young wives, which was followed by cricket and locust raids to destroy nearly all our crops for five years, and yet we were neither hungry or naked. These were days that tried the souls of both men and women, and yet the love and gratitude of any one of my children today more than repays all, and I know that both men and women in plural marriage were happy in the assurance that they were obeying the command of God and the council of His servants.

And without the consent and approbation of him who held the keys of that priesthood, no one had the right even to speak upon the subject of plural marriage to the women he would marry, and even then, he ought first to obtain consent of her parents before having the right to speak to her upon the subject. And this was ever the law so far as I understand it. And for all plural marriages or sealings there was the one only that held this right, which he, if necessary, could delegate to others.

And then with regard to a man's right to take a second wife without the knowledge and consent of the first, I will only say, if his first wife be like the Sarah of old, there would be no such necessity, but if other wives, then see D. & C. Sec. 132:64-65.

And now your question as to the cause of the early persecutions of the Saints. To answer this question, we should go back to its inception to find cause for the hate that is ever behind to incite persecution. Between the present and former dispensations there is a striking analogy. Jesus appeared to the learned, haughty, dignified and opulent Jews as the "poor illiterate carpenter's son of Nazareth," a despised "Galilean," who claimed to be the Son of the Highest, the Great Jehovah, that "without him there was nothing made that was made," that he held "all power both in Heaven and on Earth," that he could "destroy the temple and rear it up in three days," etc. while the multitude turned from them to follow Him the "lowly Nazarene," hence their envy and jealousy which ripened into hate and in their nailing Him as a malefactor to the cross, and just so it has been in our day.

Joseph Smith, of lowly birth, a farm boy of common class, poor, illiterate and without distinction other than being religiously inclined; he attended revivals, was in these anxious circles honestly seeking religion and to learn which was the right church; and calling upon the Lord in simple faith that he might know. Both the Father and the Son, in a pillar of light descended, and in teaching him commanded that "he join no religious sect, as their creeds were all an abomination in His sight."

And this blow, by an ignorant son of poverty at fourteen years of age, in the face of all Christendom, was an insult to the dignity of all priestly learning, greatness and wealth; with all their millions in Bible, missionary and other societies for converting the world, all their greatness defied and denounced by an ignorant boy, their contempt led to hatred and persecution. And when that same boy became a man, he claimed having revelations, and that an angel had delivered to him golden plates containing the history of a fallen people, and that God, through him was about to restore the ancient gospel in its purity, which, if true, would blot out all their greatness. And so inspired by hate, they made lies their weapons with which to fight the truth; both of which are attributes of the devil, whose servants they were, as "blind leaders of the blind." The leaders blinded by envy, jealousy, self interest and hate while the multitude were blinded by the popular prejudice and cry of "away with them," and all going together to the pit; just as the Master saw, and upon the cross "prayed His Father to forgive them as they knew not what they did." Our Prophet Joseph like the Master, was held in contempt by learned priests, bigots and hypocrites, and like Him, was scorned, despised, and derided by the rich; and by all Christendom was hated without cause, and persecuted unto death by those who would not know him.

It is true that the Prophet seemed to lay the foundation of our Church with a military spirit, and so, unlike the present, he taught us resistance to all oppression: to defend our liberties with the sword. But I can now see as the temple of truth and love is built higher by the Master's hand that resentment brought to us only calamity and the reverse of our hopes. And I can also see now that unnecessary offences were at times given to strengthen the prejudice or hate of our enemies; for that was the infancy of the Church and its days of child-like enthusiasm and great hopes. And at times, no doubt, leading elders made child-like boasts to irritate our enemies.

But of that period and experience, as compared with today, you can realize but little, and so I do not marvel at your criticisms upon the common manner of disposing of the question of "causes," for all is now so changed.

And as since, before 1830 the Lord began, through the Prophet Joseph, to turn the keys of knowledge to flood the world with new light and life, or to plant in the "three measures of meal" that "leaven" through which all the world will yet become "leavened," which has since its inception been working in the world's thought to produce great change, politically, religiously, socially, financially and scientifically — the increased light that came to earth through the keys of knowledge turned by the Prophet Joseph for which he was derided, hated, and killed, but towards which all searching eyes of inquiry are now turning with new thoughts leading towards the great truths of the gospel.

While many principles of our religion are being counterfeited by the world to throw dust in the eyes of the thoughtless, that they may not discover that this is the great day of "God's preparation" for regenerating the earth with a Zion for its Capitol City.

"The Prophet and his hobbies." The Prophet fully realized that arrayed against him, or the truth, was combined all the religious, political, financial, educational and social powers of the world. And all this power he had to meet with wisdom that came alone from God. He had not time or place for "hobbies", but stood boldly to defend the truth with such weapons and helps as came to him of the Lord.

P. P. Pratt, through his "Voice of Warning to all the people, published at an early day in Kirtland, was a primary exponent of the Prophet's theology. And the Prophet's reply to journalists who early, in Nauvoo, asked him for a copy of the "Mormon creed" has since become our "articles of Faith." And if the Prophet did have a "hobby" it was to provide for the poor and to defend the liberties of the people, for which he organized the Nauvoo Legion, and for which he laid down his life. And the principle of his government or influence over his people is explained in his reply to a church dignitary, I think a Catholic Bishop, who at Nauvoo Mansion asked him "by what power he governed so great a people?" He replied, "I do not govern them, I teach them correct principles and they govern themselves," which was a "hobby," if he had any.

"The Prophet's teaching of love" was not to work upon the sympathies and sensibilities of the people, but by his great example and self-sacrifice, and in showing us that while all the world were against us, our only hope was in our union, and that union was only possible as the fruit of our love for each other. And in teaching us the "Fatherhood of God, and the Brotherhood of Man," we could begin to see why we should "love God supremely, and our brothers as ourselves." He taught us that God was the great head of human procreation—was really and truly the father of both our spirits and our bodies: that we were but parts of a great whole, mutually and equally dependent upon each other, according to our conditions. And in our love of God we show, as do the members of our bodies, naturally a greater love and protection for our head. But this reasoning could not be fully understood by all, and as I have said before, in the infancy of the church, our minds and views were more narrow, and we were more petulant, resentful and perhaps more vindictive then than now, that the principle of charity and love are seen to be the life spring and core principle of our gospel. And now that we see the temple of charity, union and love, reared above its foundation, once guarded by the "Nauvoo Legion," commanded by the Traitor, "Joab, General in Israel," we are led to feel that those were the days of childhood's mistakes, yet all leading to great purposes as was the call of Judas to the apostleship. And we are as a people today, in wisdom, stature and power with God, just what we have grown to be through accumulating experience in the Father's care.

"Early day marriage among the Saints." Replying to your question, relating to early day marriages in the Church, I will say, that there were no arbitrary rules relating to marriage, other than that the ceremony be in strict accordance with statute law of the state. And as no one of the elders at a very early day took to themselves the right to perform that ceremony, it was left to the Justice of the Peace, until Elder Seymour Brunson at Kirtland, assumed that prerogative and was patronized until others followed his example; and I remember of no marriage by the Prophet until at Nauvoo. And for marrying with the outside, the rule from the first was as now, strongly against it by council, but tolerant as to common fellowship, while all the wise understand that such marriage is of no eternal worth.

In reply to your question on "Early proselyting and attitude of the Church toward other denominations," "I must say again, that in the rise of the Church all advantages of wealth, education and popularity were with our enemies; while the few poor, unlearned elders, called of the Lord, were at every disadvantage. But in having the truth and a trust in the Lord, and they at times, through their faith and zeal, enthused by the spirit of their callings, were led to use the gospel truths as a battering ram, to demolish creeds and hypocracy, as fabrics "built upon the sand," instead of first rearing in view of all the gospel temple of truth and love, as a home of refuge for the honest in heart, when their houses built upon the "sand" should fall.

And our labors then were perhaps not always in the wisdom and charity that the experience and learning of subsequent years has brought. And in proportion as we were derided, persecuted and held in contempt by a hireling priesthood, whose creeds we knew were but an abomination, and all their ministry but grauds, and so we regarded their show of sincerity as hollow mockery and pretence, all for popularity or gain. And of all the sects, we regarded the

Catholic church as the great head of priestcraft and hypocricy. And so far as I am personally concerned, I am hardly rid of that view and feeling yet, that they are really but "garnished sepulchers" filled with the bones of a dead and rotten past.

And right here a full chapter could be written of young men, who, while yet but boys, went forth in ignorance, and through their humility and in the spirit of their calling, soon became mighty both in word and in deed, and for a season would be as brilliant stars of our hopes, but through forgetting the Lord, in remembrance of their own greatness, too many, like bright meteors, sank from sight to rise no more, in fulfillment of His word that "no flesh should glory in His presence;" while others, trusting in their own strength, were led into sins and were swallowed up in their transgressions, after a labor in faithfulness for a season.

"Pioneers and Oregon." With others, from the Prophet at an early day, I took in the idea of our pioneering or exploring, to find somewhere in the west a place of safety for the Church. And while some thoughts would be of valleys in the mountains, an oasis in the "Great American Desert," others did talk of Oregon, but not in the Prophet's day did any properly organized company start. But at his death the star of our hope for a home of peace began more plainly to rise in the Great West, somewhere to be found. But where, we knew not. Among the speculations as to where, Oregon was talked of, and then of Van Couver's Island, which, with its great advantages for Mormon safety from persecution, was pointed out by our professed friend Stephen A. Douglas, who came to the Nauvoo Mansion in 1845, then kept open by myself, soon after which the praises of Upper California began to be rehearsed and sung. But by Brigham Young, to my knowledge, there was never a pointer given as to our destination as a people. And although in organizing the Pioneer Emigration, I was appointed captain of fifty wagons, and was among the first to cross the Mississippi, and camped on Sugar Creek, I yet heard no suggestion by our leader as to where we were going, nor did I know of a "Scout, mountaineer, or guide" being in our camp for one day, or for anyone to give a word to point or direct our way but Brigham Young. And never until after our arrival in Salt Lake Valley, did I see Fremont, Kit Carson, Peg Leg Smith or Captain Bridger, all of whom I saw after our Modern Moses guided alone by revelation, had led us to the Salt Lake Valley.

"Of changes and mistakes," I hardly feel inspired to write, for change is everywhere and in everything, and liability of change and mistakes is with every one, and if the Master "learned obedience" through experience, how much more need of experience have we? I believe that the mistakes of a true man will be as steps upon which he will rise to greater wisdom, exertions, and to broader views. And why should not the experience of yesterday make us the wiser today? We are not always in the same mind and feeling: for when prompted by hunger, He cursed the tree that bore Him no fruit; and when angry with scourges he drove from the Temple "money changers" and kicked over their tables. But this was not His mood when at the grave of Lazarus He so wept that the guests exclaimed, "Behold how He loveth him;" nor when in view of calamities to come He wept over Jerusalem; and does it not look like a mistake that He chose as one of His apostles a Judas to betray Him?

And now all of this, to a great degree, finds a parallel in the life of the Prophet Joseph. He was already to fight for the rights and liberties of his friends, and his heart was ever full of sympathy and tears, to sorrow with those he loved; and he too chose among his counsellors and friends those who did betray and bring him to death. And no man, seemingly, could make greater mistakes in selection of associates than did the Prophet; and this, with the many other things of which he was accused, his enemies held as evidence that he was a fallen prophet. And even the Lord not only at times admonished him for neglect of duty; but speaks of his "sins" and "transgressions," which would imply that he was not always equally enlightened and guided by inspiration. And in the earliest days he did so make mistakes that the Lord at one time witheld from him the keys of his calling. And he does not in his own history hesitate to say that after conversing with both the Father and the Son, and being administered to by holy angels, that he made great mistakes and was overcome in transgression and sins. And as to mistakes through want of properly discerning the "times and seasons" of prophetic events, we were over seventy years ago taught by our leaders to believe that the coming of Christ and the millenial reign was much nearer then than we believe it to be now. And mistakes through imaginations and groundless hopes have been all along the line of our experience as a Church. And are not our reverses, disappointments and mistakes permitted to be monitors and guides for the future? And I do know of things done and of principles taught by the Prophet Joseph that our Prophet, Joseph F., would not today accept as an example for him to imitate. And is not our growth in wisdom the cumulated fruit of our experimental or active life?

"President Brigham Young." Of Brigham Young as President of the Church, I will again bear this as a faithful testimony that I do know and bear record that upon the head of Brigham Young as chief, with the Apostleship in full, was by the voice of the Prophet Joseph in my hearing, laid the full responsibility of bearing of the kingdom of God to all the world. And I do further bear this as a testimony, faithful and true, to the Church and to all the world, that at a conference of the whole Church, at Nauvoo, subsequent to the Prophet's death and return of the absent Apostles, that I sat in the assembly near to President Rigdon, closely attentive to his appeal to the conference to recognize and sustain his claim as "Guardian for the Church." And I was perhaps, to a degree, forgetful of what I knew to be the rights and duties of the apostleship, and as he closed his address and sat down, my back was partly turned to the seat occupied by Apostle Brigham Young and other Apostles, when suddenly, and as from Heaven,I heard the voice of the Prophet Joseph, that thrilled my whole being, and quickly turning around I saw in the transfiguration of Brigham Young, the tall, straight and portly form of the Prophet Joseph Smith, clothed in a sheen of light, covering him to his feet; and I heard the real and perfect voice of the Prophet, even to the whistle as in years past caused by the loss of a tooth said to have been broken out by the mob in Hyrum. This view, or vision, although but for seconds, was to me as vivid and real as the glare of lightning or the voice of thunder from the heavens, and so deeply was I impressed with what I saw and heard in this transfiguration, that for years I dare not publicly tell what was given me of the Lord to see. But when in later years I did publicly bear this testimony, I found that others would testify to having seen and heard the same. But to what proportion of the congregation who were present I could never know. But I do know that this, my testimony is true.

The Prophet's lost tooth, to which I alluded was, as generally understood, broken out by the mob at Hyrum while trying to pry open his mouth to strangle him with acid, which from time, until the tooth was replaced by a dentist neighbor, a year or so previous to his death, there had a whistle-like sound to accompany all his public speaking which I again plainly heard at the time of which I write.

And while I do know that Brigham Young as President of the Church, was the right man in the right place, and a great leader for Israel, I still know that he never claimed to be perfect in all of his ways, but that, like his brethren, he at times was liable to mistakes. And to some of his mistakes I am a witness, and also that he saw some of his mistakes and nobly corrected them.

And to show more fully his leading traits and general "personal character," I will go back to relate that soon after embracing the gospel in 1832, Brigham Young started with his brother from their home in the state of New York, to visit the Prophet at Kirtland, and on their way called upon us at Pomfret, N. Y., who had received the gospel just before them, and remaining overnight with my sister's husband, Lyman R. Sherman. And while at evening in animated conversation upon the gifts as promised to accompany the gospel, the spirit came upon Brother Sherman in mighty power, and he opened his mouth in an unknown tongue, to the great surprise and joy of all, and I think that Brother Brigham also at that time received the gift; Brother Lyman R. Sherman being the first known to have spoken in the gift of tongues by the power of God in this dispensation. And on Brother Brigham arriving in Kirtland at the Prophet's home, being called to lead in family prayer, as a surprise even to the Prophet, he opened his mouth in a strange tongue, the first heard by him, which he said at once was in the language of our first parents. And he, at that time, made the Prediction upon the head of Brigham Young that "at some period he would become the leader of the Church, and that there would be but one danger to beset him. and that would be his love of wealth." These things were told me by Brother Sherman at near the time of their occurrence, who remained almost as the right hand of the Prophet until the day of his death. And while I am witness that after the Prophet's death that Brigham Young became Israel's great leader, a Prophet, Seer, and Revelator, to the Church in all the world, I yet know that he was a great financier and at times did manifest a love for wealth, and did make mistakes, some of which he may not have lived fully to rectify. But with all of his mistakes, private or public, his voice was ever the voice of the true shepherd to Israel. And in looking for mistakes, I feel admonished to look after my own personality, which, with all his faults, might perhaps leave me, in comparison, too small for a full claim to notice.

From him young manhood, all through his after life, in close observation, I saw him through every calling, rise to become Israel's great chief, holding every key of Priesthood and power pertaining to the Kingdom of God on the earth and the salvation for the dead. And I saw, too, that through his great capacity as financier, with his love of riches, that he became as the Prophet had foretold, possessed of great wealth, which, although it may have had an influence to a degree upon his children, it had none to draw him from the love or duties of his high calling, in which, at times, he seemed fully tested, and the confidence of the people was towards him from his first assuming the Presidency.

His great influence as a leader seemed to lie in his quick discernment, his ready decisions, and in his right judgement, in placing men and things in their proper position, and to their best possible use; while his intuitive magnetism, his kindly sympathy in afflictions, his noble bearing as a brother, friend and as a man in its true and full sense, inspired confidence, respect and love in all who really knew him. And as for comparing him with others filling the same position, I can only think of them all, and each, as strong and mighty pillars in the Great Temple of our Hopes, equal in strength and use, but each molded by the Master hand in symmetry and beauty to a difference in form and mind but not in Priesthood and purpose.

"Brigham Young, his interest in education." Upon this question I will not prolong remarks. With Brigham Young from 1832 until his death in 1877 I was often closely associated, and I know him to have been a pioneer, a promoter, and a true friend to education, and although he was not himself cultured in scholarship or refined by classic education, yet he by nature was highly cultured and refined both in habit, demeanor and conversation, and no one could associate with him and not be impressed by his refining influence. And so far as the influence of music and drama tend to civilize and elevate, or refine society, credit should be due to Brigham Young as the pioneer chief in their promotion and establishment in the heart of the "Great American Desert," to give musical tone and inspiration to all its divisions into states.

But we should not forget that Brigham Young was the leader of a people, driven before the cannon and bayonet, of a heartless and cruel mob, who fled across the Mississippi in winter, leaving their homes without opportunity to provide food or clothing; and plundered of all they could not carry, and to go they knew not where; and to save the lives of all of these many thousands now devolved on Brigham Young, even to look after the possibilities for transportation, to learn the way, to open roads, to see that all had food, and then protect them from the tomahawk, scalping knife and bullet; and when in the Valleys, to measure out land, to formulate laws, and to counsel the people how to save a pittance from swarms of crickets and locusts that ravaged their field.

And for some years, President Young, with all the people, were devotedly seeking to save the souls of the people alive, from starvation, with hope of a better day for education.

But enthused by the spirit of our leader, in every way-station on the road, in every town or ward settled after arriving in Utah, about the first house built by the people was for public school and meeting purposes. And that Brigham Young opposed education, with desire to keep his people in ignorance, is a monster in falsehood, for he was not only the pioneer in education in the mountain states, but so long as he lived he assisted it liberally with his means, and the Brigham Young Academy and College, in Utah, will continue to bear fruit to the honor of his name after his traducers with their falsehoods, are buried in forgetfulness, under the contempt of God and all just men.

"What I know of the objects and purposes, in raising the Mormon Battalion." To show you that I did know the motive of President Young in sending the Battalion, I will say that as one of that special Council organized by the Prophet, of which I have written, and of which President Young being the head, I still hold my seat and still had a voice in all general movements relating to our exodus as a people from Nauvoo. And I will say that this council, as a legislature of the people, did continue under the Presidency and became the Colonial Council, or legislature of the State of Deseret. And I was present at the arrival of Colonel Little and company at Garden Grove, with the requisition, by Govt. for five hundred volunteers for the American Army, served upon the fleeing Mormons as a test to their loyalty and patriotism by Senator Benton of Missouri. It was well understood at the time, as the subject was fully ventilated by the council, and all comprehended it as a great sacrifice and that there was no reward or benefit offered by the government in any degree.

It was a test of the people's and our Prophet's loyalty and patriotism while under arrest; and this patriotism and loyalty was now to be placed upon the altar at a great disadvantage. And would we stand the test—even as did our Father Abraham answer this great question?

At Garden Grove all of the enlistment was filled, and now, this was unequalled patriotism and valor of the Sons of Zion, who sacrificed aged parents, wives and children, sweethearts and other dear ones, by leaving them homeless, unprotected, and to the mercy of the wild and naked plains.

That such a privilege was sought for by the Mormons, should be stamped as a monstrosity in falsehood. But that it was a great and far-reaching test of loyalty all will admit, which was to establish the truth of Mormon love and loyalty to that heaven-inspired and God-given Constitution of the United States, which will yet give guarantee of liberty and equal rights to all people of the earth and nations shall "learn war no more," and shall learn to better comprehend that great principle of the Fatherhood of God and the Brotherhood of Man.

I do not think of more to write.

/s/ Benjamin F. Johnson

AUTHOR'S NOTE: This letter was written to Elder George S. Gibbs, secretary to the First Presidency of the Church, at their request. In 1903, when it was written, Benjamin F. Johnson was one of few still living who had participated in many of the early events of the Church and who also had a close relationship with the Prophet Joseph Smith. The above was taken from the original letter except where portions of the letter were missing. In these instances a reproduction of the letter given to Charles S. Sellers was used. Brother Sellers discussed this letter with Benjamin, who gave Brother Sellers a copy of the letter.

Bibliography

Arizona Historical Review, A Quarterly. Phoenix, Arizona: Arizona State Historian.

Arrington, Leonard J. *Great Basin Kingdom.* Cambridge, MA: Harvard University Press, 1958.

Babbitt, Julia Johnson, Letter to Benjamin Johnson.

Bailey, Raymond. "Emma Hale, Wife of the Prophet Joseph Smith." thesis. Brigham Young University, 1952.

Bilderback, James C. *Masonry and Mormonism, Nauvoo, Illinois 1841-1847.* thesis. University of Iowa, 1937.

Brundage, E.E. affidavit. 24 Sep 1960. copy in author's possession.

Cannon, George Q. *Treasures of Pioneer History.* comp. by Kate B. Carter, Salt Lake City: Daughters of Utah Pioneers, 1956.

Conference Report. 71st Semi-Annual Conference. in Church Historian's Library.

Dastrup, Ila. "Mormon Colonization: A Type in the Western Movement." thesis, Brigham Young University.

Fielding, Robert Kent. "The Growth of the Mormon Church in Kirtland, Ohio," a Thesis presented to Indiana University. Bloomington: 1957.

Fields, Clarence L. "History of the Kirtland Temple." thesis. Brigham Young University, August 1963.

Gentry, Leland Homer. "A History of the Latter-day Saints in Northern Missouri 1836-to 1839." dissertation. Brigham Young University, 1965.

Hammond, F. A. letter to George Q. Cannon. 6 Oct 1854. *Deseret News*, 4 Jan 1855.

Hansen, Ralph. "Administrative History of the Nauvoo Legion in Utah." thesis. Brigham Young University. 1954.

Hinckley, Helen. "Religion and Nineteenth Century Western Colonization." thesis Brigham Young University, 1928.

Historian's Library, Salt Lake City.

Historical Record, The. Andrew Jensen, ed.

History of Hawaiian Mission, Church Historian's Office, Salt Lake City.

History of Spring Lake Ward, Nebo Stake, in Church Archives.

Holland, Melvin. "A History of Mesa." thesis. University of Arizona, 1933.

Horne, John F. Affidavit, Mesa, Arizona, 23 September 1962.

Huff, Emma N. comp.*Memories That Live - Utah County Centennial History*, Springville, UT: Art City Publishing Co., 1947.

Hunter, Milton R. *Brigham Young The Colonizer.* Salt Lake City: Deseret News Press, 1940.

———. *Utah - The Story of Her People.* Salt Lake City: Deseret News Press, 1946.

Huntington, O.B. *Deseret Evening News*, Oct. 16, 1897, on file at Church Historian's Library, Salt Lake City, 7-8.

Hyde, Orson. letter to Benjamin Johnson. 4 Dec 1858. in author's possession.

Jensen, Andrew, ed. *The Historical Record.*

Jensen, Andrew. *Encyclopedia History of The Church of Jesus Christ of Latter-day Saints.* Salt Lake City: Deseret News Publishing Company, 1941.

Johnson, Benjamin Franklin. "A Life Sketch." unpublished article. in Church Historian's Office, Salt Lake City.

———. "A Prophecy Fulfilled."

———. letter to "An Old Friend" 19 November 1853.

———. diary. in Church Historian's Office, Salt Lake City.

———. letter to *Deseret News* 17 Oct 1855.

———. letter to George S. Gibbs, 1903, Church Historian's Office, Salt Lake City).

———. letter to Anthon H. Lund. 12 May 1903. in Church Historian's Office.

———. letter to Brigham Young. 4 Jan 1867. in Church Historian's Library, Salt Lake City.

———. letter to Brigham Young. 4 Jul 1859. Church Historian's Library, Salt Lake City.

———. letter to Brigham Young. 17 Feb 1859. in Church Historian's Office, Salt Lake City.

———. letter to Brigham Young. 22 Sep 1857. on file in Church Historian's Library.

———. letter to Brigham Young. 25 Feb 1857. Church Historian's Library.

———. letter to *Deseret News.* 15 Jan 1893.

———. letter to *Deseret News.* 25 Jun 1902.

———. letter to George Q. Cannon. 15 Oct 1854. *Deseret News*, 4 Jan 1855.

———. letter to George S. Gibbs. in Church Historian's office.

———. letter to Grover Cleveland. 15 Jan 1886, Church Historian's Library, Salt Lake City.

———. letter to Harriet Johnson 5 Nov 1852. in author's possession.

———. letter to Harriet and Susan Johnson. 30 Sep 1862. in author's possession.

———. letter to Harriet Johnson. 10 Jan 1851. in author's possession.

———. letter to Harriet Johnson. 22 Apr 1854. in author's possession.

———. letter to Harriet Johnson. 24 Dec 1855. in author's possession.

———. letter to Harriet Johnson. 28 Jan 1854. in author's possession.

———. letter to Harriet Johnson, 22 March 1856.

———. letter to Harriet Johnson. in author's possession.

———. letter to Harriet Johnson. 17 March 1853. in author's possession.

———. letter to Heber C. Kimball. 28 Mar 1854. *Deseret News*, 22 Jun 1854.

———. letter to Heber & Lizzie. 11 June 1902.

———. letter to his "Brother." 19 Oct 1854. in author's possession.

———. letter to J. Horner. 4 Jun 1853. Church Historian's Office.

———. letter to Joseph Cain. *Deseret News*, 19 Mar 1853.

———. letter to President Anthon H. Lund. 12 May 1903. Historian's Office, Salt Lake City.

———. letter to S. W. Richards. 29 Mar 1853. *History of Hawaiian Mission*. Church Historians Office Salt Lake City. 1.

———. letter to Wilford Woodruff. 24 July 1888. In Church Historian's Office, Salt Lake City.

———. letter to Harriet. 25 Jan 1852. In author's possession.

———. manuscript. Church Historian's Office, Salt Lake City.

———. *Mormonism as an Issue* . Church Historian's Library, Salt Lake City.

———. *My Life's Review*. Independence, Missouri: Zion's Printing & Publishing Co., 1947.

———. "Show us a Sign." *Early Scenes in Church History* . Salt Lake City, 1882.

———. "What I Know of 'Mormonism' and It's Enemies, or A Few Jots from a 59 Years Experience in 'Mormonism,'" on file at Church Historian's Library, Salt Lake City.

Johnson, Benjamin Farland. "A Sketch of the Life of Benjamin Franklin Johnson written by his son." unpublished. in Church Historian's Office, Salt Lake City.

———. "Memories that Live." Historian's Office.

Johnson, Ellis H. affidavit. 22 Jul 1959. in Church Historian's Office, Salt Lake City.

Johnson, Hattie. letter to Luella and Neal LeBaron. 28 Jan 1965. In Author's possession.

Johnson, Joel H. diary. 1802-1882.

———. *Voice from the Mountain*. Salt Lake City, 1887.

———. Johnson, Julia. letters to her mother.

Johnson, Samuel Joseph. affidavit. 8 Oct 1960. in Church Historian's Office.

Johnson, George Washington. diary. manuscript at Brigham Young University Library.

Journal History. Church Historian's Office.

Journal of Discourses. 26 vols. Liverpool, 1851-86.

Journals of the House of Representatives, Council, and Joint Sessions of the First Annual and Special Sessions, 1851 and 1852. Salt Lake City, 1852.

Kirkham, Francis W. *A New Witness for Christ in America* . Independence, Missouri: Zion's Printing and Publishing Co.

LeBaron, Harriet Naomi Johnson. "Biographical Sketch of the Life of Harriet Naomi Johnson LeBaron." unpublished. in author's possession.

LeBaron, Homer Neal. Interview. 27 Sep 1960. copy in author's possession.

———. interview. 15 Jul 1966.

LeBaron, William Farland. letter. 29 Sep 1964. in author's possession.

———. interview. 29 September 1964.

Lundwall, N. B. *Temples of the Most High*. Salt Lake City: Bookcraft, 1952.

Maricopa Stake History. in the Church Historian's Office, Salt Lake City.

Maricopa Stake Quarterly Historical Report. 22 Jul 1882. in Church Historian's Office, Salt Lake City.

Martineau, James H. *Deseret Evening News*, 4 Aug 1894.

———. "Is There Power in Prayer?" *Improvement Era*. 8:337-340.

McBride, Ralph. "Utah Mail Service Before the Coming of the Railroad, 1869." thesis, Brigham Young University, 1957.

McClintock, James H. *Mormon Settlement in Arizona.* Phoenix, Arizona: Manufacturing Stationers, Inc., 1921.

Millennial Star. Liverpool, ????.

Minutes of the Council of Fifty. Special Collections, Brigham Young University Library.

Neff, Andrew Love. *History of Utah, 1847 to 1869.* Salt Lake City: Deseret News Press, 1940.

Nephi Ward History, Church Historian's Office, Salt Lake City.

Nibley, Preston. *Exodus to Greatness.* Salt Lake City: Deseret News Press, 1947.

Nibley, Preston. *Stalwarts of Mormonism.* Salt Lake City: Deseret Book, 1954.

Nix, Norma G. "Tribute to B. F. Johnson." 15 March 1955.

Openshaw, Rose A. "Highlights of the Life of Julia Hills and Ezekiel Johnson, Parents of Patriarch Benjamin Franklin Johnson" 1958.

———. "Grandfather Johnson had a Birthday," June 1957.

Pioneer Heritage. a periodical.

Pomeroy, Cassandra Johnson. "Bed Time Stories," *The Ezekiel Johnson Bulletin,* XII, 2:(Jun 1965) 3.

Riggs, John L. affidavit. 22 Sep 1960. in the Church Historian's Office, Salt Lake City.

Roberts, B.H. comp. *A Comprehensive History of the Church of Jesus Christ of Latter-day Saints.* 6 vols. (Salt Lake City: Deseret News Press, 1930)

Robinson, Joseph E. letter to C. S. Sellers. Mesa, Arizona 28 June 191? (the year is illegible).

Romney, Thomas Patten. *Mormon Colonies in Mexico.* Salt Lake City: Deseret Book, 1938.

Santaquin Ward History. 1856–58.

Sellers, Charles S. "A Last Witness." *Improvement Era.* 14:545.

Shumway, Ernest Widtsoe "History of Winter Quarters, Nebraska, 1846-1848." thesis, Brigham Young University, 1953.

Smith, John. patriarchal blessing. 10 Dec 1869. in author's possession.

Smith, Joseph Fielding. *Essentials in Church History.* 13th ed. Salt Lake City: Deseret Book, Deseret News Press, 1958.

Smith, Joseph, Jr. *History of the Church of Jesus Christ of Latter-day Saints.* 2nd ed. rev. edited by B.H. Roberts. 7 vols. Salt Lake City: Deseret News, 1932-51.

Spring Lake Villa Ward History. in Church Historian's Office, Salt Lake City.

Terry, Jessie Jolley. "The Life Story of Julia Hills Johnson."

The Canning Industry. 5th ed. Washington, DC: National Canners Association, 1963.

Tullidge, Edward W. *History of Salt Lake City.* Salt Lake City, 1886.

Warrum, Noble. *Utah Since Statehood.* Chicago-Salt Lake City: S.J. Clark Publishing.

Whitney, Orson F. *History of Utah.* Salt Lake City,1892.

Woodruff, Wilford. letter to Benjamin Johnson. 7 December 1882.

Young, Brigham. *History of the Church of Jesus Christ of Latter-day Saints—Period II.* Salt Lake City: Deseret News, 1956.

Index

0 26575 51715 6